PINOLE
THROUGH TIME

JEFF RUBIN AND GEORGE VINCENT
PINOLE HISTORICAL SOCIETY

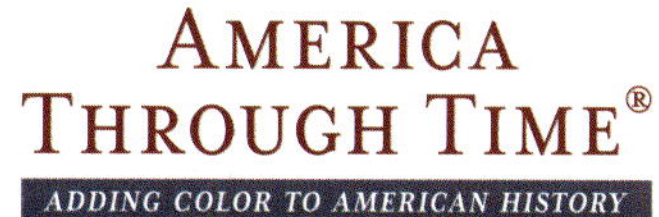

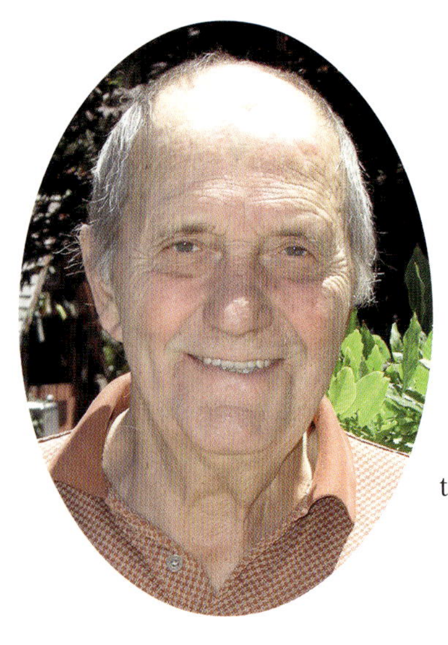

This book is dedicated to the late Dr. Joseph Mariotti, co-founder of the Pinole Historical Society, historian, and passionate environmentalist. He saved the Fernandez Mansion, Pinole's most historic building, from demolition. His contributions to Pinole will be noted for generations to come.

America Through Time is an imprint of Fonthill Media LLC

Fonthill Media LLC
www.fonthillmedia.com
office@fonthillmedia.com

First published 2015

ISBN 978-1-63500-023-8

Typeset in Mrs Eaves XL Serif Narrow
Printed and bound in England

Connect with us:
www.twitter.com/usathroughtime
www.facebook.com/AmericaThroughTime

INTRODUCTION

"Nothing ever changes in Pinole."

This long-held gem of local folklore has deep roots in perceptions of those living here, passed down through many generations of Pinoleans.

During its formative years, Pinole was a sleepy stage stop along the dusty road connecting the growing cities of Martinez and San Pablo. Early histories described Pinole in simple terms as a "prosperous village" or "hamlet by the bay." The outside world, to a large extent, bypassed Pinole, and the one-horse town evolved a quiet, almost unnoticed way of life unique unto itself.

This self-satisfying image became the cornerstone of a home-grown heritage proudly retained and reinforced from parent to child, transcending many generations. This popular vision was sustained by the daily rhythms of life surrounding Pinole's early inhabitants.

Generations went to the same Pinole-Hercules School #1 having the same teachers. Births and baptisms were handled by the same doctors and churches. Courtships and marriages grew between former playmates, classmates, or neighbors, who rarely moved from the same place.

Most menfolk labored for the same Hercules Powder Company employer whose workers gathered at day's end at the same Antlers, Club Alibi, or Tommy's Three Bells taverns.

Residents were entertained yearly by the same summer Holy Ghost Festival Parade. This was led by the same Pinole Municipal Band, whose members were the same familiar figures seen on Pinole's streets.

Even the town's gossip had the ring of sameness to it.

It was no wonder, then, that this culture of small-town sameness, repeated for almost two centuries, created and nurtured a mind-set of a comforting and harmonious environment in which to live. To the census takers, this Pinole became legally known as Township #11.

To those born here with memories stretching back to a not-so-distant past, the yesterdays were fondly recalled as "Those good times in Old Pinole."

However, even the oldest old-timers of bygone years witnessed dramatic changes and upheavals in their surroundings. Those "good times" came with the unhappy price of disappearing familiar scenes and places. The aged Fernandez warehouses and Southern Pacific Depot were gone from the bay front. The old downtown lost the Golden West Hotel, as well as a skating rink, movie house, and opera house. Pinole Valley surrendered the smells and sights of its tomato fields and ranching culture to the building sounds of new homes.

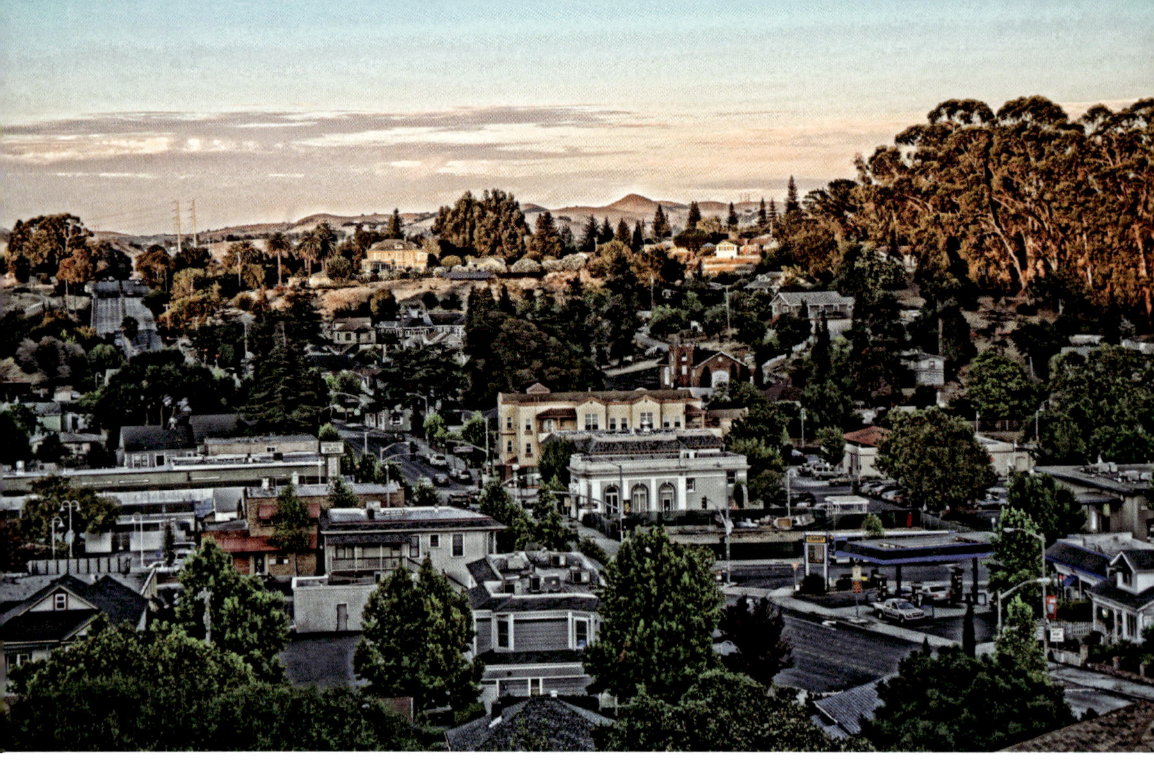

Downtown Pinole from Shale Hill: El Sobrante photographer Larry Neptune took this photo of downtown Pinole in 2010. Creatively using Photoshop, he made the photo look like a painting.

This book makes the connections between times past and present in Pinole. It is a visual primer opening Pinole's rich history to a new public. The central message is one calling for the preservation of vintage and current Pinole landscapes, as well as lamenting legacies already lost to the wrecking balls of time and neglect.

The story of Pinole is presented in a kaleidoscope of images depicting the physical changes as Pinole matured from a rural outpost into a proud city. The good times and the places of Old Pinole are now joined with the faces of "New Pinole."

Only a few Pinole landmarks and homes of the past survived the ravages of time and the modernization demolitions of the 1950s and 1960s. The Bank of Pinole celebrates its centennial anniversary in 2015. It survived the 1989 Loma Prieta Earthquake, which led to leveling of the bank's neighbors made of brick. The 100 year-old structure is a prime example of a community treasure now needing protection from the more destructive forces of politics and apathy.

Ideas and attitudes change very slowly. The notion that nothing ever changes in Pinole may still exist. However, the true reality of an ever-changing Pinole also exists within the memory walk taken in *Pinole Through Time*.

George R. Vincent

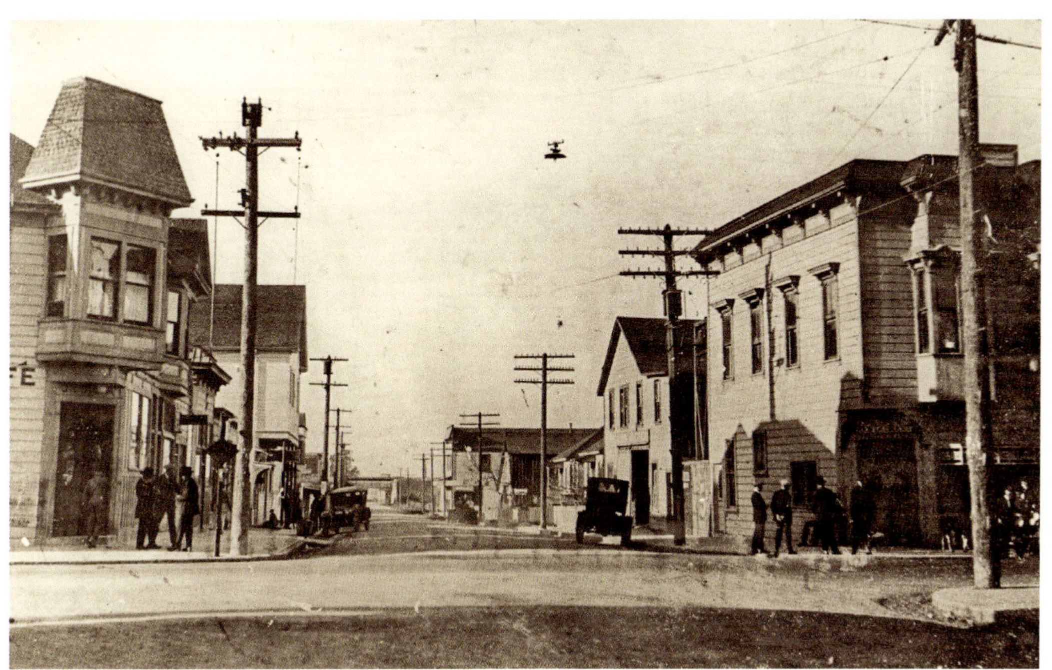

TENNENT AVENUE LOOKING NORTH: Early in the twentieth century, downtown Pinole had fourteen saloons; the Swenson and Lewis Saloon (left corner) and the Stats Hotel and Saloon (right corner) were two of them. This area, known as the Four Corners, was the hub of Pinole's business and social life. After a brick building was built on the Stats Hotel site, Pontes and Barroca's Central Grocery operated there for many years. Antlers Tavern now occupies the Swenson & Lewis site in 2015, and Tina's Place occupies the Stats site. The entire west side of Tennent Avenue, including Forester's Hall—the large white building—was destroyed in a massive blaze in 1908.

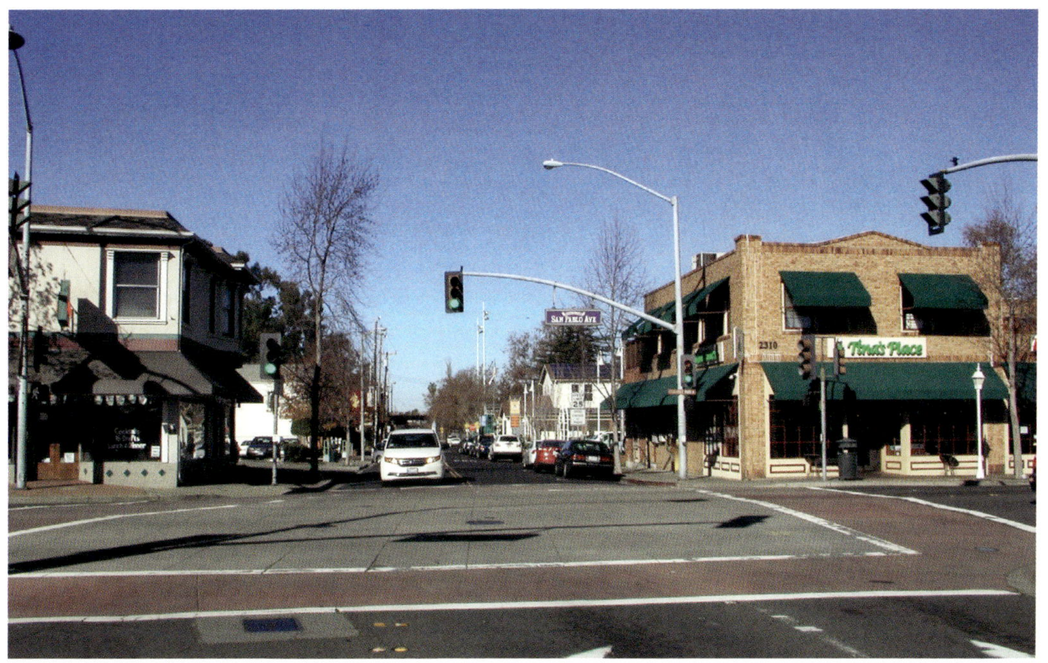

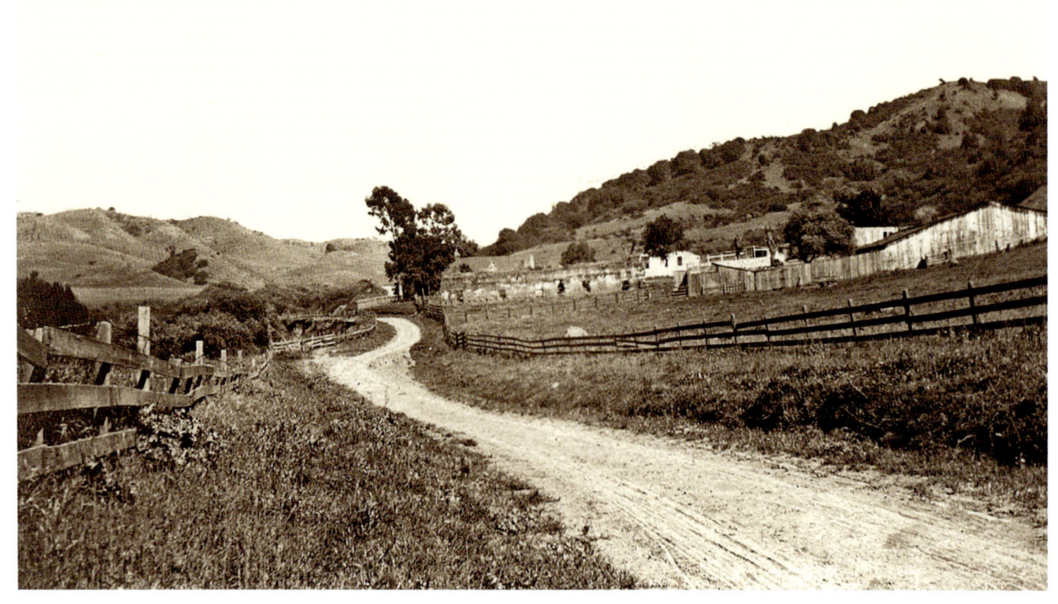

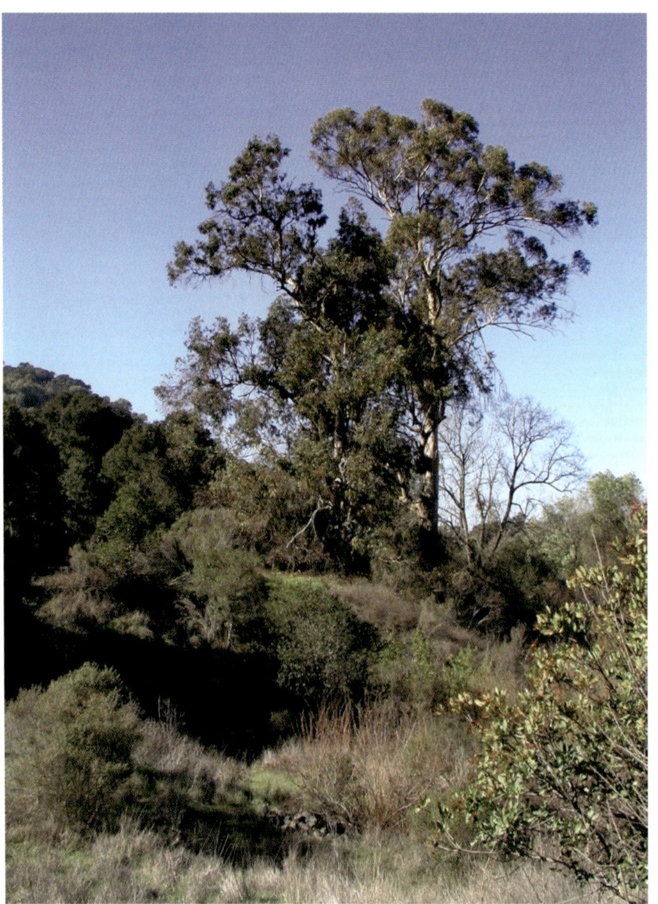

THE MARTINEZ ADOBE: Don Ygnacio Martinez, a retired Mexican military officer, built his Pinole estate on a 17,000- acre land grant he received from his government in 1823. He named his holdings Rancho El Pinole, and brought his wife, Maria Martina, and most of his 11 children to live in the large adobe home he had built there. The site now includes Pinole Valley Park and a popular walking trail on Adobe Road, which led to his home. This eucalyptus tree was planted 100 years ago by Ignacio Martinez, Don Ygnacio's grandson. It's a short walk past the dog park and the caretaker's residence.

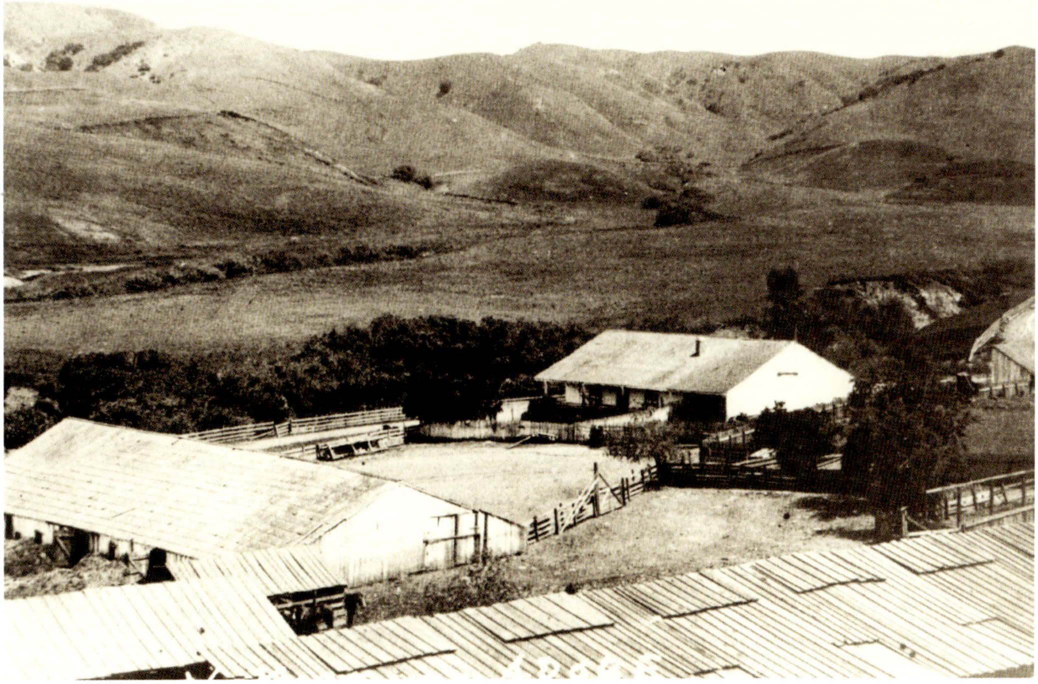

THE MARTINEZ ADOBE: Don Ygnacio Martinez and his family were called Californios, people of Spanish-speaking heritage born in California. Fewer than 100 years later, the Martinez Adobe stood in ruins and all of Don Ygnacio's land had been sold, much of it to Bernardo Fernandez. The land on which the Adobe stood is now Pinole Valley Park, with two soccer fields, a baseball field, a children's play area, and two dog parks

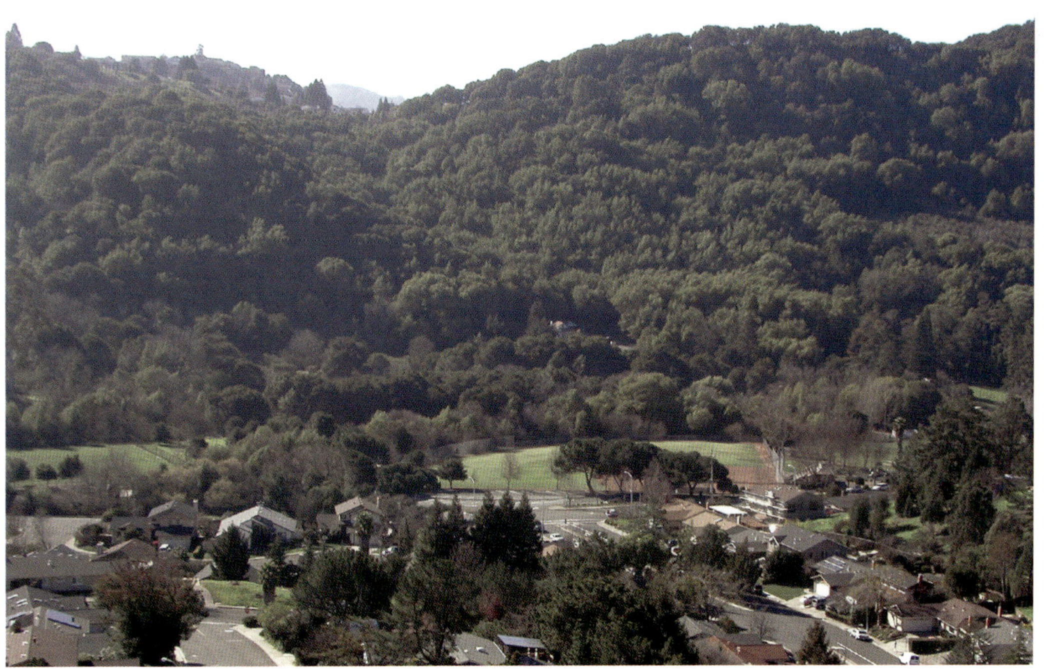

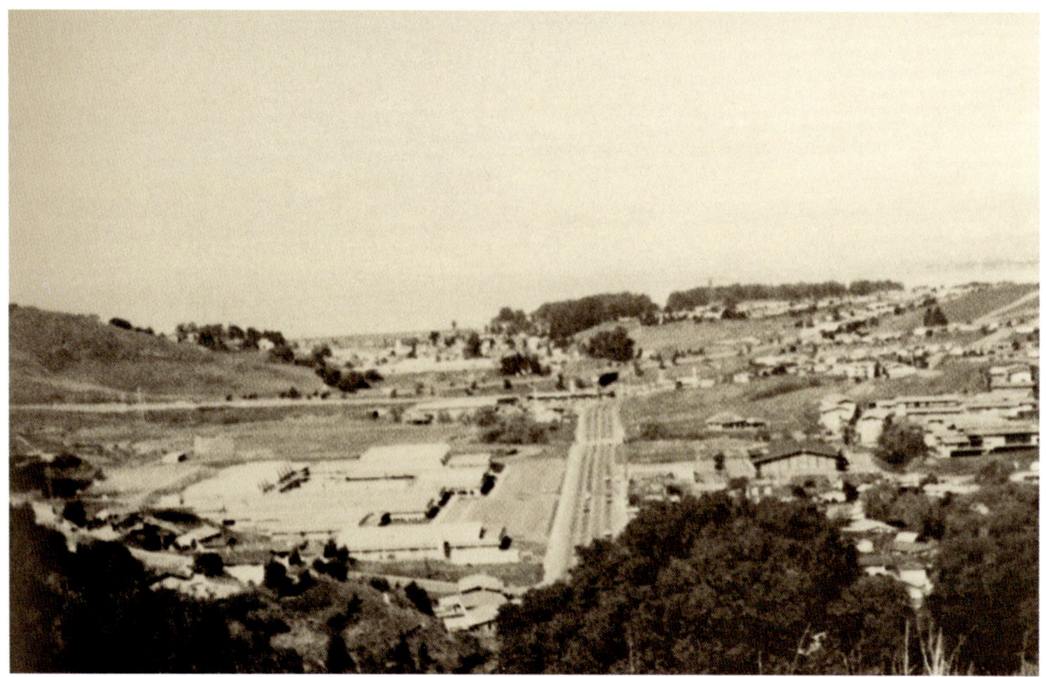

LOOKING NORTH FROM PINOLE VALLEY: The valley had little commercial development in this photo taken from the 1970 Pinole Valley High School yearbook. The high school had been open just a few years. The Lee Bros. supermarket, which had its ribbon cutting on February 16, 1960, dominated the east side of Pinole Valley Road. The supermarket is gone, replaced by a storage facility. The Pinole Library is a significant addition to the landscape, along with the remodeled Pinole Valley Shopping Center and other retail centers.

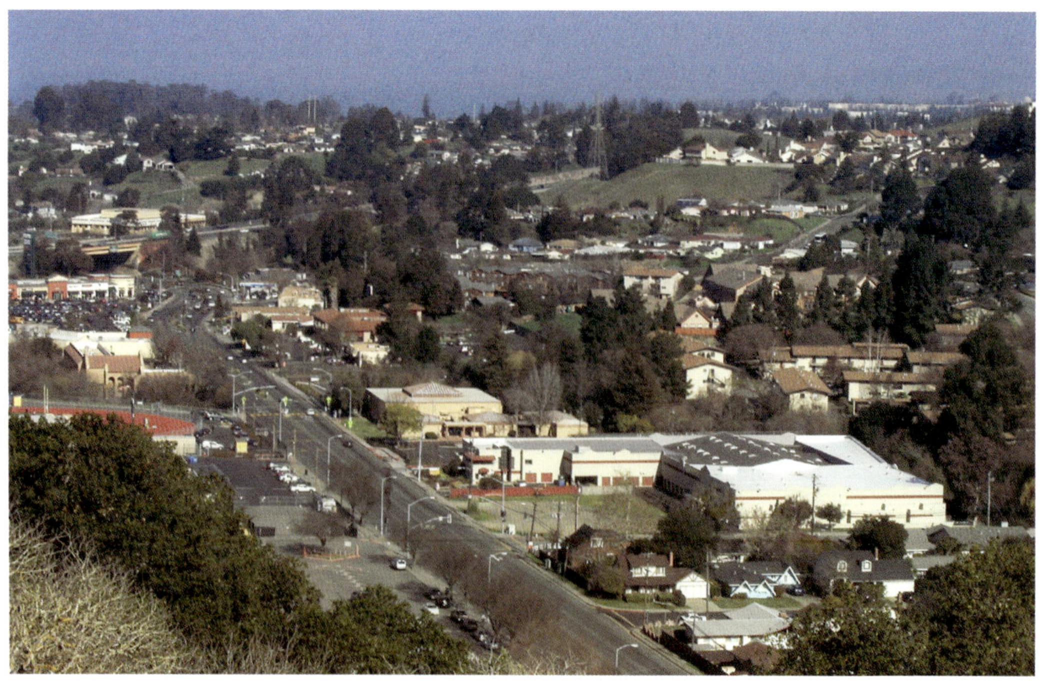

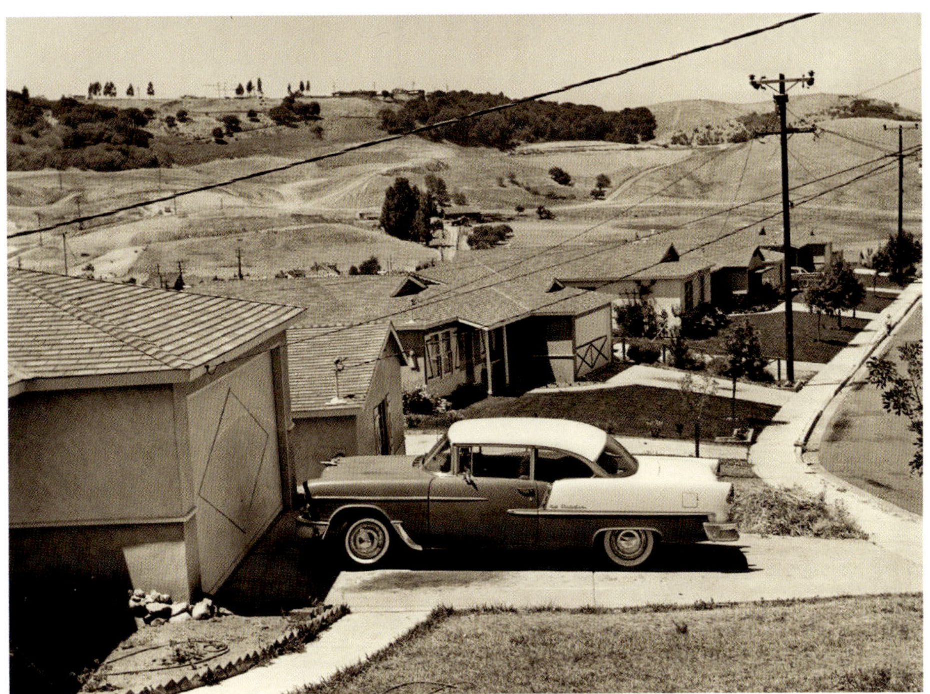

ROSE RANCH FROM PALOMA STREET: In 1961 the Pinole Estates development off Estates Avenue was among the first in Pinole Valley. New homes in the hills east of Pinole Valley Road looked down on the Rose Ranch, the future site of Pinole Valley High School and much of the commercial area that exists today. In the distant hills to the west Shea Drive and the streets perpendicular to it, along with Elizabeth Stewart Elementary School, have yet to be built.

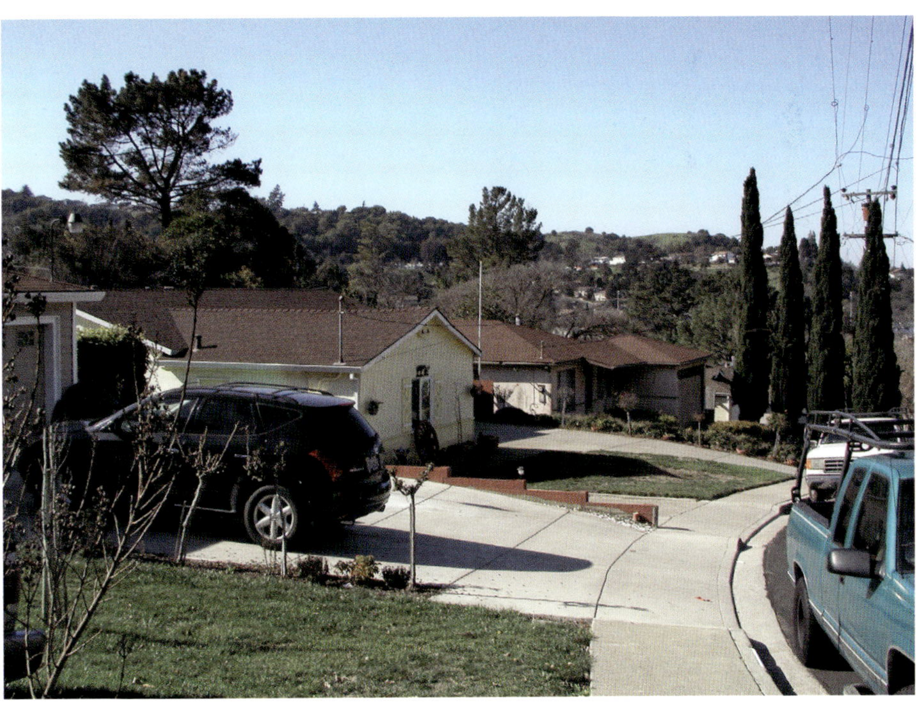

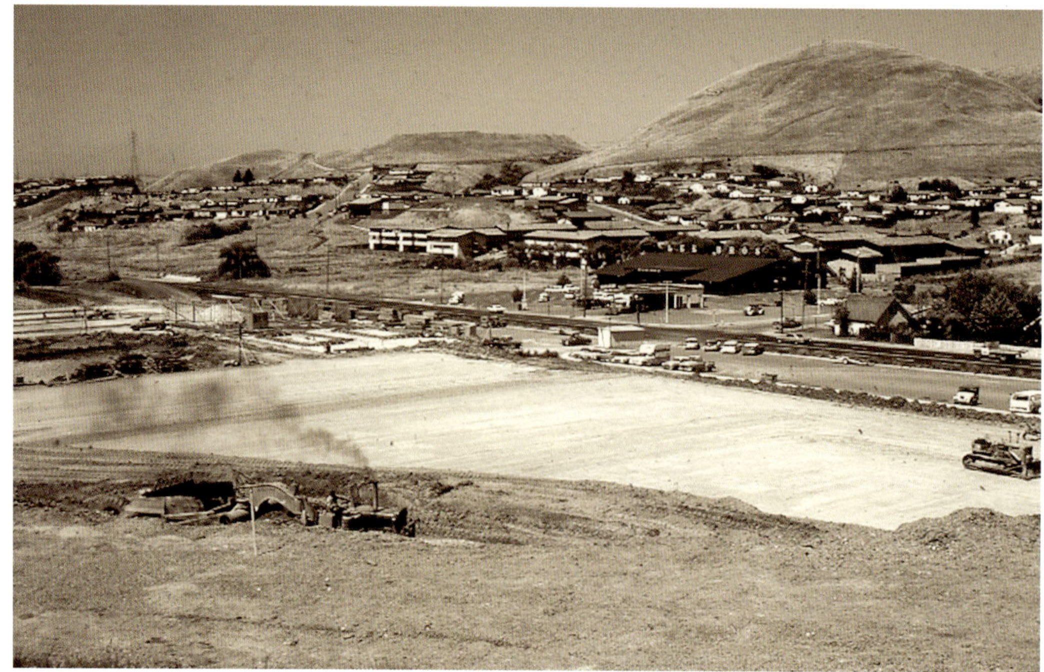

PINOLE VALLEY HIGH SCHOOL LOOKING EAST: In 1965, grading had started for the first Pinole Valley High School, which opened in 1967. There was virtually no development along Pinole Valley Road, or, for that matter, anywhere south of Interstate 80. What was a new PVHS then is now old; the demolition of the school had begun (below), courtesy of an Earl Combs photo, and a new PVHS will rise on the same site. The once-empty landscape along Pinole Valley Road is now filled with shopping centers, restaurants, a church, and the Pinole Library.

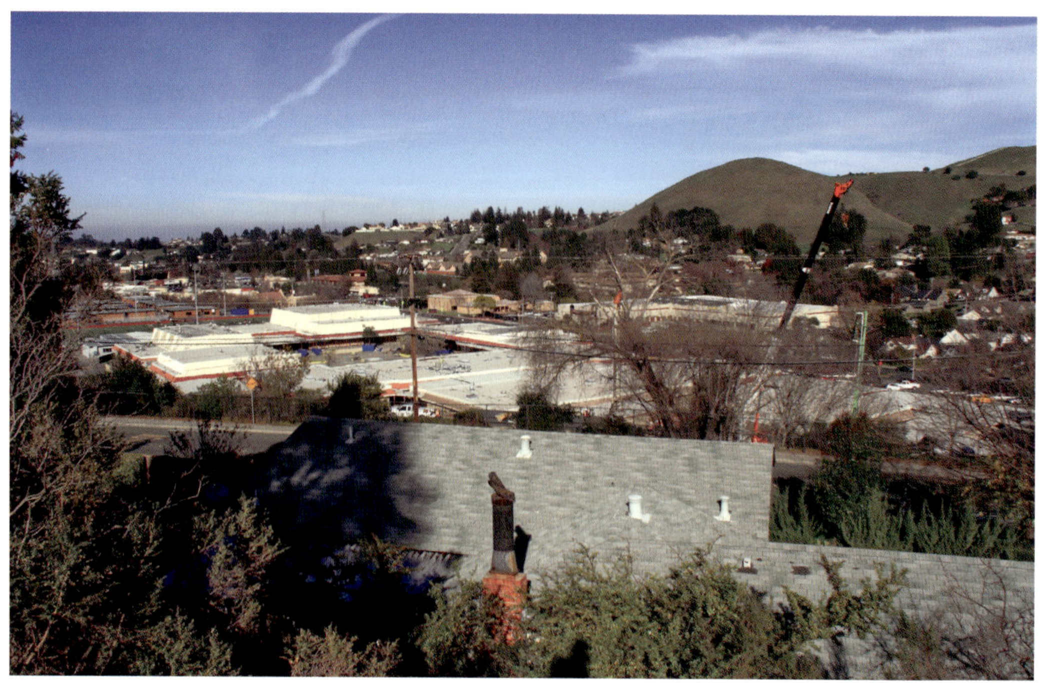

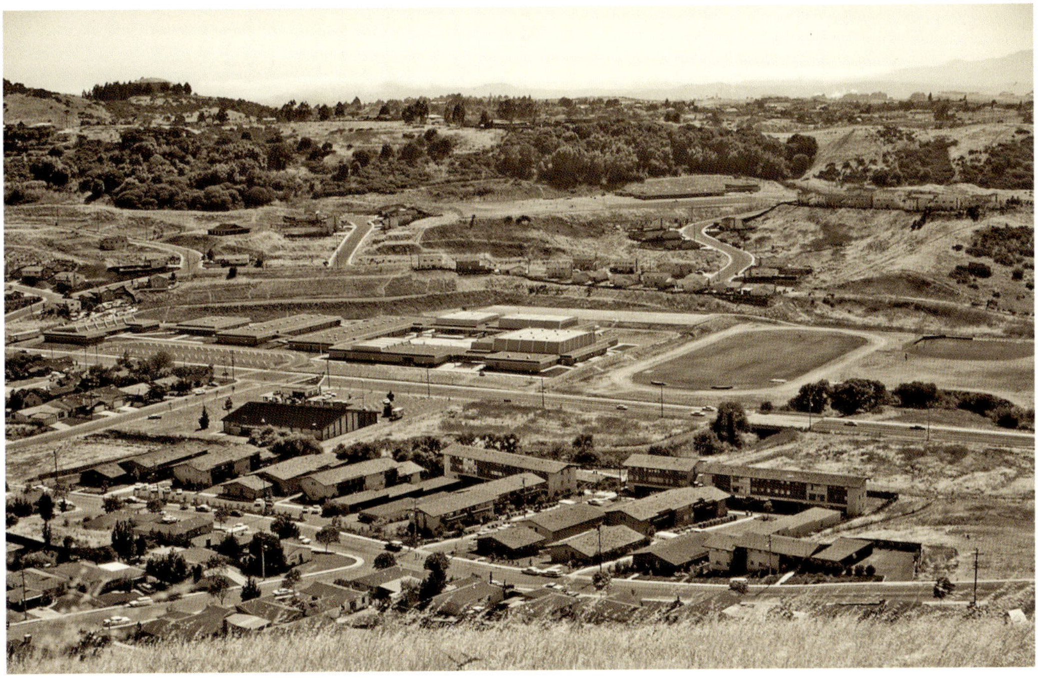

PINOLE VALLEY HIGH SCHOOL LOOKING WEST: By 1966, construction of the Pinole Valley High School campus was nearly complete, with the outline of the football and baseball fields visible in this Earl Combs photo taken from Faria Hill. The Lee Bros. supermarket is the only development on either side of Pinole Valley Road. PVHS students are now attending classes in portable buildings (center, right), as a new campus will rise after the demolition of the old school. The hills behind the school are now filled with private homes.

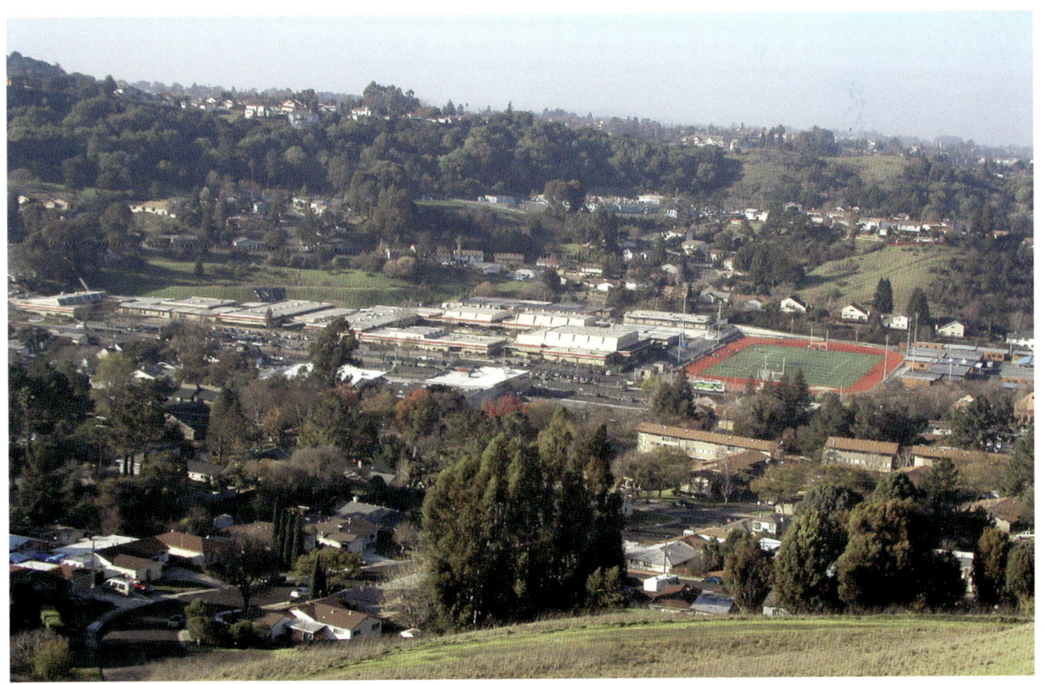

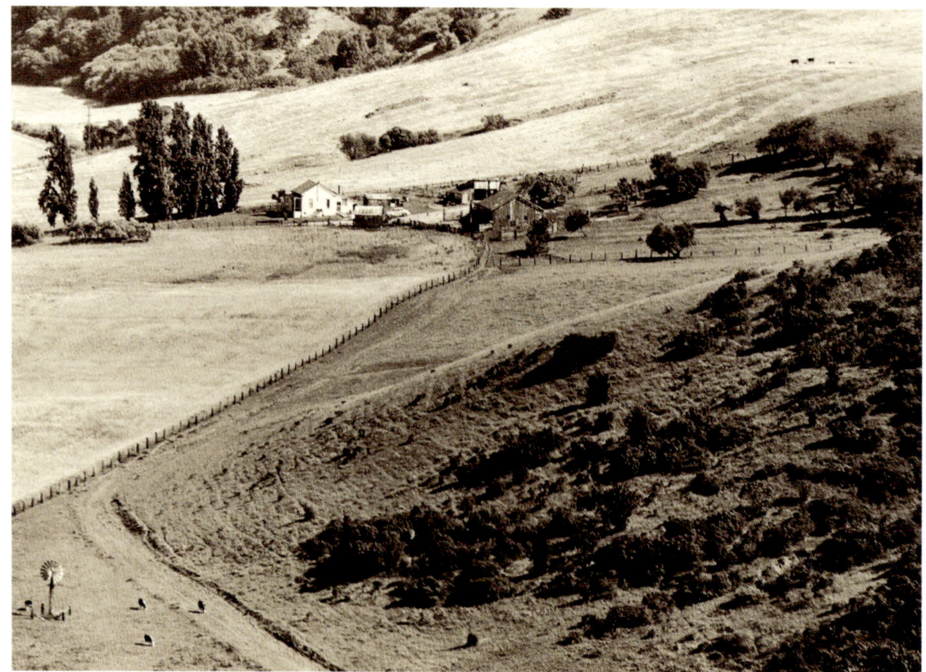

ROSE RANCH/PINOLE VALLEY HIGH SCHOOL: The Antone Rose family came to Pinole from the Portuguese Azores in the 1880s. The Roses settled one mile northwest of the old Martinez Adobe on ranch land where Pinole Valley High School sits today. Walt Peterson took this photo of the ranch in 1956, just prior to the land boom that transformed Pinole Valley into tract homes. Pinole Valley High School opened in 1967. Students are now housed in brown portable buildings next to the football field; the old campus has been demolished to make way for a new school.

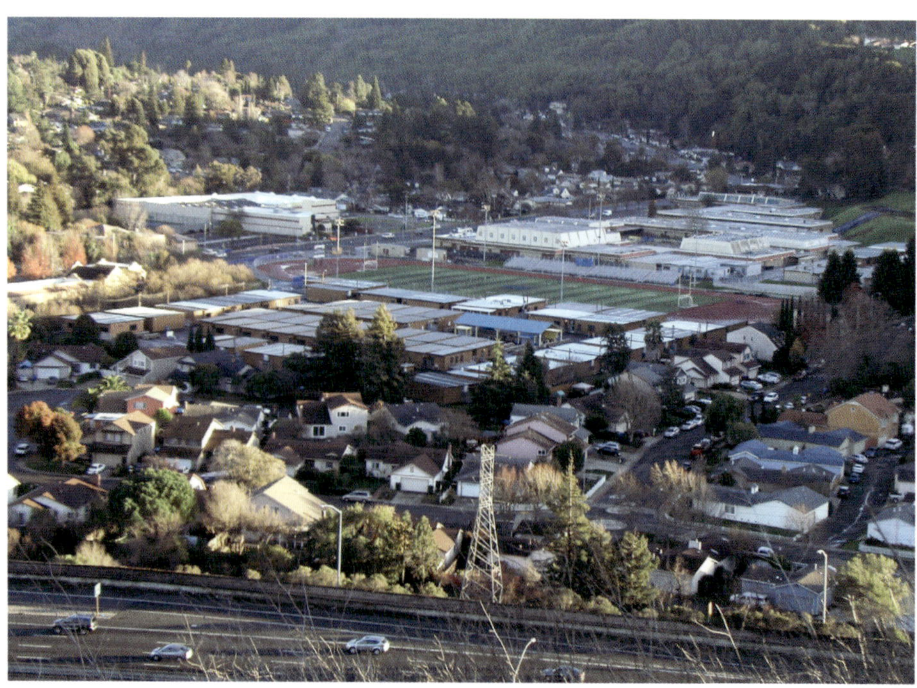

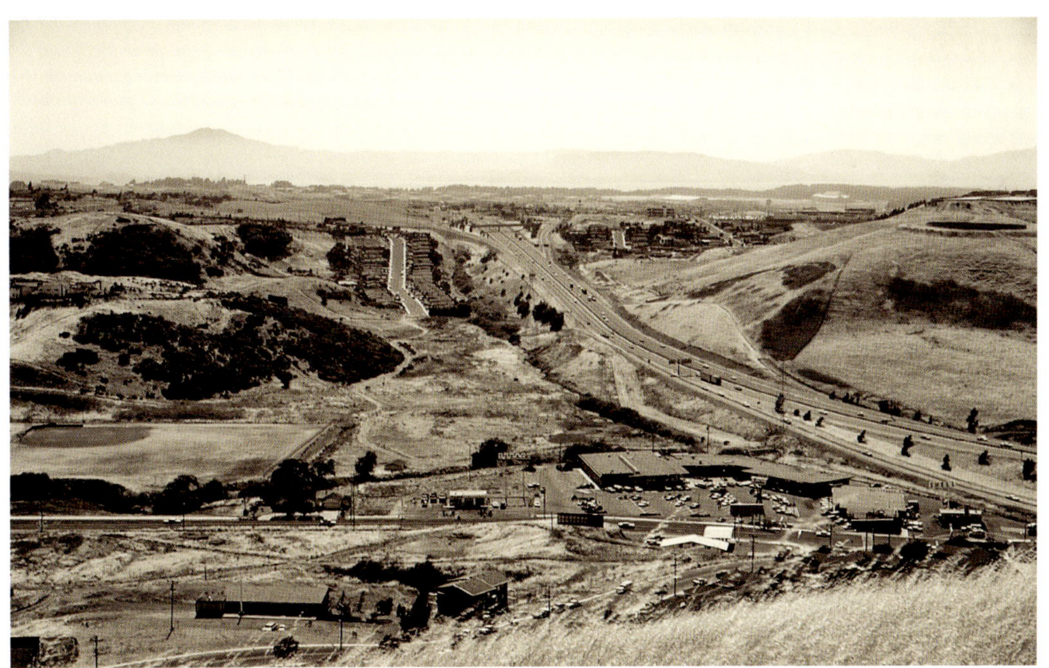

PINOLE VALLEY SHOPPING CENTER: The original Pinole Valley Shopping Center, photographed here in 1968 by Earl Combs from Faria Hill, was built in stages, from the supermarket in 1959 to the in-line stores in the 1960s. It was Pinole's first shopping destination away from the downtown area. Much of Pinole Valley Road was still undeveloped then; that would soon change, as the valley's ranches disappeared and were replaced by private homes. In 2015, a completely remodeled and expanded Pinole Valley Shopping Center is a major destination, with restaurants, Walgreens, Mechanics Bank, Trader Joe's, and specialty stores.

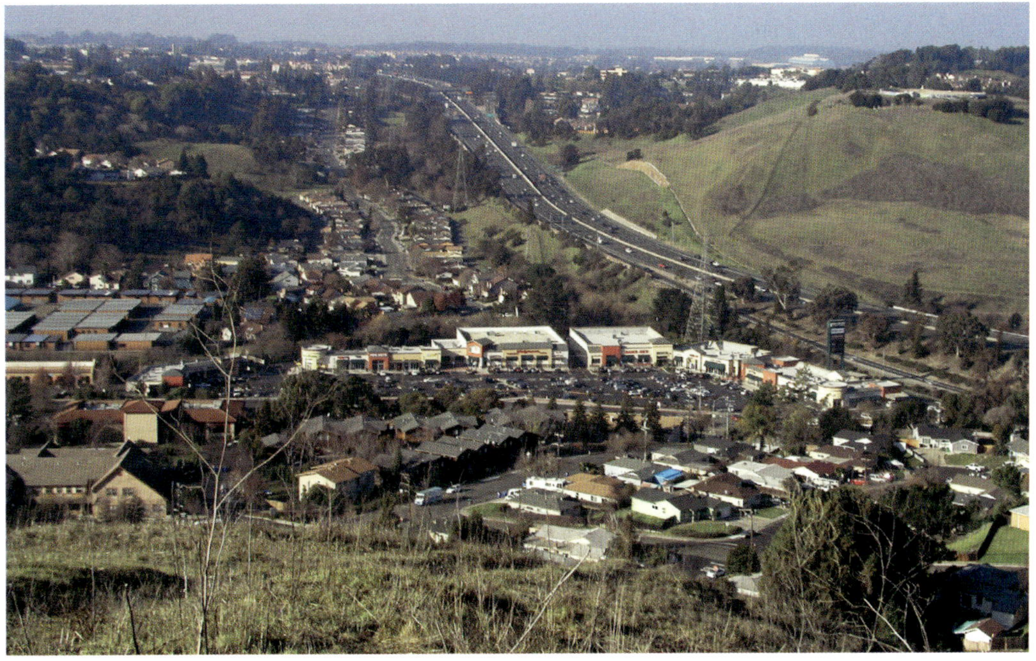

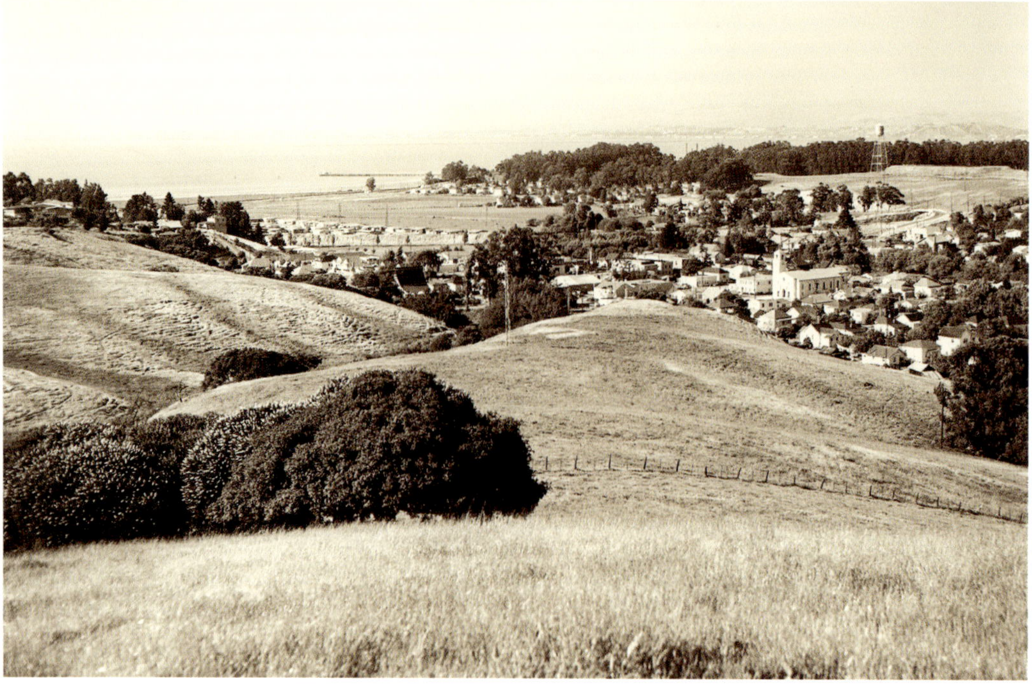

DOWNTOWN FROM MARIOTTI'S RESERVOIR: Pinole's western hills and the distant Hercules flatlands were undeveloped when this photo was taken by Walt Peterson in the 1960s from the reservoir owned by Dr. Joseph Mariotti, an orthopedic surgeon and team physician for the Pinole Valley High School football team. Lush hills gave way to single-family homes, townhomes, and condominiums in the early 1970s. Today, nearly every inch of once-vacant area in both cities has been developed.

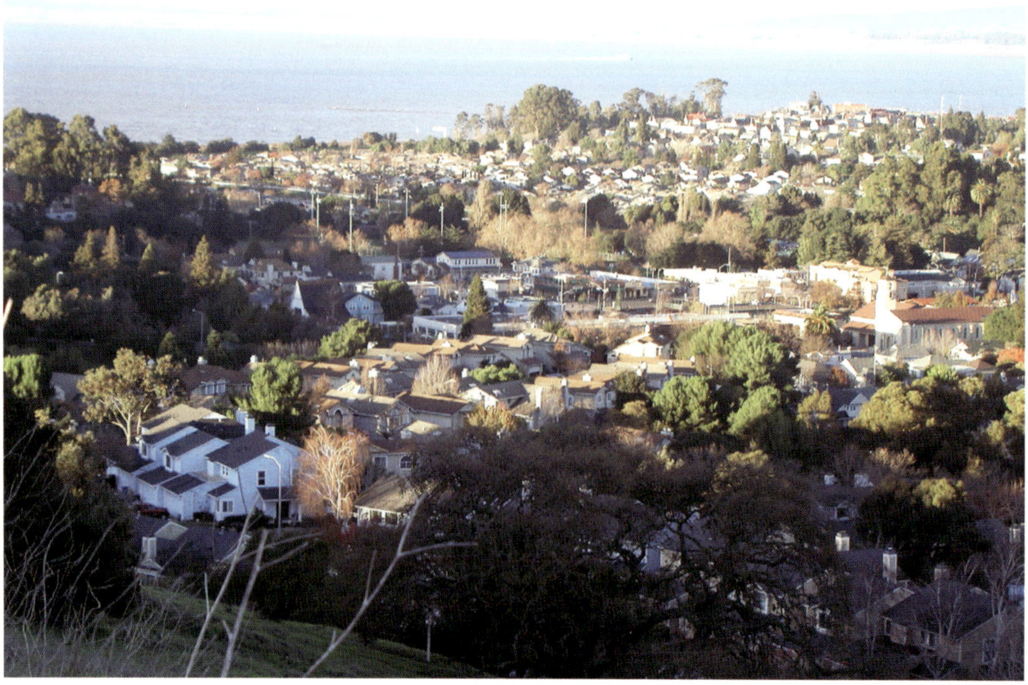

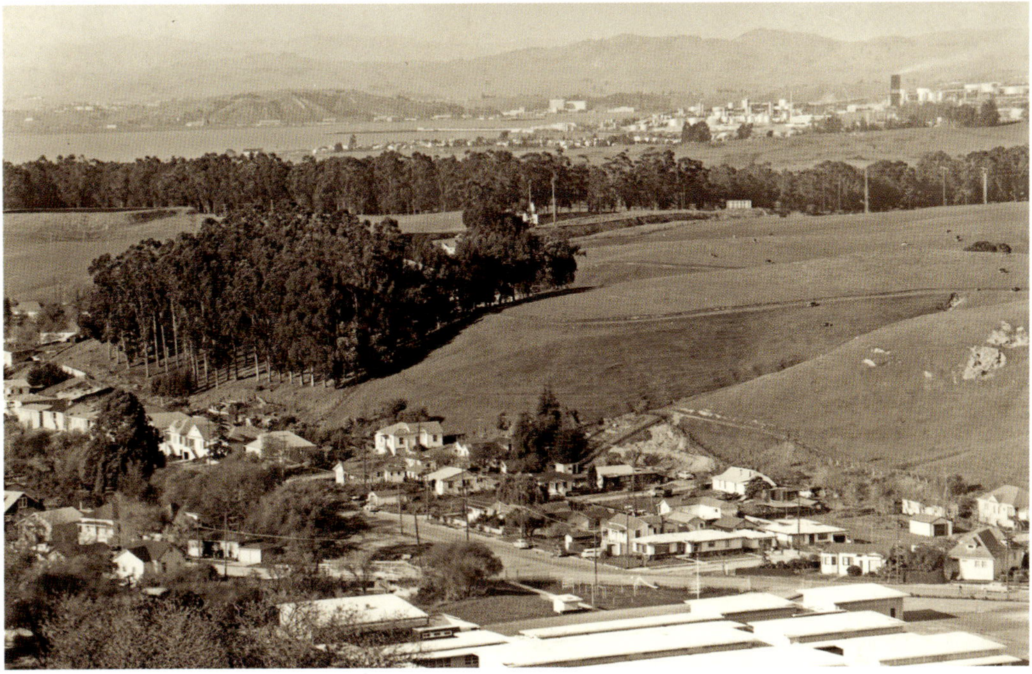

LOOKING EAST FROM MARIOTTI'S RESERVOIR: Barren hills framed the giant eucalyptus trees guarding the Pinole-Hercules School #1 in this 1960s photo taken by Walt Peterson from Dr. Joseph Mariotti's reservoir. The recently constructed Margaret Collins Elementary School, opened in 1950, is in the foreground. Though some patches of green remain, most of the hillside area is now residential, with many homes enjoying sweeping vistas of San Pablo Bay and Marin County. The eucalyptus trees that once protected the school now provide shade for Pinole Grove Senior Housing.

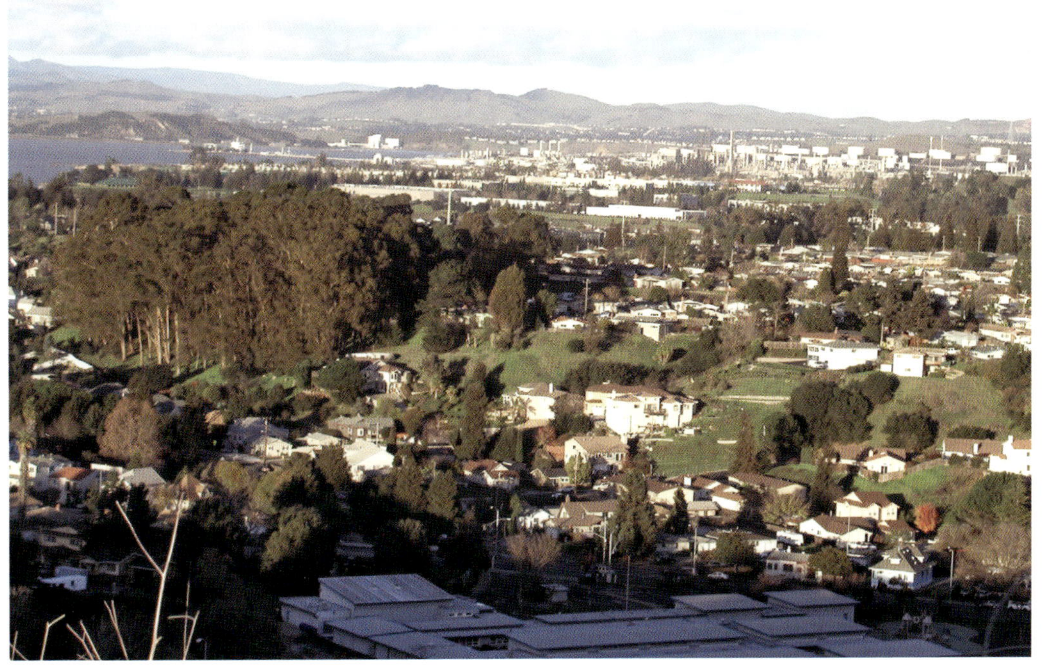

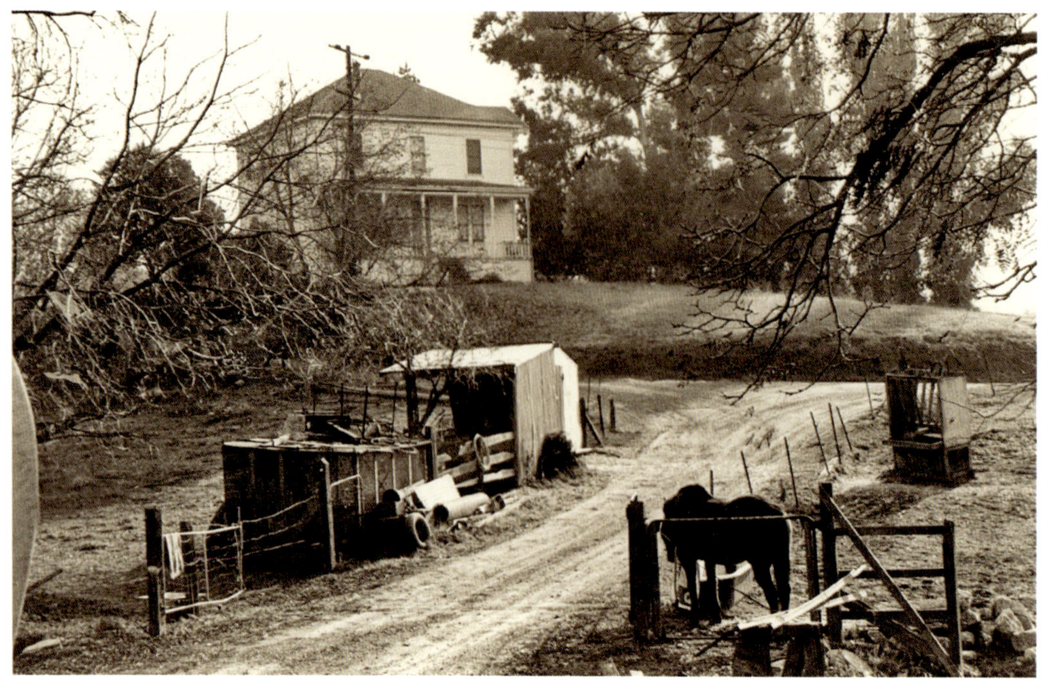

FARIA HOUSE/KAISER PERMANENTE MEDICAL OFFICE BUILDING: The Faria House is one of Pinole's iconic buildings, built in 1880 by Dr. Samuel J. Tennent as a wedding gift for his son, James. Joseph Dutra and Maria Nunes Faria, immigrants from the Azores, bought the home in the early 1900s and generations of Farias were reared here. They had eighteen children, eleven of whom survived to adulthood. The house was moved to Heritage Park in downtown Pinole in 2005 to make way for the Kaiser Permanente Medical Office Building, which opened January 12, 2009.

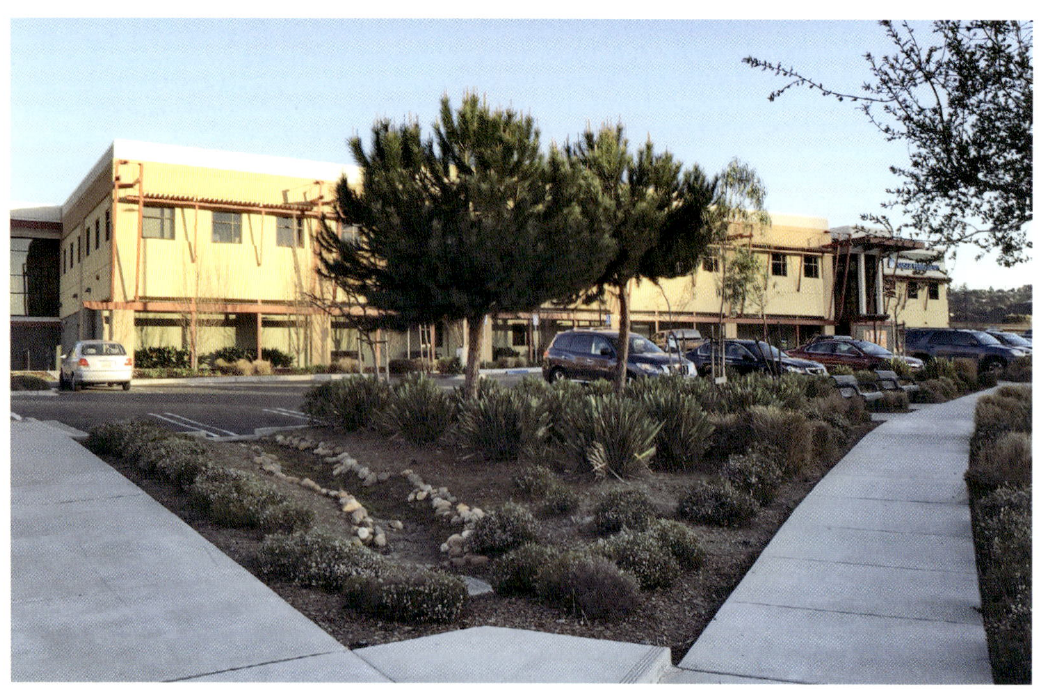

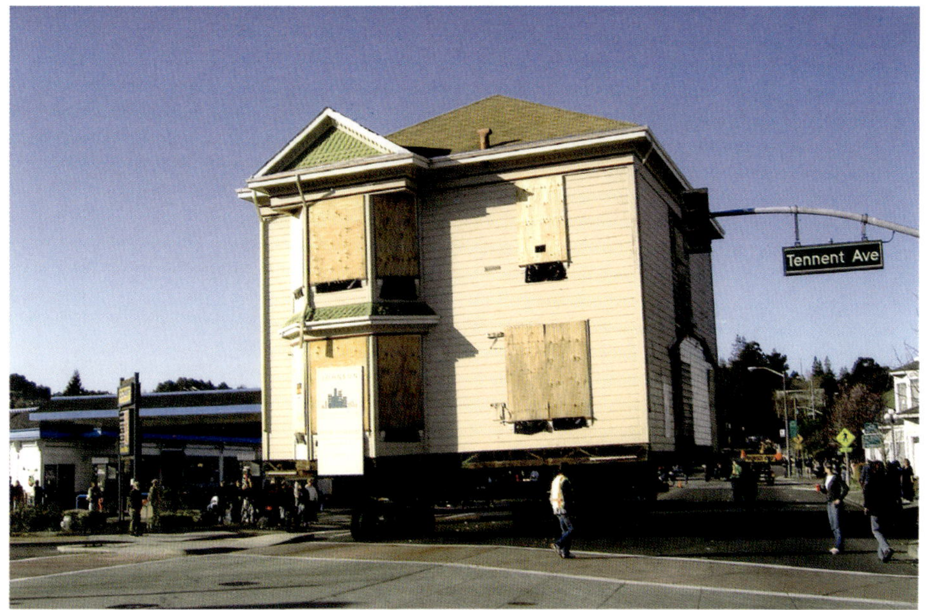

FARIA HOUSE MOVE: The move of the Faria House to downtown Pinole in 2005 was a citywide event that attracted numerous onlookers along its one-mile journey. Hoisted onto a flatbed truck, the 1880 home built for the son and daughter-in-law of Dr. Samuel J. Tennent inched its way north down Tennent Avenue before turning west on San Pablo Avenue, on the way to its new residence in Heritage Park. The vacant building, photographed by Larry Neptune, was recently painted, and the Pinole Garden Club tends to its rose bushes.

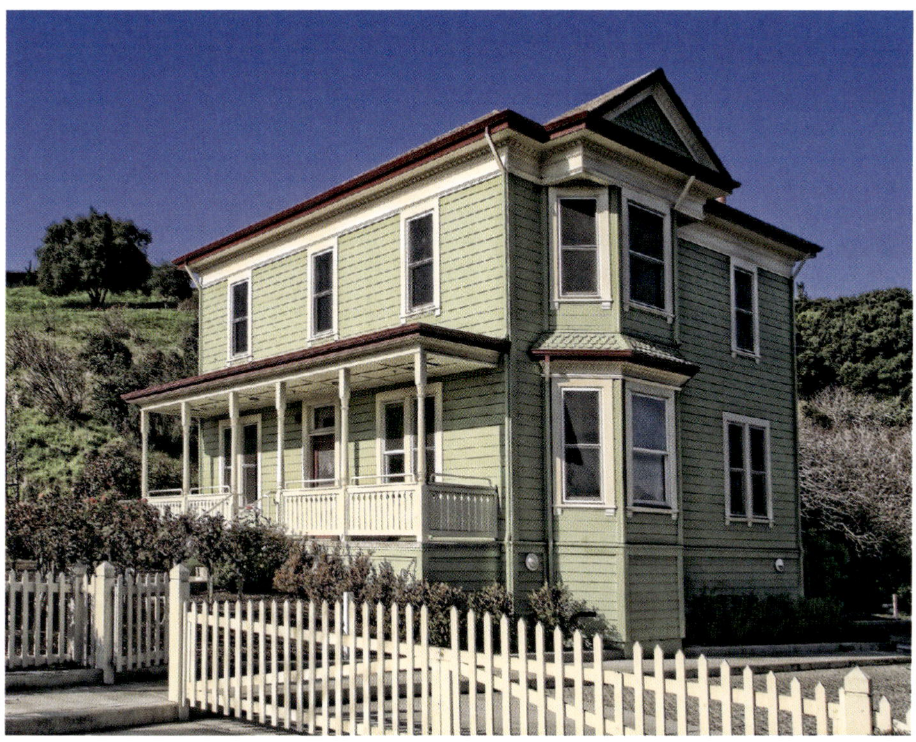

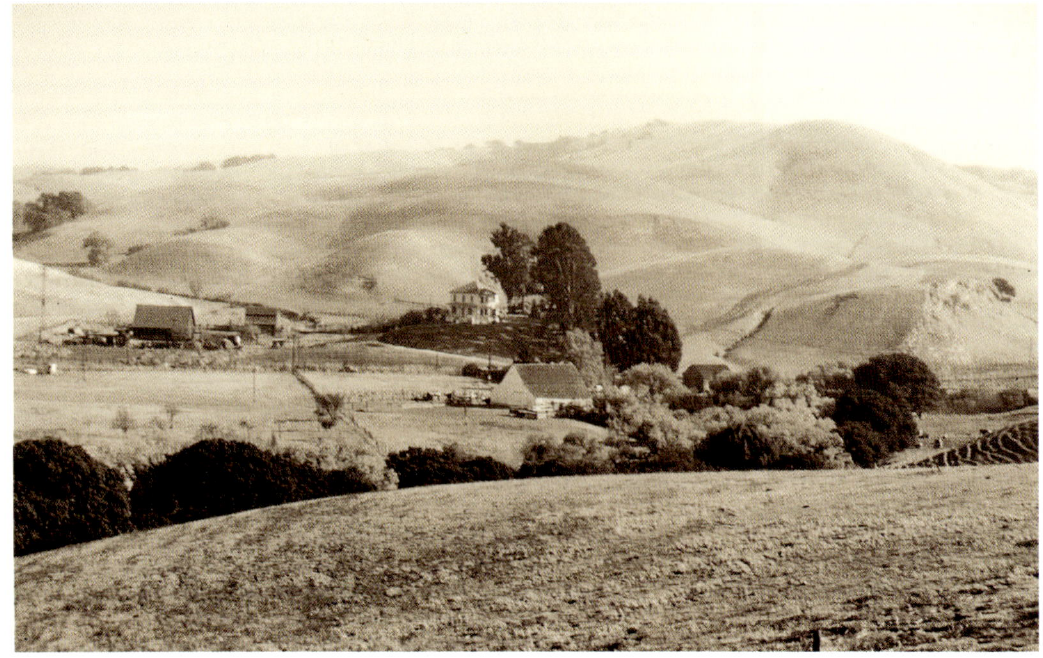

Cessilini and Faria ranches: The Tennent/Cessilini ranch (foreground) was across Pinole Valley Road from the Faria House and ranch (background). It was part of El Rancho Pinole and was 1/11th of the rancho inherited by Rafaela Martinez after Don Ygnacio Martinez's death in 1848. Rafaela married Dr. Samuel J. Tennent in 1849, and a year later they returned to the site and built the first frame home in Pinole. Bill Faria raised dairy cows on his parents' ranch in the 1920s and 1930s. He was a tomato farmer in the Willows Flats in Hercules in the 1940s and a cattle rancher in the 1950s. A Kaiser Permanente Medical Office Building occupies the Faria site today.

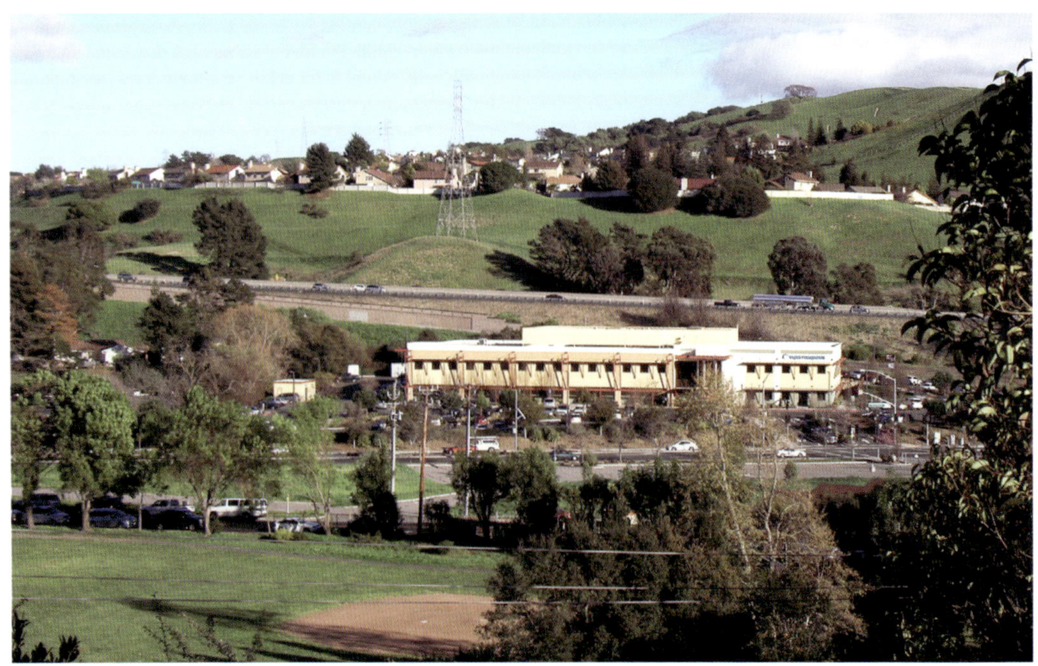

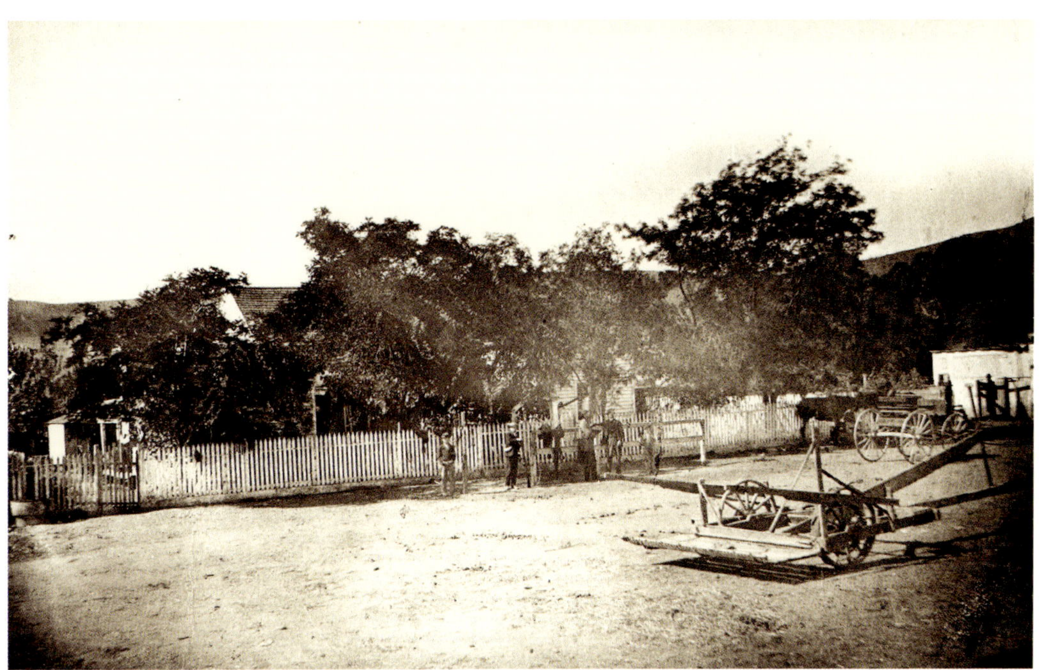

TENNENT/CESSILINI RANCH: Dr. Samuel J. Tennent's descendants sold the property in the early twentieth century and the original house was taken down. The ranch was a dairy for the Joe Silva family. Jimmy Cessilini married Silva's daughter, Albertina, and a Spanish-style home was built in the 1920s. The ranch and orchard extended into present-day Pinole, with the large barn used for storing bales of hay needed to feed their many horses and livestock in the winter. The bunkhouse behind the home and slaughterhouse remained with the barn into the 1980s. Pinole Lanes, a bowling alley, occupies the south end of the ranch property in 2015.

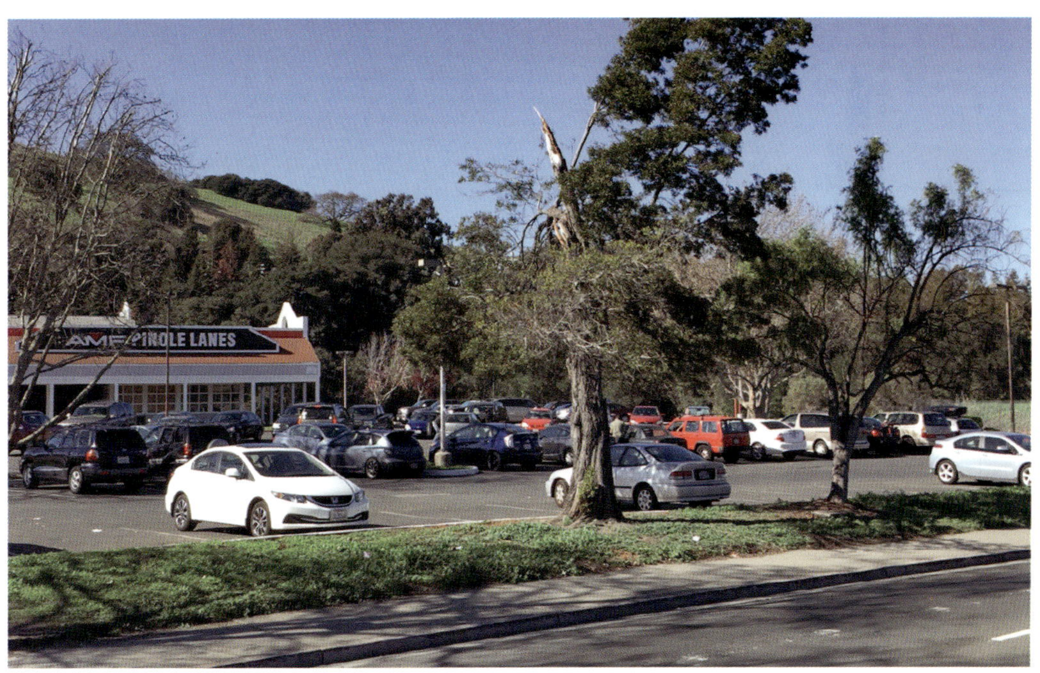

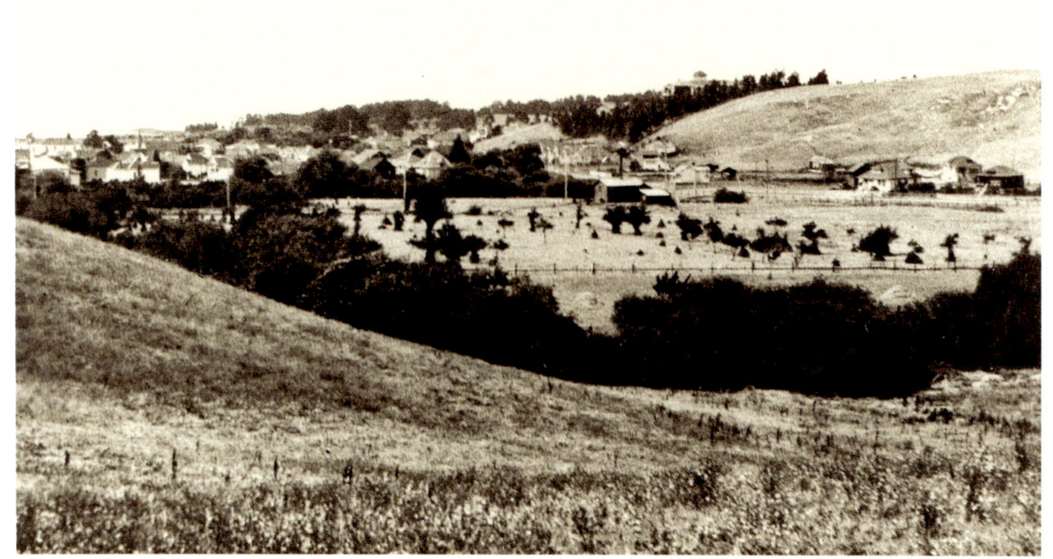

PINOLE VALLEY ROAD FROM HENRY AVENUE: Pinole began to spread south from its main downtown area as its population grew and homes were built along Pinole Valley Road. The Pinole-Hercules School #1, the Old School, can be seen behind a grove of eucalyptus trees, but Linda Heights just below and to the right of the school, had yet to be developed in the 1930s, when this photo was taken from what would become Henry Avenue, named for Henry Ellerhorst, a member of a pioneering Pinole family. Margaret Collins School, homes on the hills, and a trail along Pinole Creek dominate the landscape in 2015.

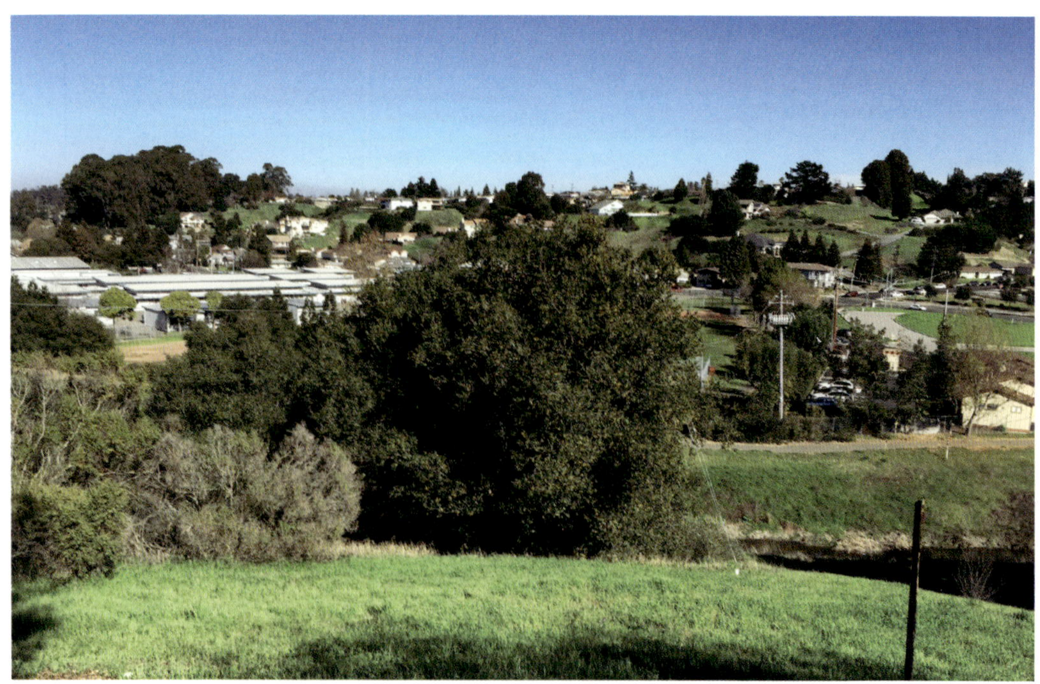

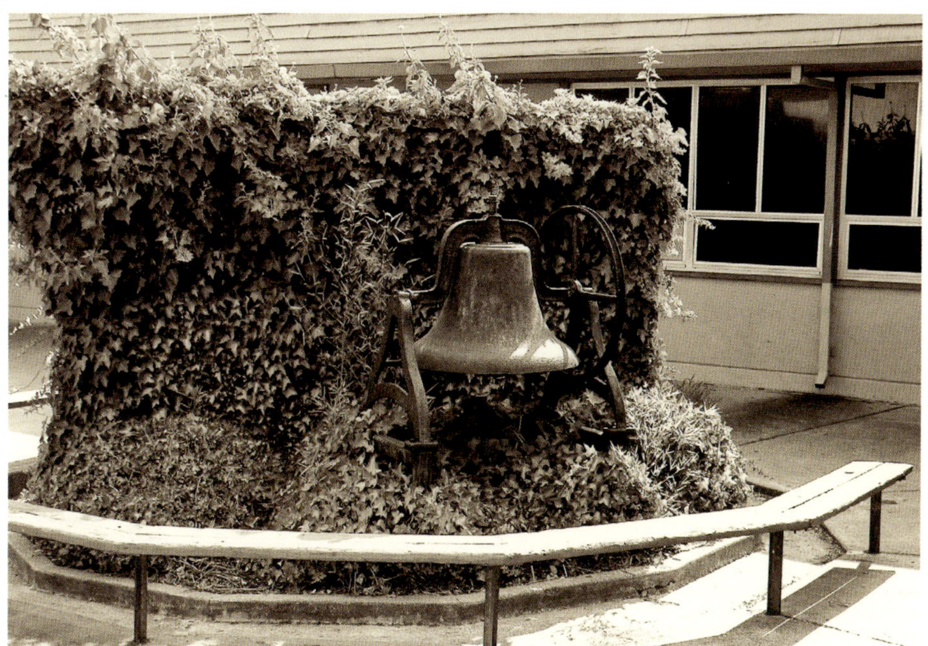

PINOLE-HERCULES SCHOOL #1 BELL: Manufactured by The C. S. Bell Co., of Hillsboro, Ohio, it is the last remnant of the school that rang generations of students to class from 1906 to 1966. The school was demolished in 1968. Its 2014 installation at Collins Elementary School concluded a five-year effort by the Pinole Historical Society to have the bell refurbished and displayed for the public to enjoy, as it is here by several of the school's graduates. The West Contra Costa Unified School District rescued the rusted and pock-marked bell from its outdoor location at Pinole Middle School and stored it until late 2013, when the district had it sandblasted, power-coated with a satin black finish, and sealed.

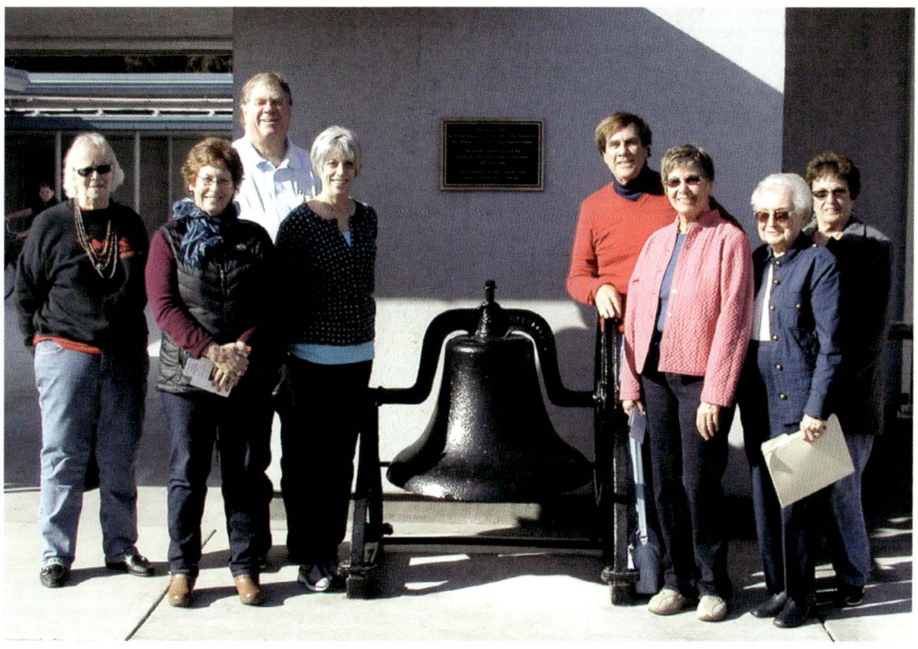

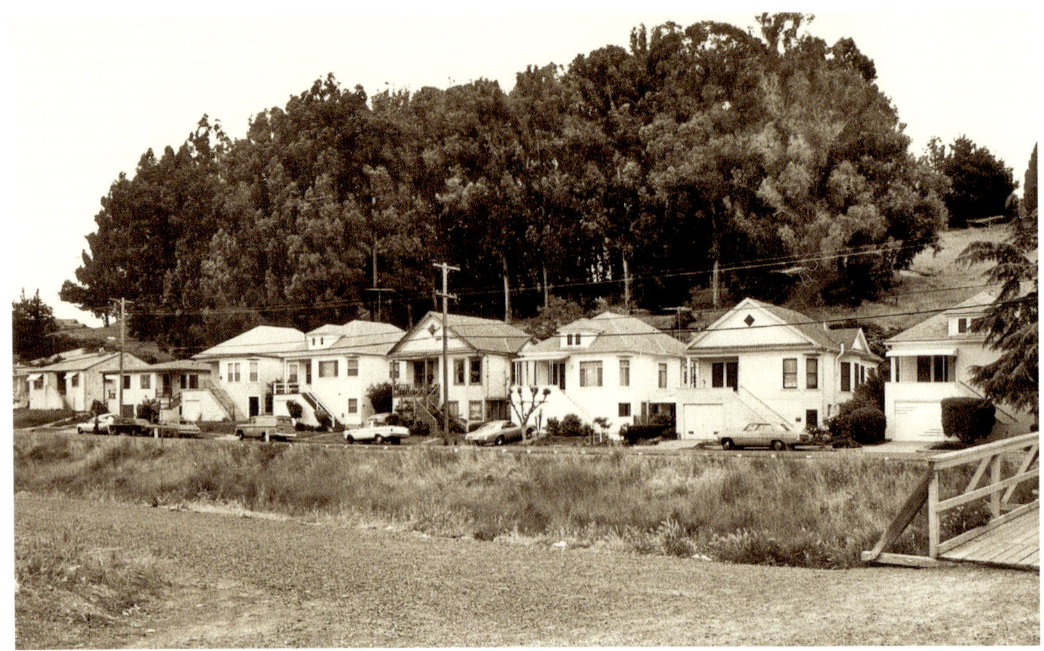

BRANDT COTTAGES: Along the east side of Pinole Creek along Valley Avenue at the foot of School Hill are the six Brandt cottages. Carolyn Sybil Meineke Brandt owned the land and commissioned a local builder to build these six cottages in 1906. Brandt and her husband, Frederick, owned ranch property extending to today's Fosters Freeze and Green Lantern, north to Pinion Avenue and the Sportsman's Club and Santa Fe tracks. After Frederick's death, Carolyn sold the ranch to the Buckley family, moved to downtown Pinole, and had these two-bedroom dwellings built. They were nicknamed "honeymoon cottages," and rented for $15 a month. These are among Pinole's most well-known preserved homes from the turn of the twentieth century.

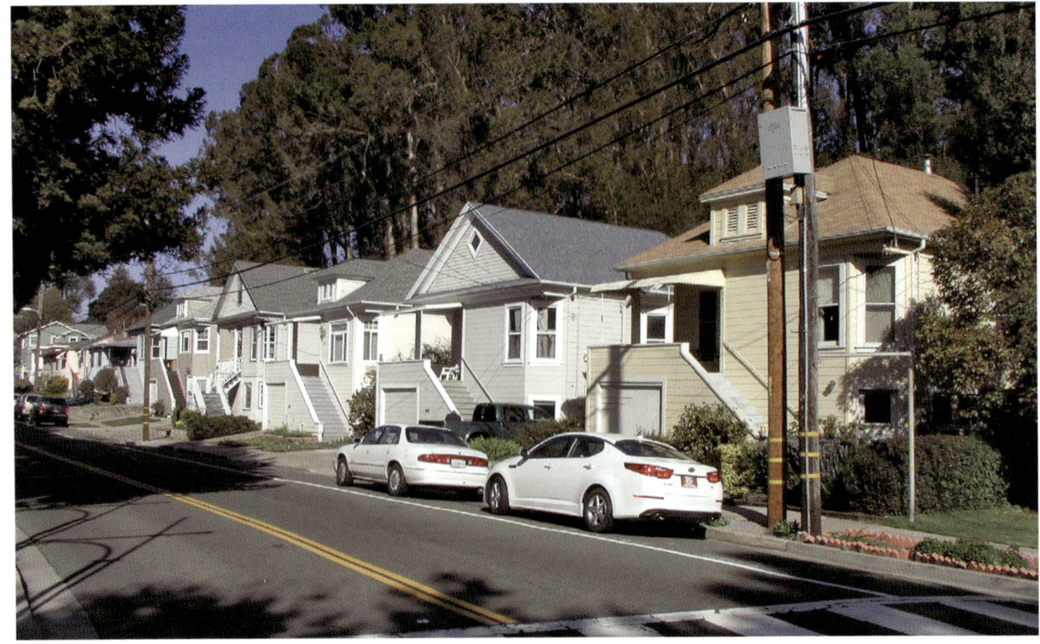

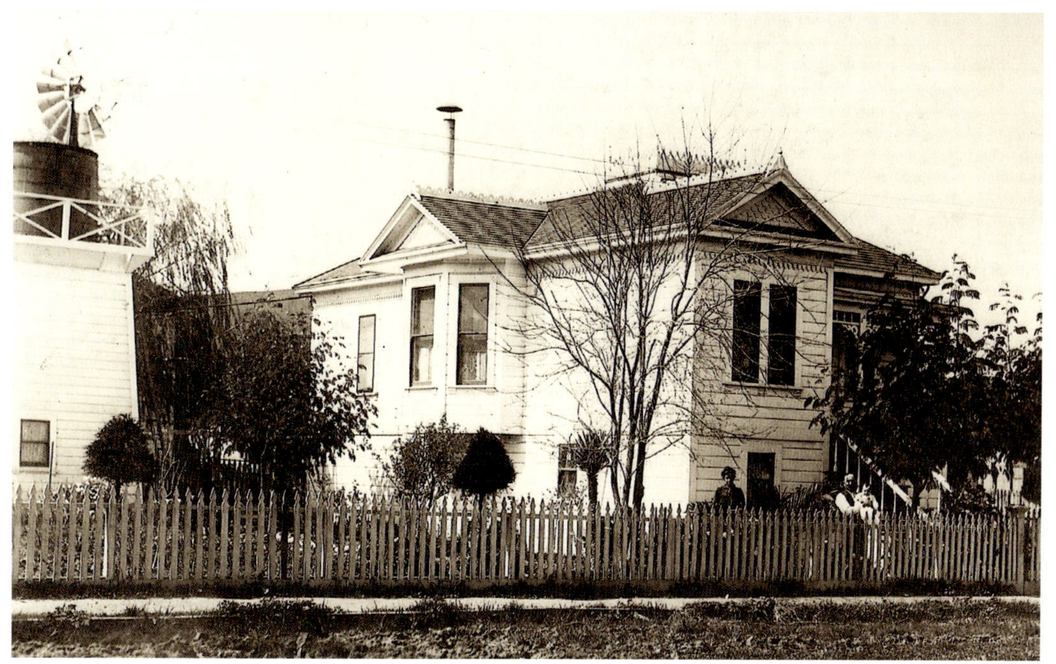

DALESSI HOME: John and Mary Dalessi (shown here in 1908 with their son, John) raised their three children on the corner of Tennent Avenue and Peach Street (1108 Tennent). John was born in Switzerland in 1863 and his native tongue was Italian. He immigrated here in 1882. Mary was born in California in 1878. John worked as a stableman at the California Powder Works, and later was a truck driver for the Hercules Powder Company. This Italianate-style home with a roof fence was typical of the architecture of the late 1870s and 1880s. Their three children attended the Pinole-Hercules School on the Hill. The Dalessi home was demolished, and a new home was built on this site.

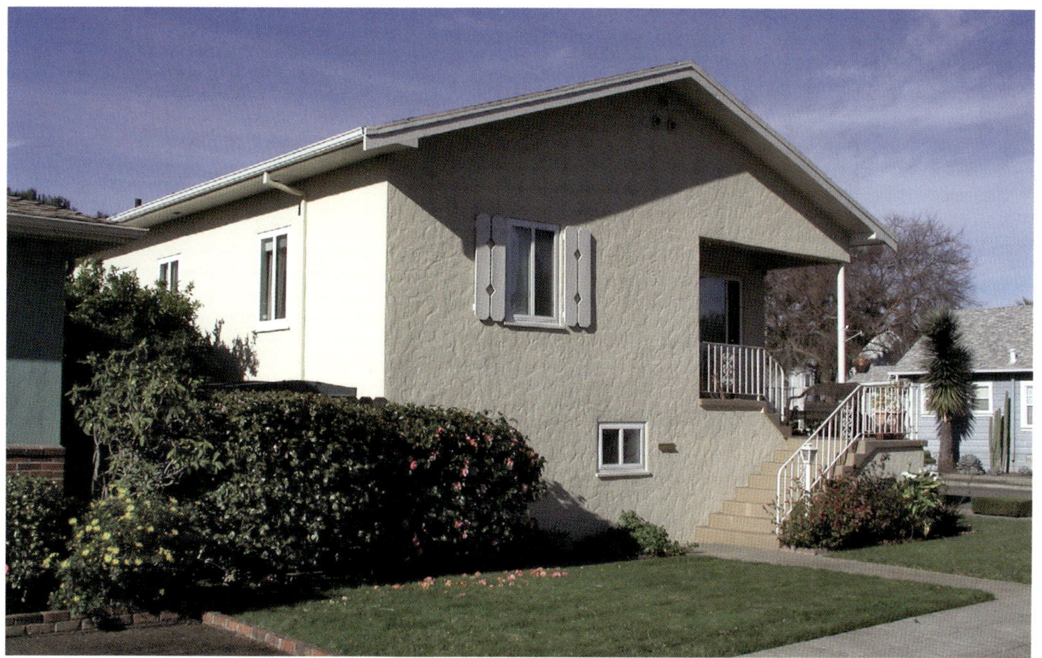

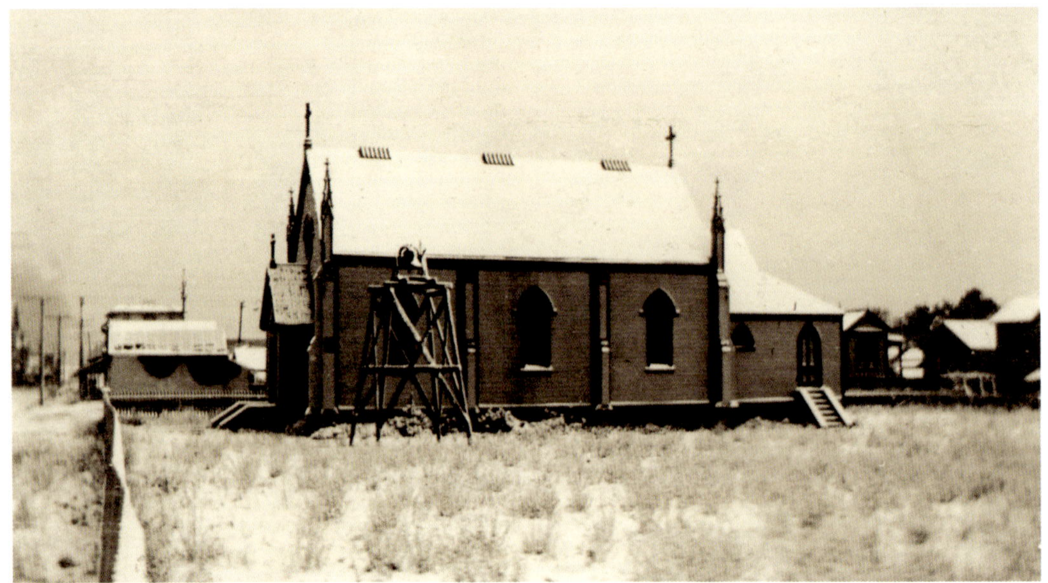

ST. JOSEPH CHURCH: The original, gothic revival-style wooden Catholic church was built in 1881 on land donated by Samuel and Raphaela Tennent. The buzzing of bees that made their homes in the walls bothered parishioners; when the church was torn down and a church rectory was built on that site, thirty pounds of honey were retrieved from the wood. A new, mission-style church opened in 1951. Many of the stained-glass windows of St. Joseph Church in this Larry Neptune photo are historical markers to the Portuguese influence in Pinole. The colorful "in memoriams" bear the names of Fernandez, Faria, Marcos, and Costa, as well as one gift of glass donated by the Portuguese organizations of Pinole.

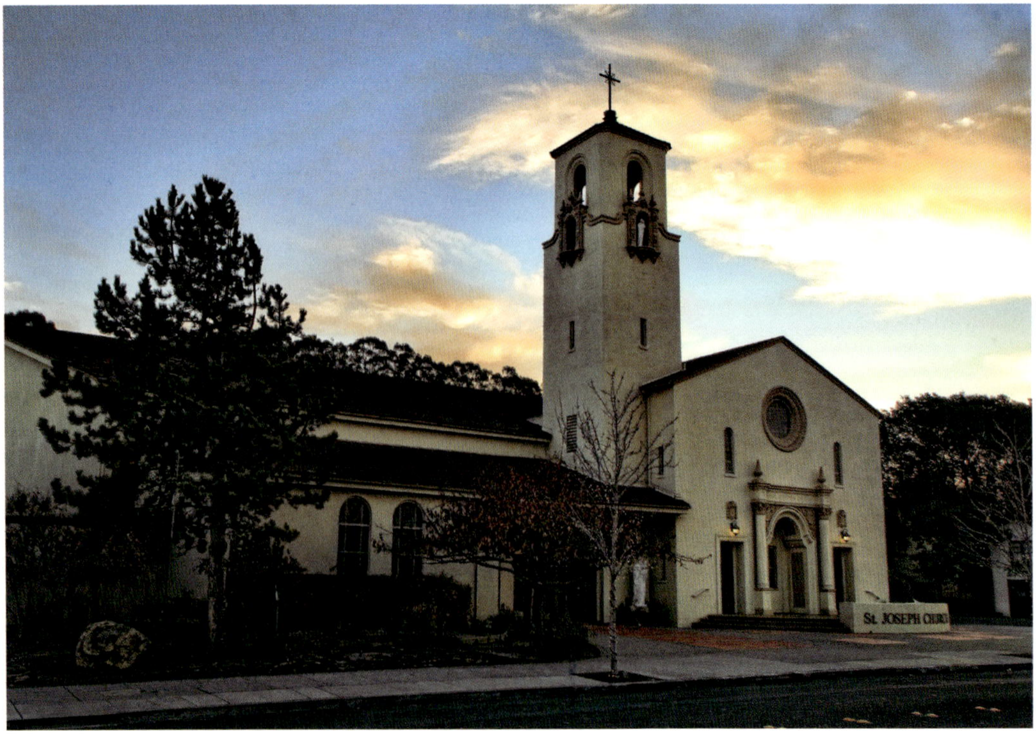

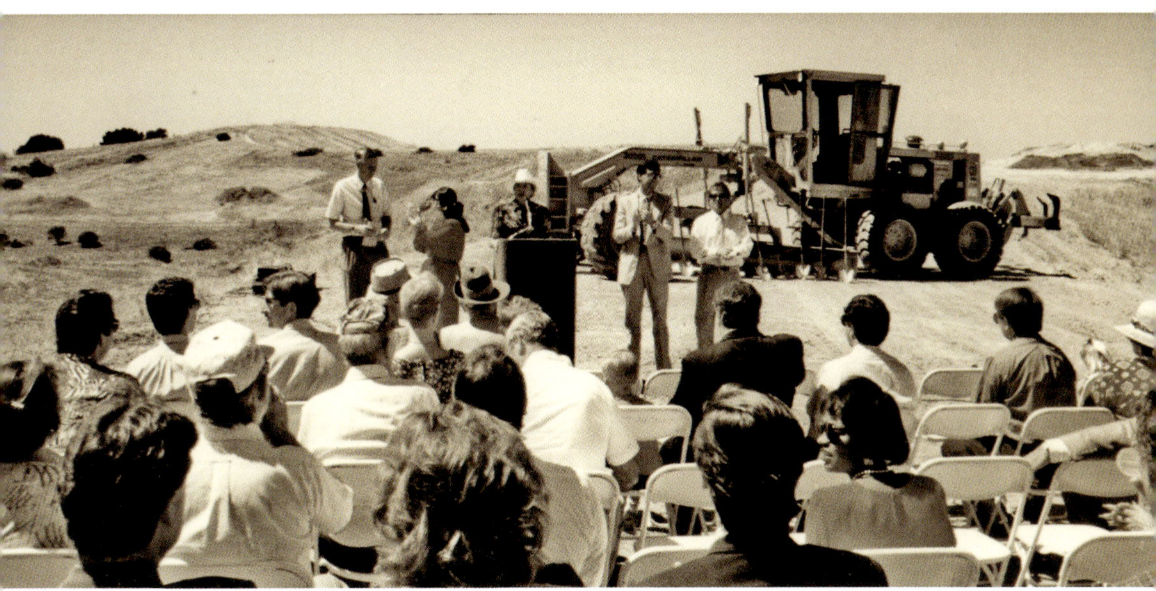

PINOLE VISTA CROSSING: Ground broke for Pinole Vista Crossing, the final development phase along Fitzgerald Drive, on June 25, 1993. The completed center opened in November 1996. The city of Richmond, realizing the economic potential of unincorporated land from Appian Way to the Richmond border, tried to annex it in the 1970s. A group of resistant voting residents blocked Richmond's efforts to acquire key properties that controlled access from Appian Way, which was in Pinole. Pinole annexed the land and Richmond, thwarted by Pinole loyalists, turned to Chevron's Tank Farm Hill, resulting in Hilltop Mall.

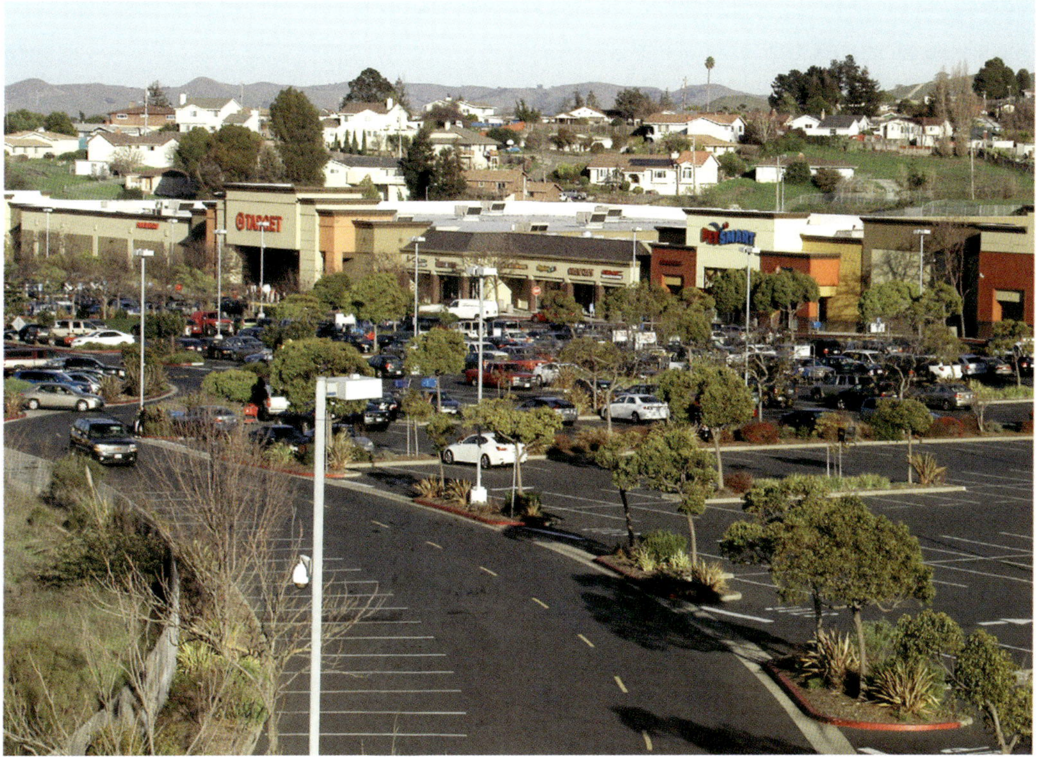

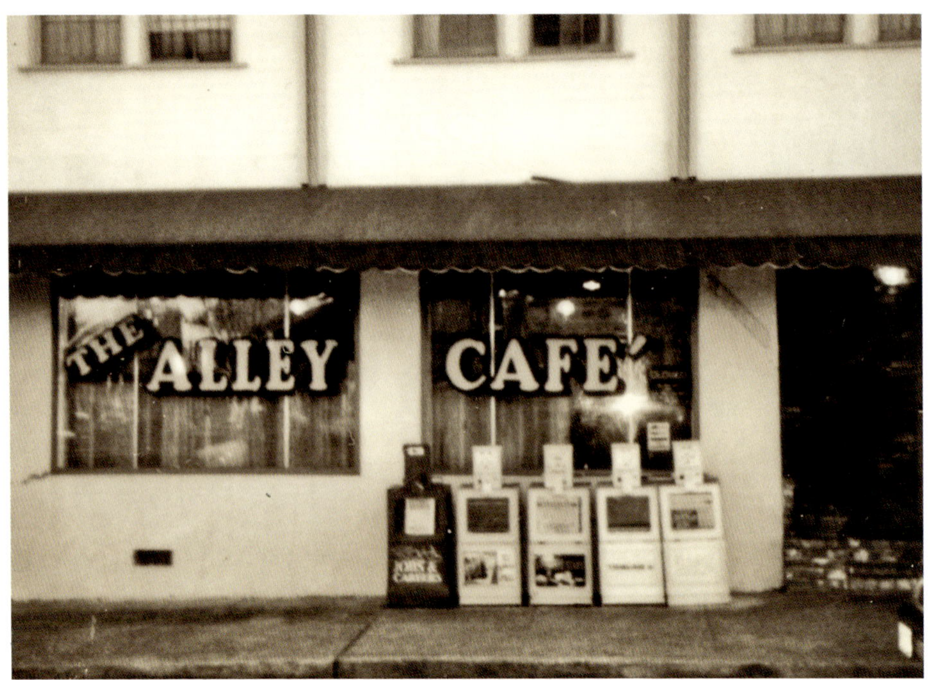

THE ALLEY CAFÉ: This breakfast/lunch restaurant has been a fixture in Pinole since 1962, when former Fire Chief Alex Clark and his friend, Bob Dutra, bought the former Greenfield's Department Store building. They sold the café, reacquired it, and then sold it again. Cori Clark's father, Dave Brandt, bought it in 1978 after the previous owner died. Cori Brandt worked for her father in the restaurant as a waitress; Dave was the cook. When Dave died in 1992, Cori (Brandt) Clark, by this time married to Alex Clark's son, Chano, took over, and was there until June 2015.

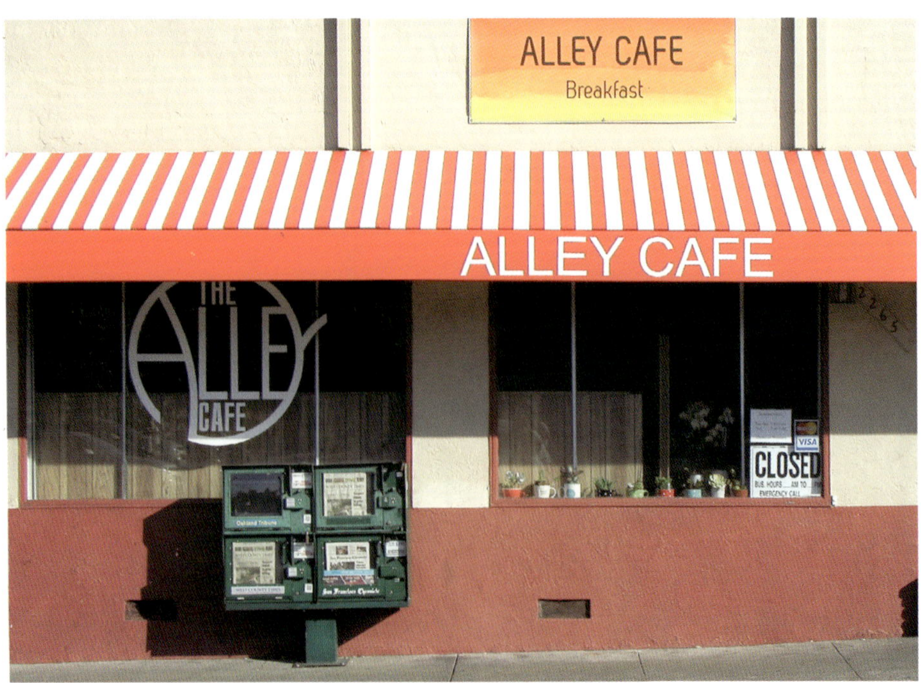

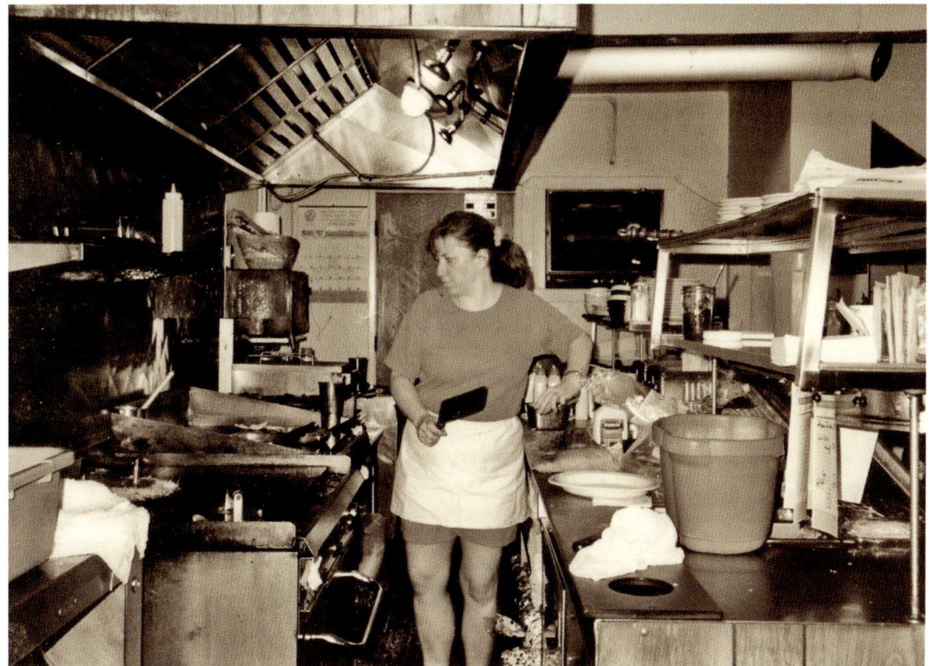

THE ALLEY CAFÉ: Not much changed at The Alley Café, including the food and the cook, until June 2015, when Cori Clark sold the restaurant. Cori fed generations of area residents, many of them who remember her fondly on Facebook. As one Facebook writer commented about the enormous portions of hash brown potatoes Cori serves: "She throws them down, oils them up, and fries the dickens out of them before they hit your plate piping hot!" Another wrote: "Where else is there only one cook for over 40 people? Cori is the bomb!"

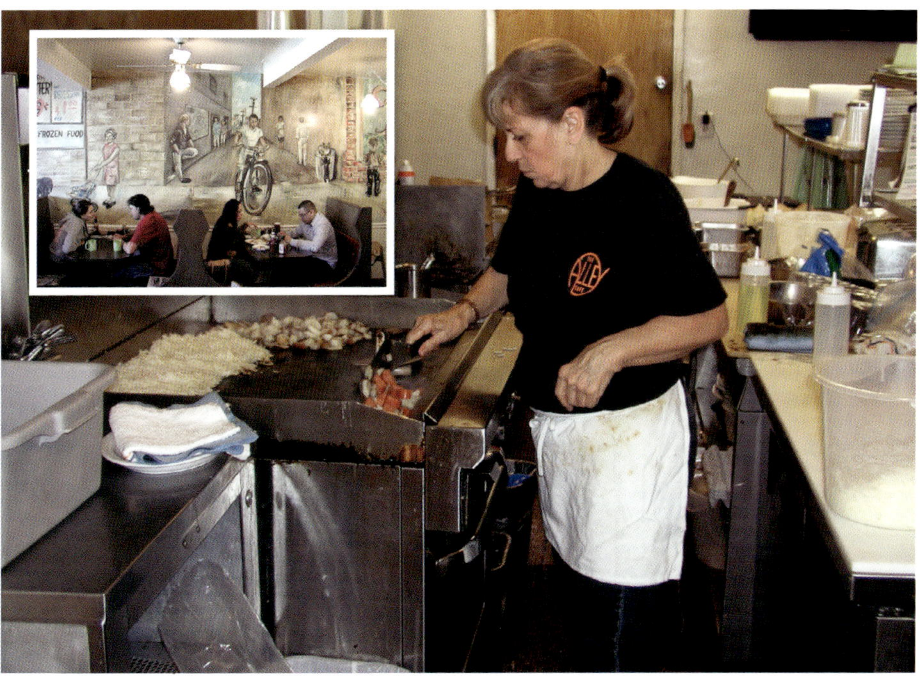

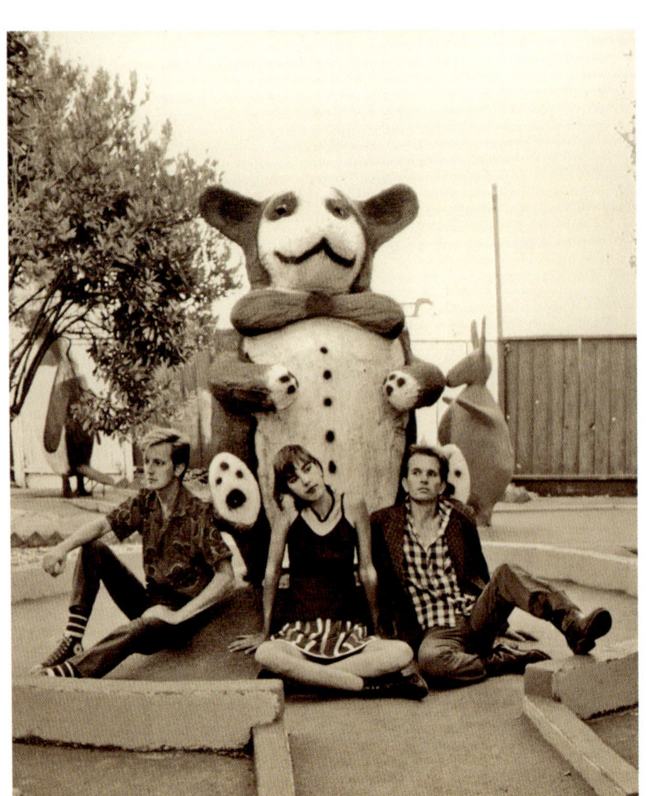

Pinole Midget Golf: For decades the playful and somewhat scary concrete creatures—Tyrannosaurus Rex, penguin, kangaroo, rooster, gorilla, giraffe, spider in a web, snake, and giant rat, etc.—greeted players at Pinole Midget Golf on San Pablo Avenue at the west end of the city. Musician Bruce Rayburn (far right), of the rock band Charm World, along with band members Greg Baker and Sally Engelfried, posed for this Harold Parish photograph that appeared on the back of Charm World's album. The heavy animals were hauled away when the property was sold in 1989—the T-Rex on a bulldozer in this photo from the *West County Times*.

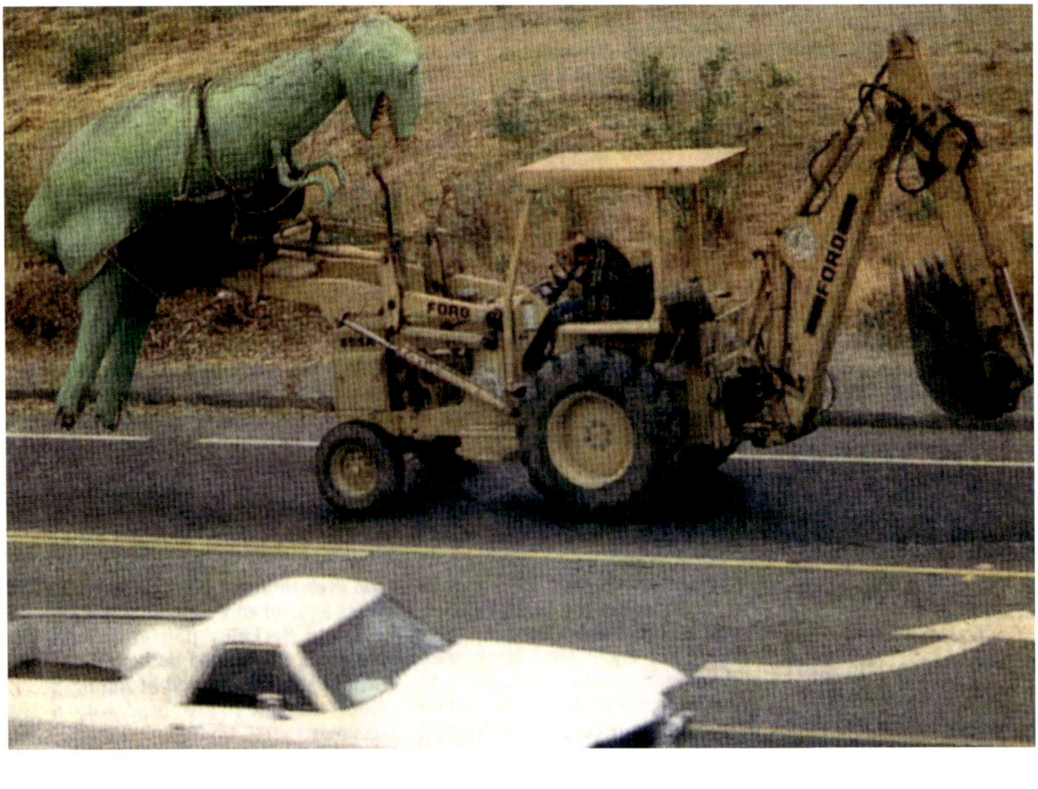

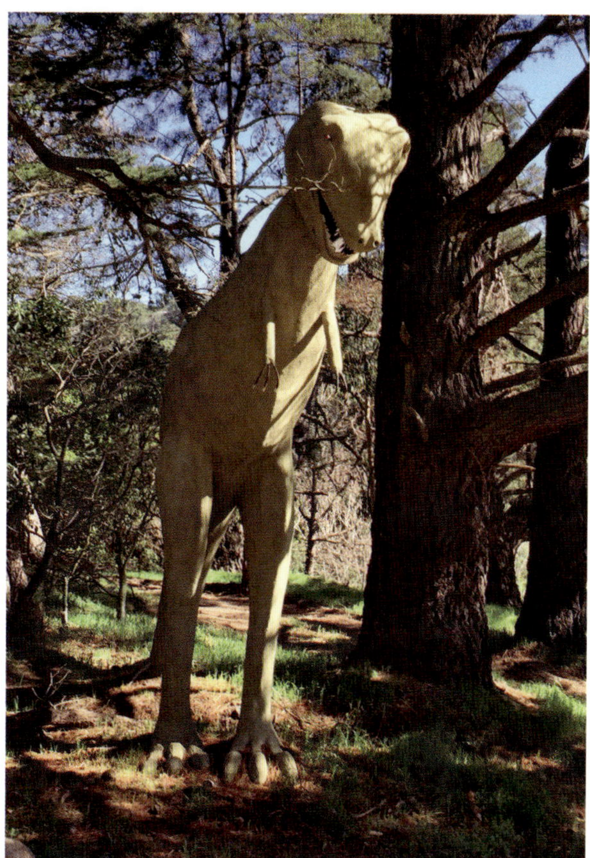

PINOLE MIDGET GOLF: Built by the Elmer Landree family in the 1960s, Pinole Midget Golf was a popular destination for many children and adults. It gained a measure of immortality when a scene from the 1973 movie "American Graffiti," where Richard Dreyfuss's character distracts the owner while the Pharaohs rob the pinball machines, was filmed in its arcade area. Dave's Auto Repair occupies this site in 2015. The T-Rex lives on private property in El Sobrante.

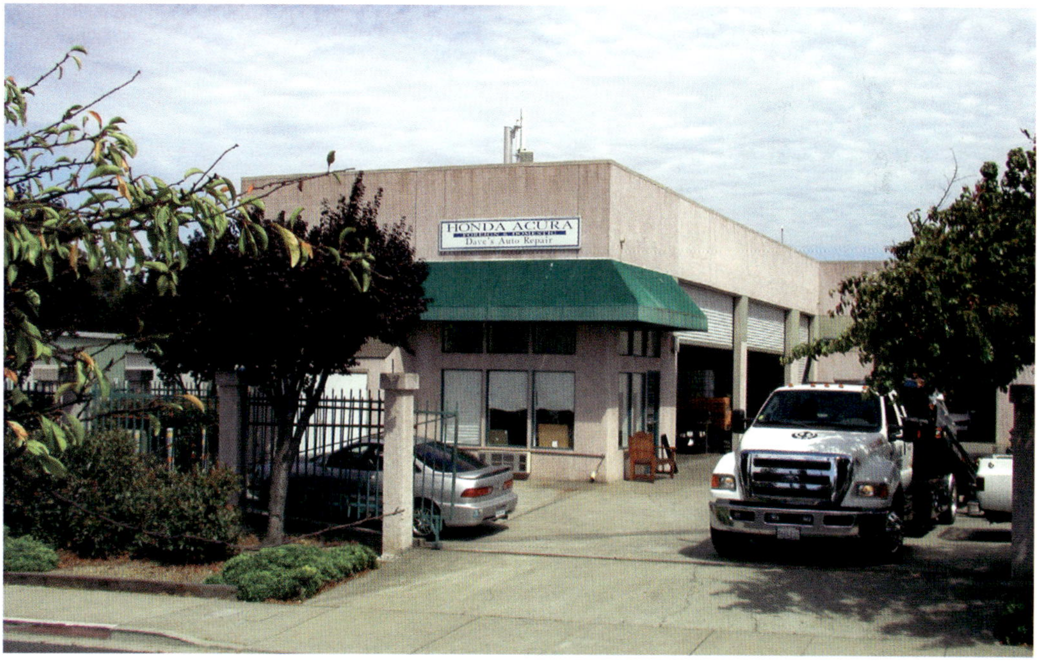

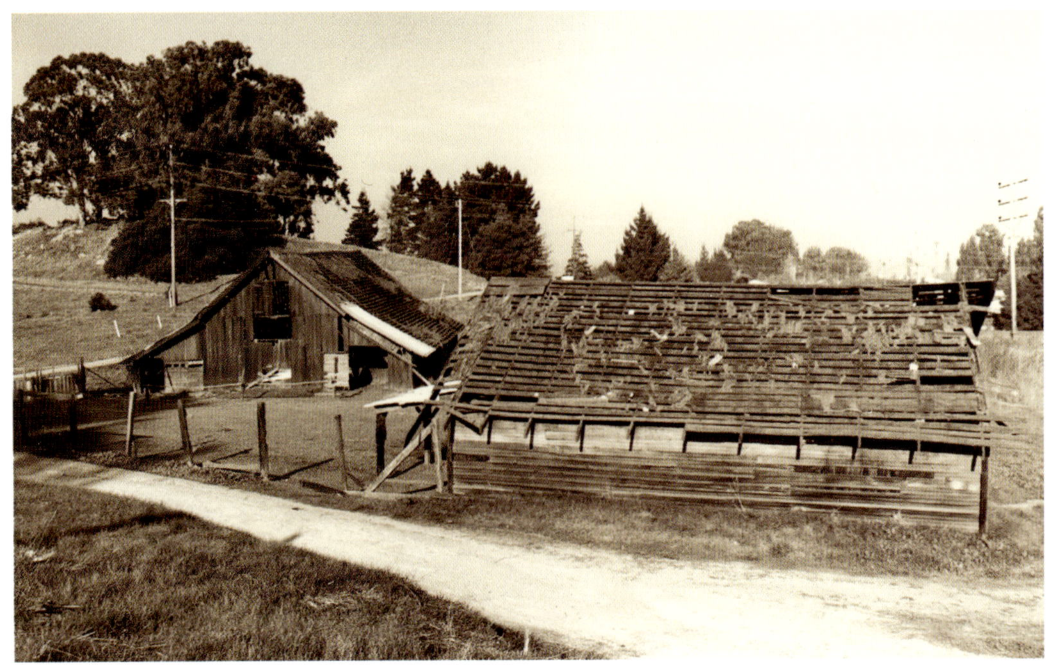

BUCKLEY RANCH: In the early 1900s, the Joseph Buckley Ranch covered 150 acres, encompassing much of the land from San Pablo Avenue down to San Pablo Bay. The Buckleys bought the ranch property from Carolyn Brandt after her husband, Frederick, died. The Buckley home was at the end of what is now Primrose Lane. The Buckley family had lived in Pinole since moving from Oakland in the early 1890s. Private homes, condominiums, and apartments now reside on the former Buckley ranch on Primrose Lane, Primrose Court, and Lopes Court. Mabel Buckley, one of Joseph's daughters, married LeRoy (Roy) LeFebvre in 1910 and had five children. Their descendants live in Pinole to this day.

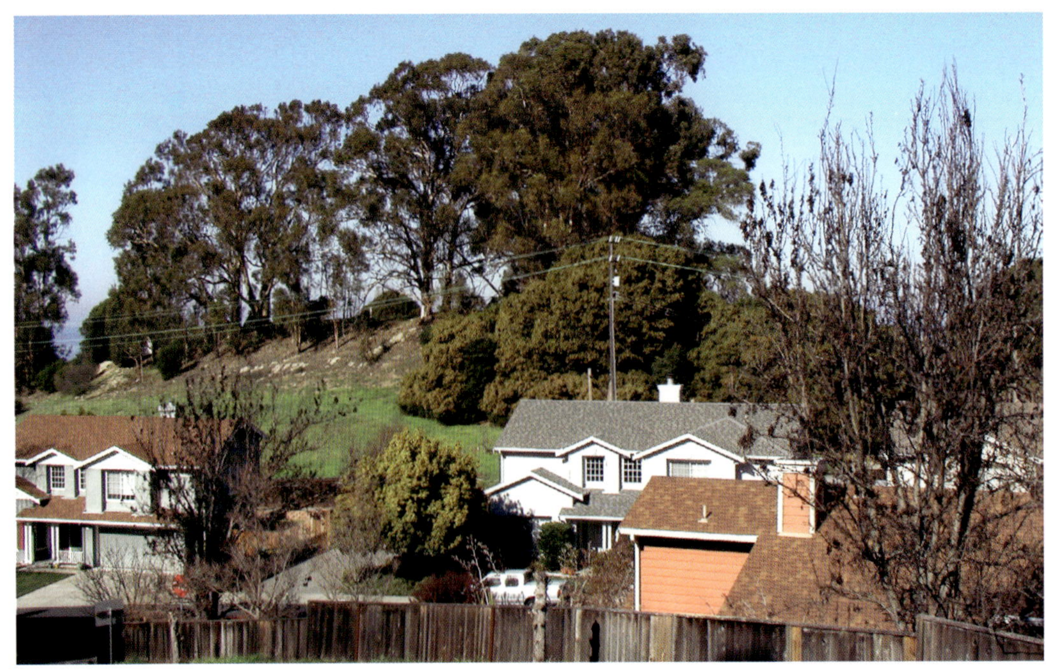

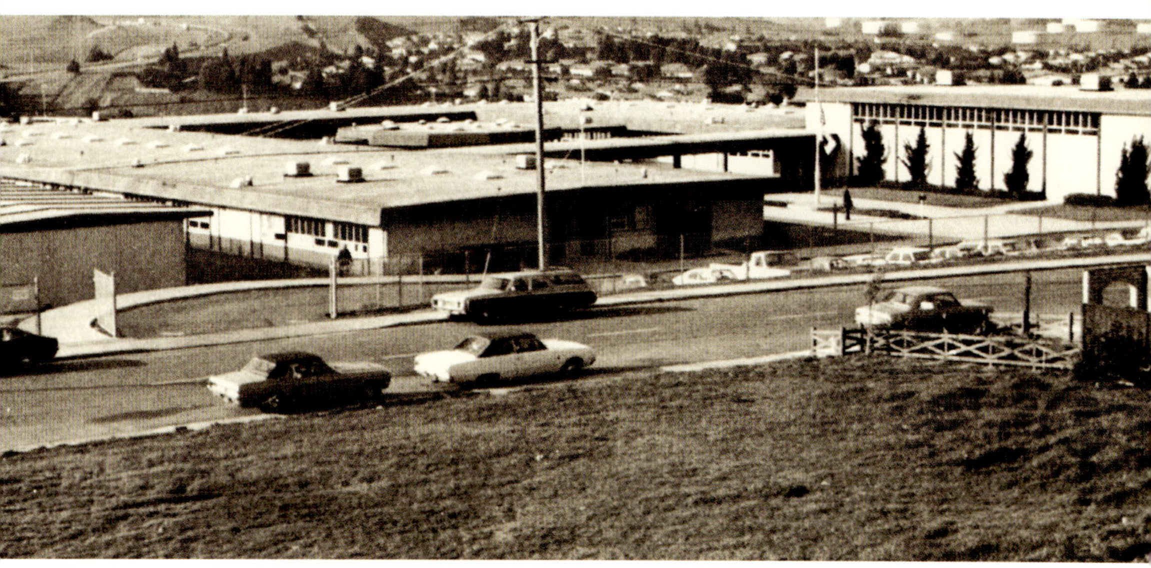

PINOLE MIDDLE SCHOOL: Pinole Middle School, at 1575 Mann Drive, opened in 1966, serving seventh- and eight-grade students. In 2006, construction began on a new campus; several buildings on the new campus opened in the fall of 2008. The administration building opened in 2011. The campus was completed in 2015 with the construction of an all-weather outdoor track and athletic field. Enrollment in 2015 was 690 students.

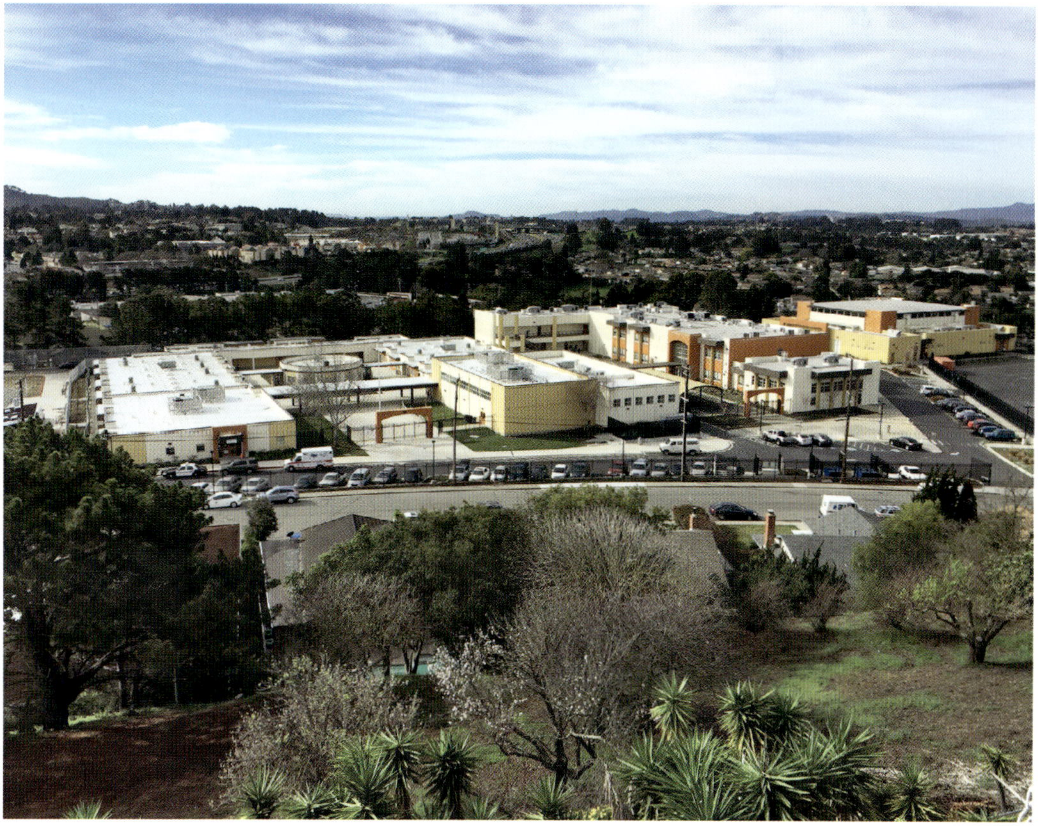

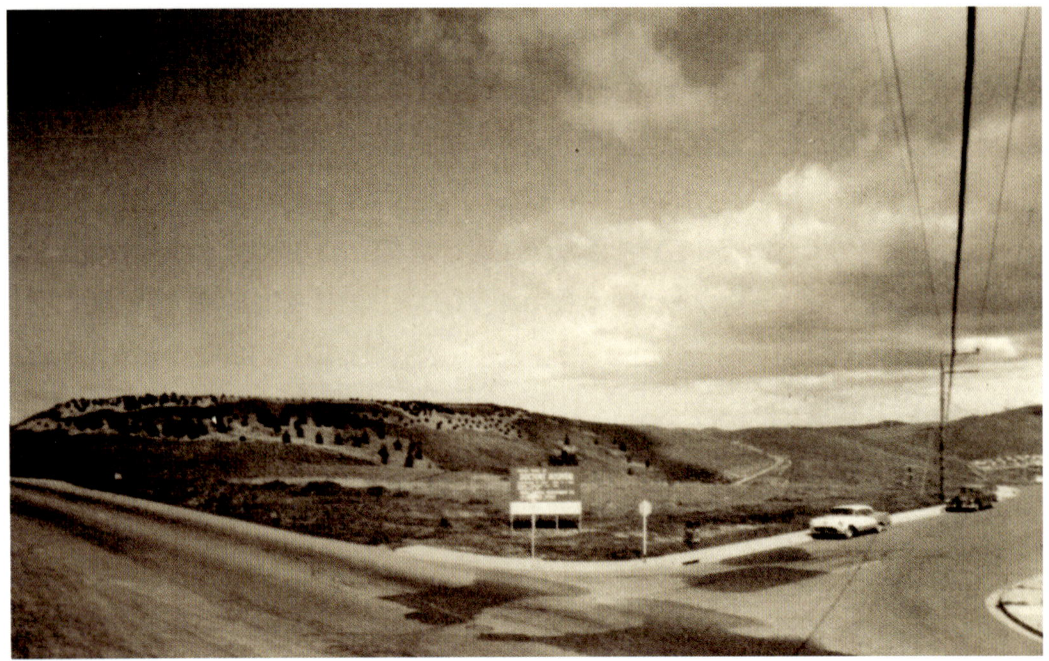

DOCTORS HOSPITAL: The land on the east side of Appian Way was pasture land for grazing cows until 1964, when a core group of six medical doctors, three dentists, and a businessman, James Fitzgerald, formed the Pinole Medical Development Company. By 1966 there were thirty-eight partners. Financing was acquired, ground was broken, and on June 28, 1967, the 150-bed, 68,000-square-foot hospital opened. Sadly, the board of directors of the West Contra Costa Healthcare District, which runs the hospital, facing a massive financial shortfall, voted to close the hospital at the end of 2006, creating a significant gap in the delivery of medical services in the community. The building (inset) remains abandoned.

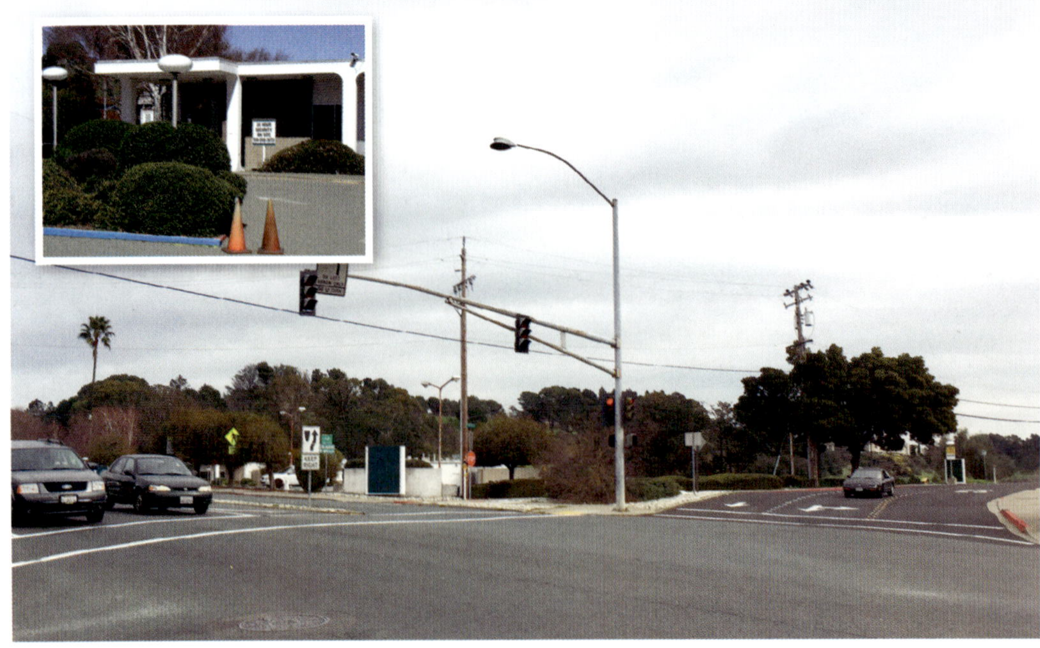

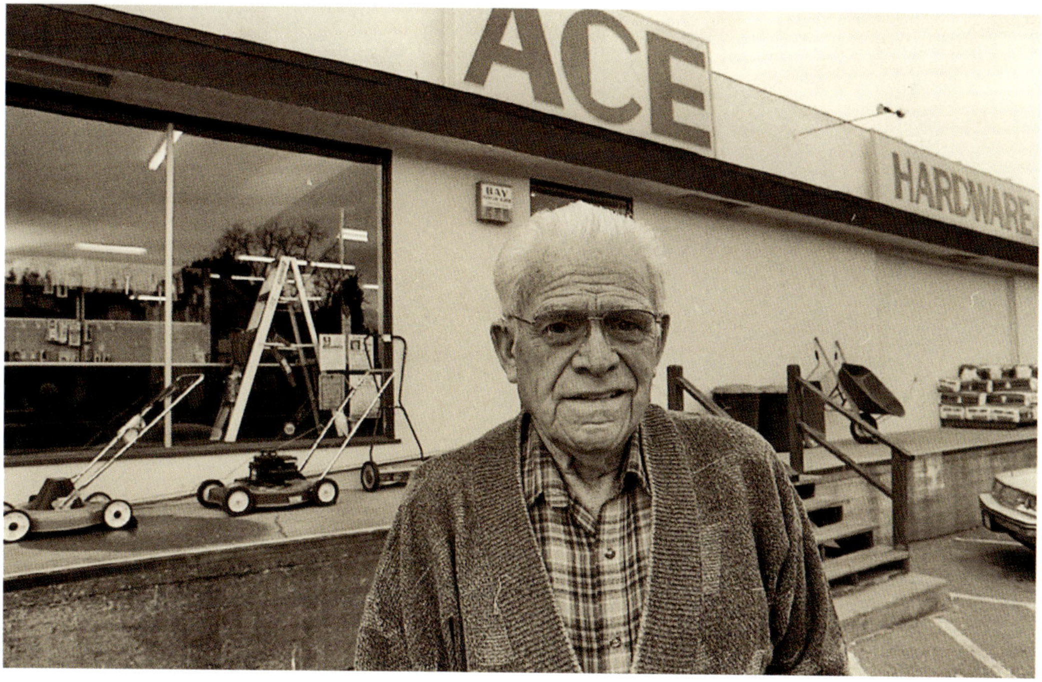

THREE BROTHERS HARDWARE/BLUE SKY SPORTS: Rene, Lucien, and Louis DeLaBriandais opened a service station and a sixteen unit auto court on their father's ten acre property on the north side of San Pablo Avenue, just east of Appian Way. Then they built an appliance/hardware store called Three Brothers. On August 1, 1989, Gregg Fehr, who had started a screen-printing business in his El Sobrante home's garage in 1980 and had small Blue Sky Sports stores in several locations in the city, moved into the former hardware store. He opened the immensely popular batting cages in 1992.

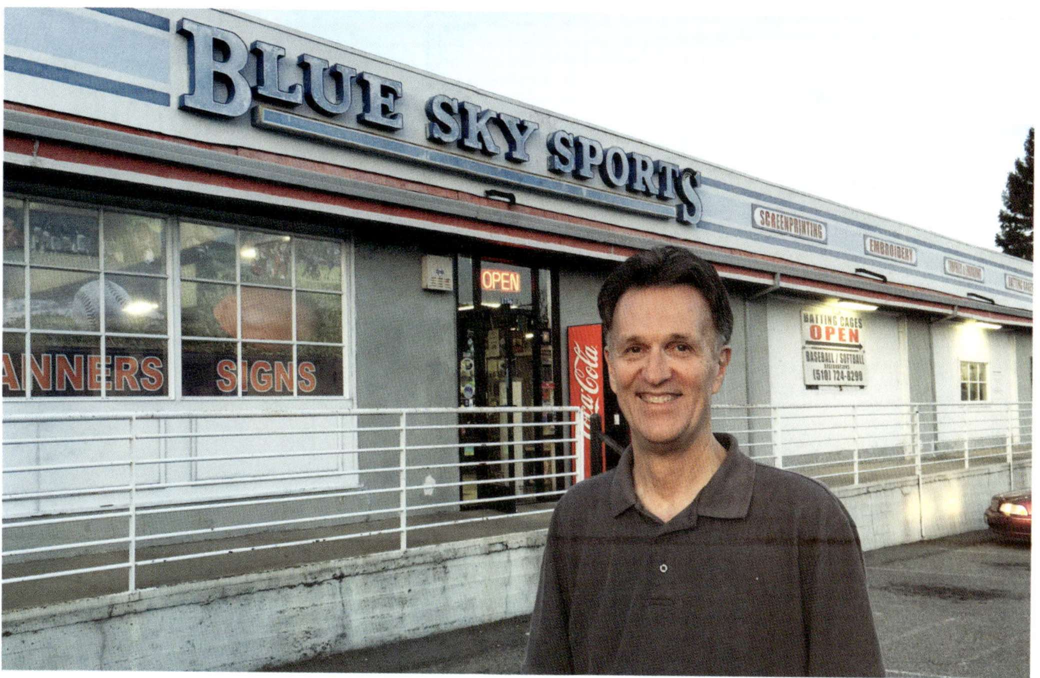

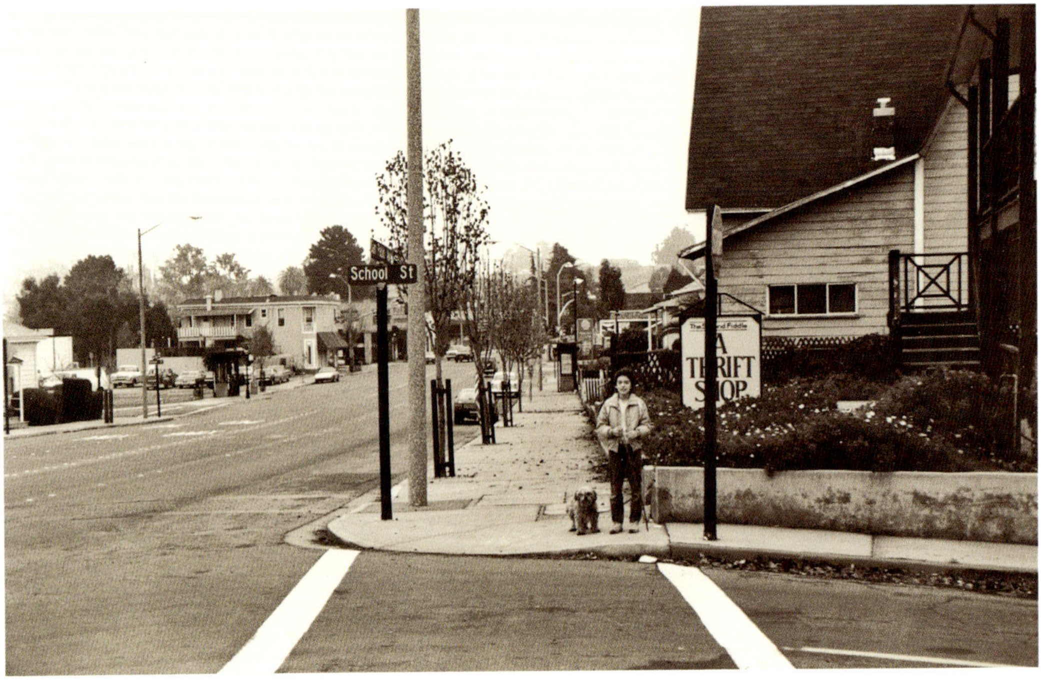

School Street: Opposite the post office, School Street, so named for the late nineteenth century/early twentieth century Plaza School that once stood on the post office site, provided motorists with a drive-thru mailbox at the intersection with San Pablo Avenue. It was a very convenient bypass to the nearly always-crowded post office. The mailbox's demise coincided with the 1998 explosion of the two-story building that housed the Second Fiddle thrift shop, seen above. The mailbox didn't blow up, but it was removed when School Street was closed and subsequently erased from the city's grid.

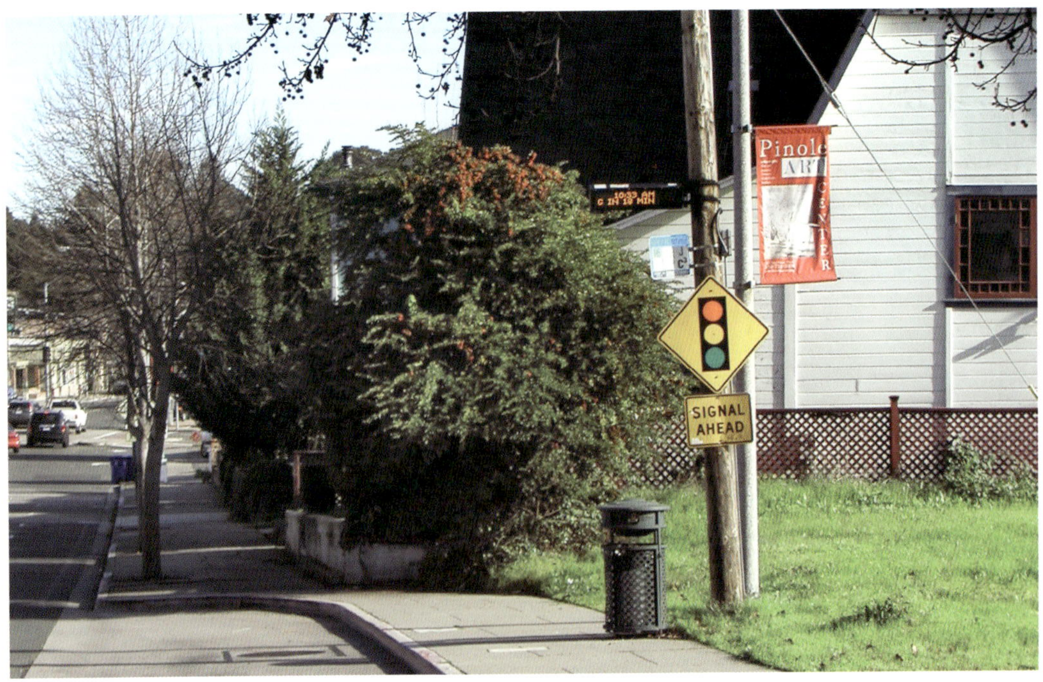

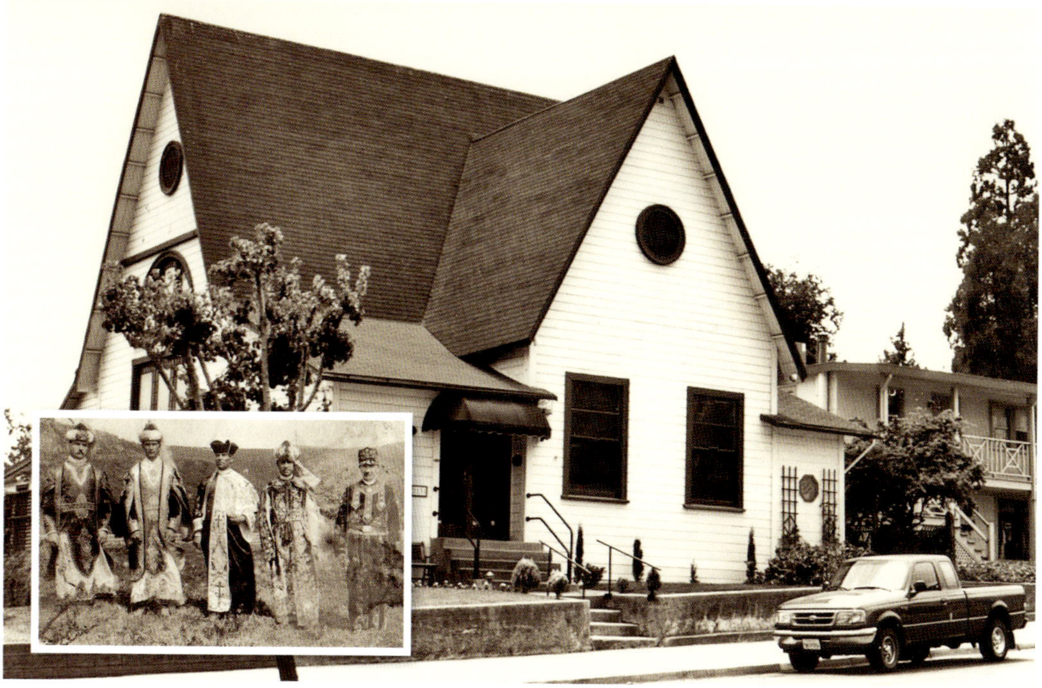

PYTHIAN CASTLE: The First Methodist Episcopal Church built this wooden structure in 1898 at 2131 San Pablo Avenue. When the church built its second home on Valley Avenue, the building was sold to the Order of the Knights of Pythias, a men's fraternal organization and secret society founded in 1864. The Pythian Knights (inset) met in "Pythian Castles," hence the local name in Pinole. This building now houses the Dennis L. Lorette Accountancy Corporation.

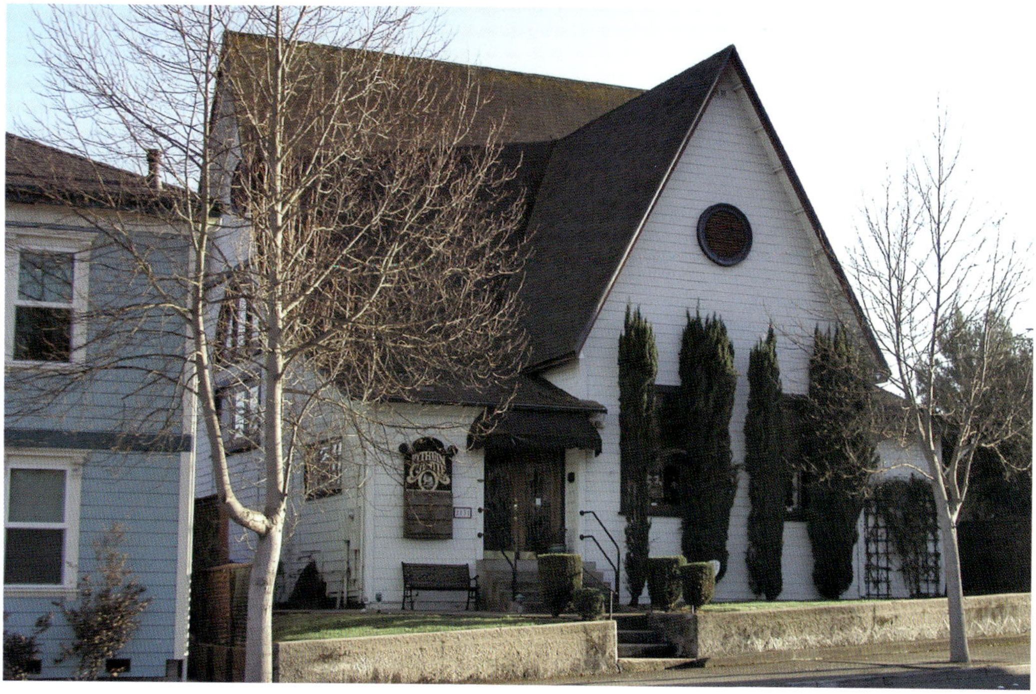

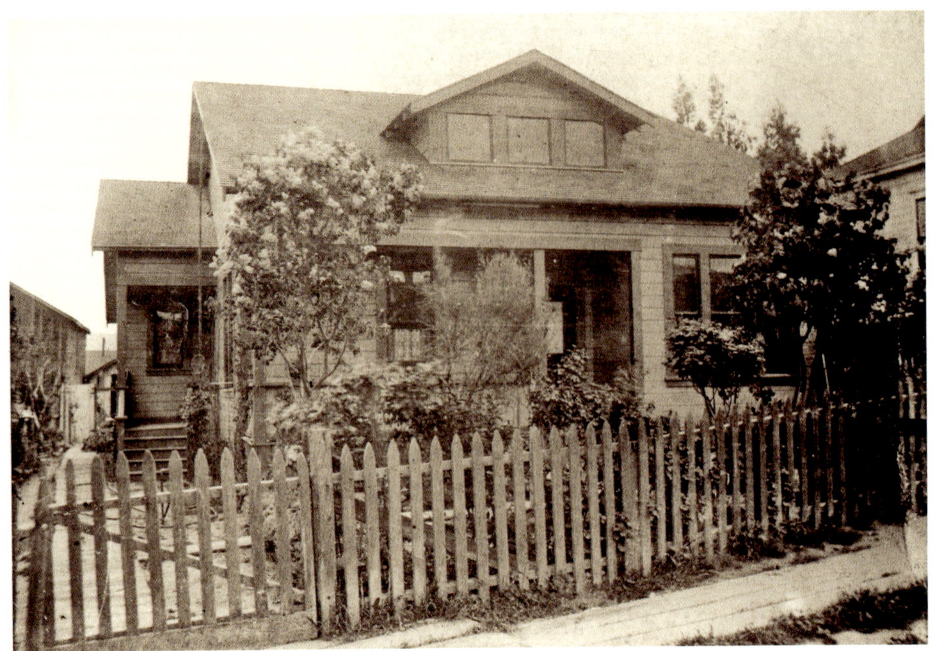

Tessie Curran Baldwin home/Garden of Gems: This home at 2235 San Pablo Avenue, originally a slaughterhouse and butcher shop, was remodeled into a residence in the 1870s for Cipriano Silvas and his wife, Maria Rosario Alvarado Silvas, who also built the Golden West Hotel on the southwest corner of Tennent and San Pablo avenues. Their daughter, Theresa, married John Curran; they reared their daughter Theresa (Tessie) at 656 Quinan Street. Tessie married Richmond Superior Court Judge Charles Baldwin and lived in Richmond most of her adult life. She inherited her grandmother's house, and lived there the last year of her life. Lee Ann Miller and her daughter, Amber Edwards, operate the Garden of Gems in this home in 2015.

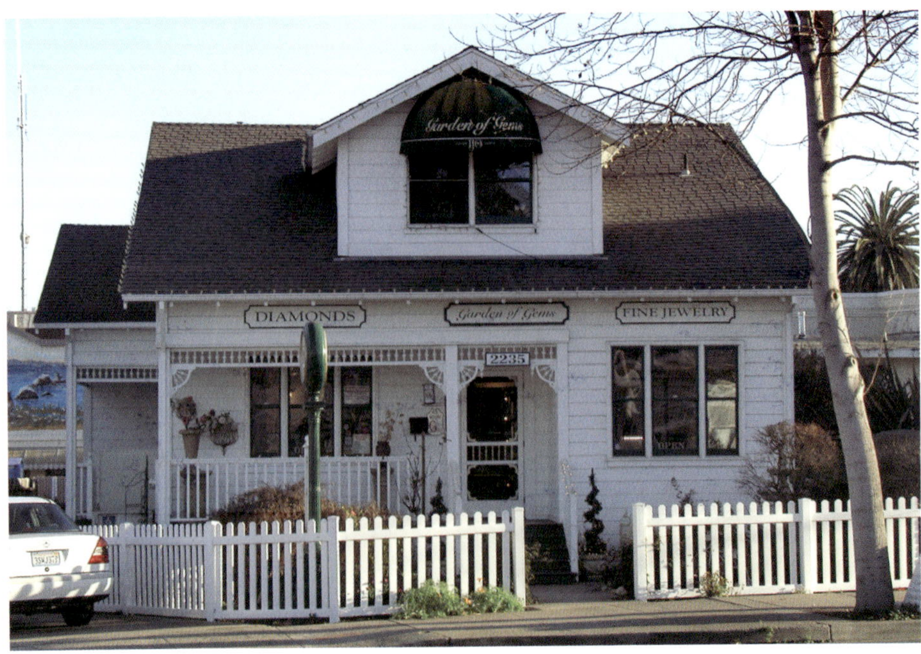

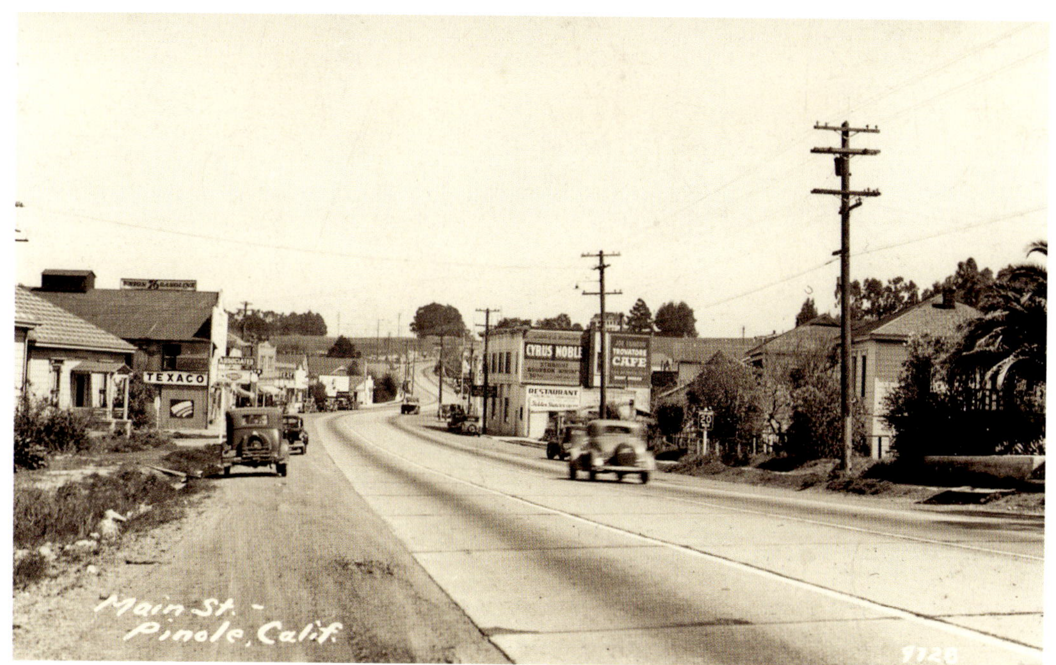

San Pablo Avenue looking east from the Faria house: There was not much traffic on San Pablo Avenue going east in the 1930s through downtown Pinole toward Hercules. The speed limit was 20 miles per hour, strictly enforced by motorcycle officer Lon Buck. The former Golden West Hotel on the southwest corner of San Pablo and Tennent Avenues was now the Joe Lunghi Trovatore Café, with the Downer Mansion seen above the café's large sign. Several gas stations and restaurants made Pinole a popular stop for residents and commuters. Downtown Pinole today looks much different, save for the Downer Mansion, Antlers Tavern, and the Bank of Pinole building.

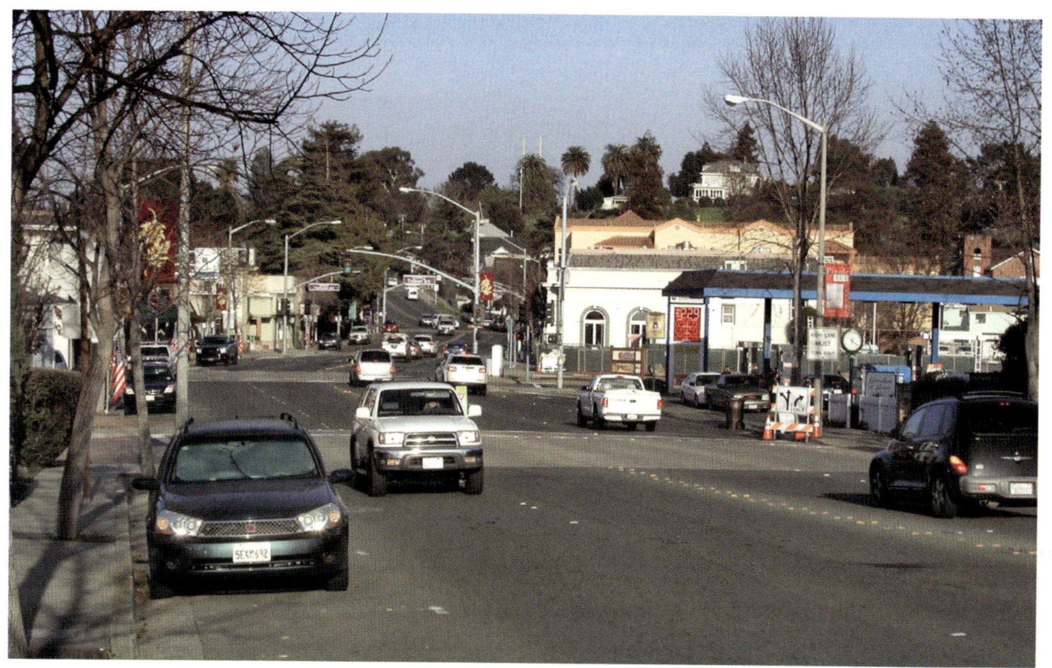

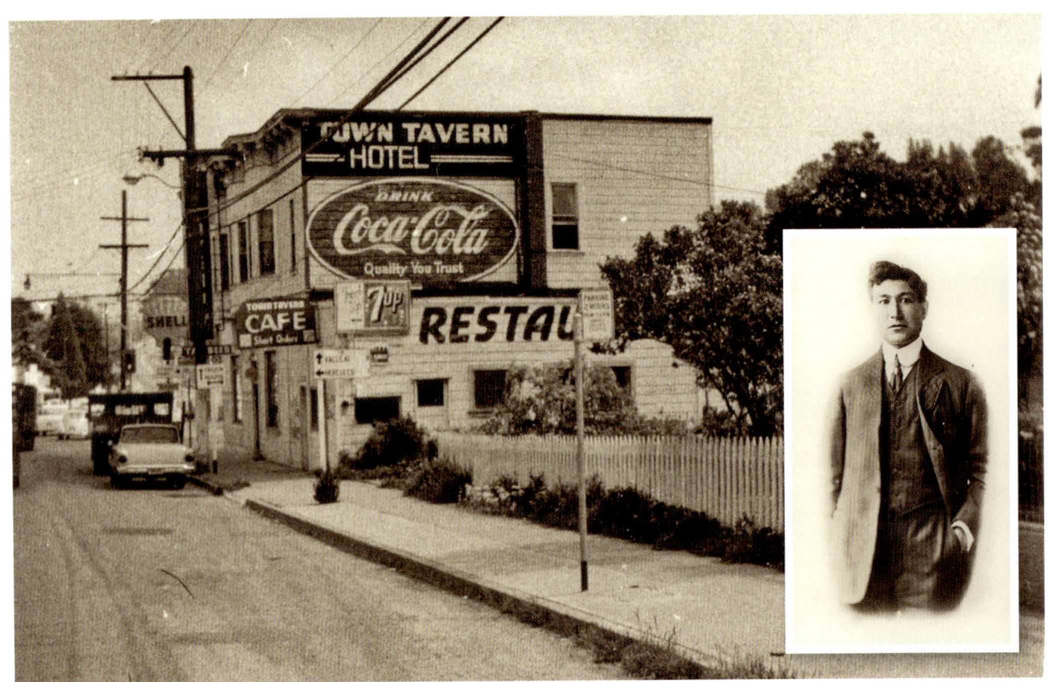

REAR OF TOWN TAVERN: In the 1950s, the former Joe Lunghi Trovatore Café was known as the Town Tavern. The building had been around since the early twentieth century, when Cipriano Silvas (inset) and his wife, Maria Rosario Alvarado Silvas, built the Golden West Hotel on the southwest corner of Tennent and San Pablo avenues, which had a saloon on the first floor run by Cipriano's brother, Jimmy, and a men's haberdashery shop. The residence behind the white picket fence is the Tessie Curran Baldwin home, now occupied by the Garden of Gems.

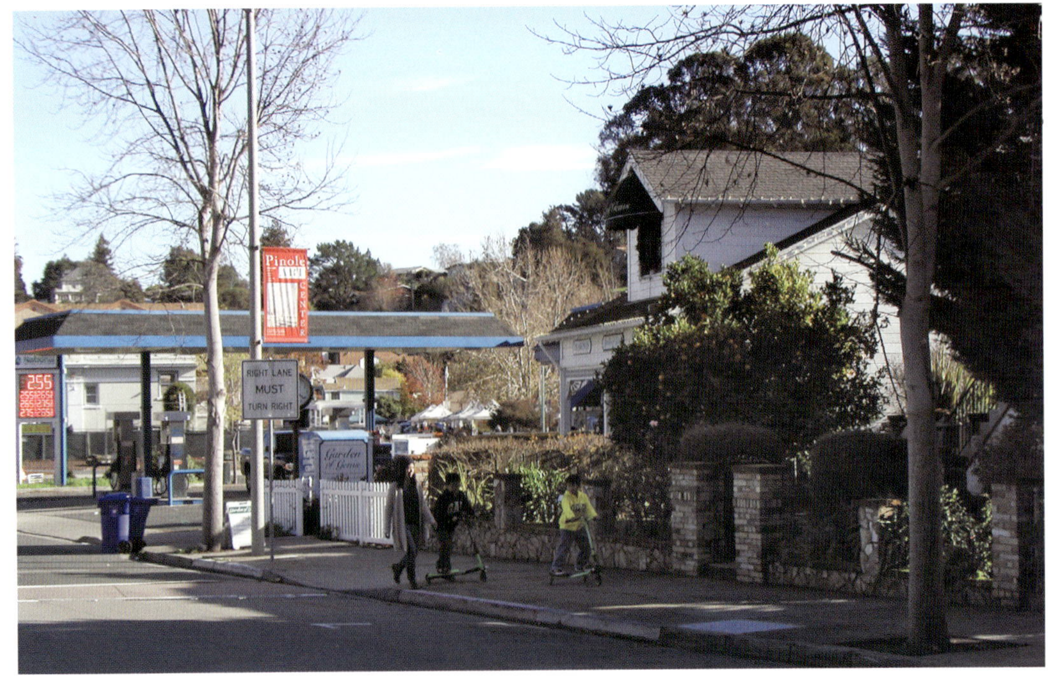

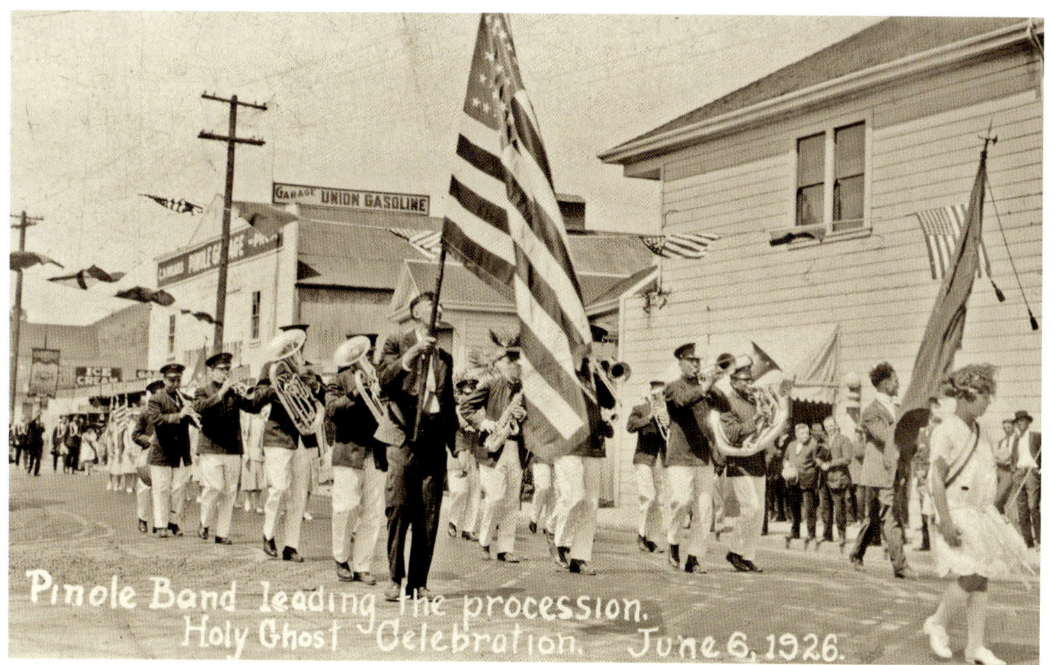

FROM QUINAN STREET TO ANTLERS: The 1926 Holy Ghost Parade proceeds down San Pablo Avenue toward Tennent Avenue. The building on the far right is Antlers Tavern. Ed Paxton owned the large Pinole Garage building in the 1940s and 1950s. His tow truck pulled cars and debris from the waters of the 1958 flood. The Pinole-Hercules Boys' Club was on the second floor of the Pinole Garage. Basketball courts were inside. People climbed a long flight of stairs on the outside of the building to get in. The Pinole Boy Scout Troop also met there. Antlers still anchors the east end of the block, while the two-story Torrac retail/office building is on the Pinole Garage site.

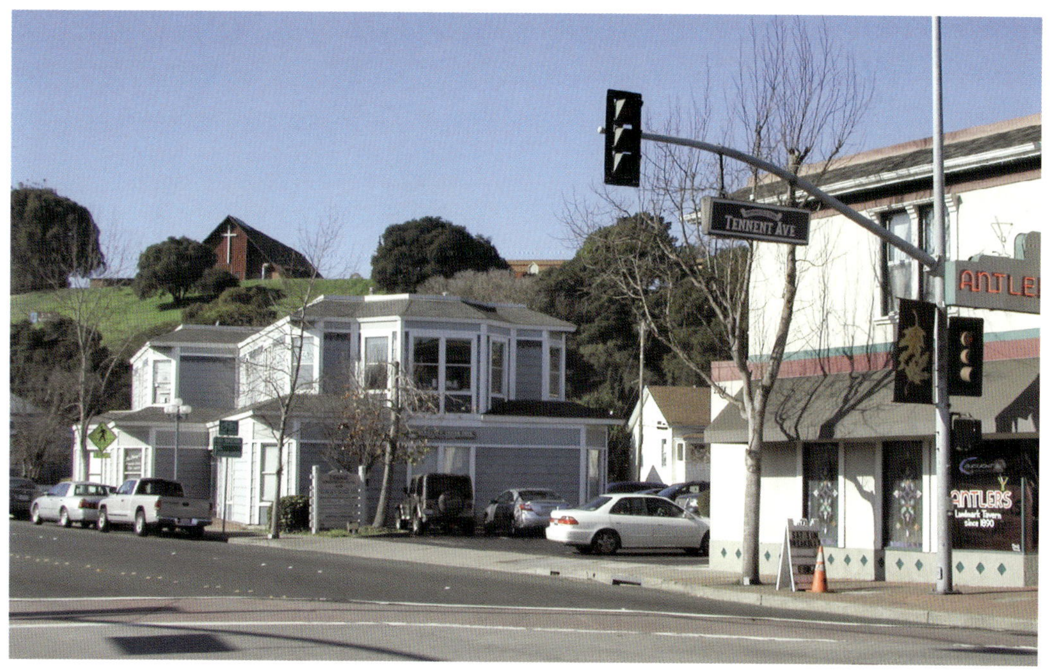

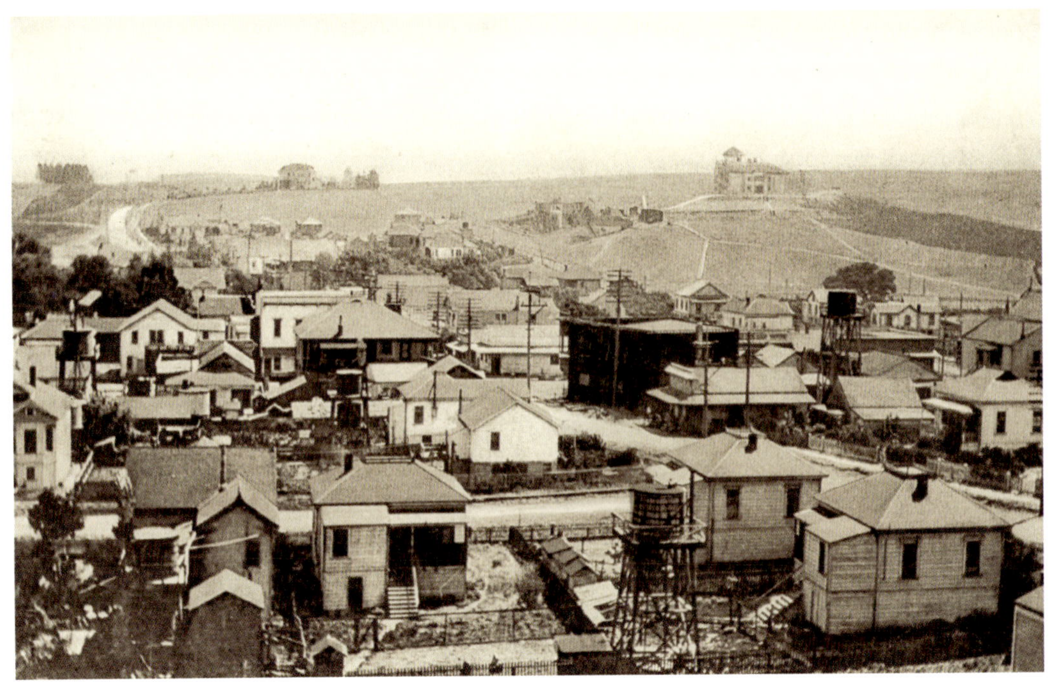

DOWNTOWN FROM SUMMIT DRIVE: Pinole's rolling hills provided magnificent vistas of the downtown area in the early 1900s. These photos showing Quinan Street and Tennent Avenue reveal the Pinole-Hercules School #1, which opened in 1906, occupying a barren hill on the east edge of the city, the Downer Mansion, built in 1900, in the distance on the Hercules border, and many of the buildings on Tennent that burned down in 1908. Notice the several water towers dotting the back yards. Many of the structures on Quinan Street survive today.

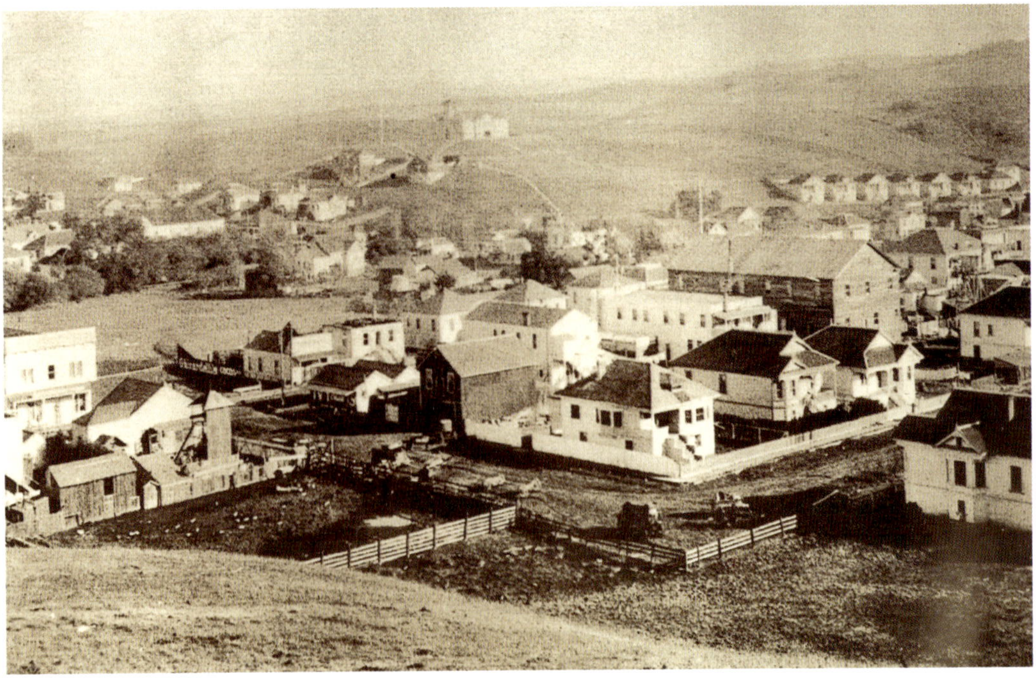

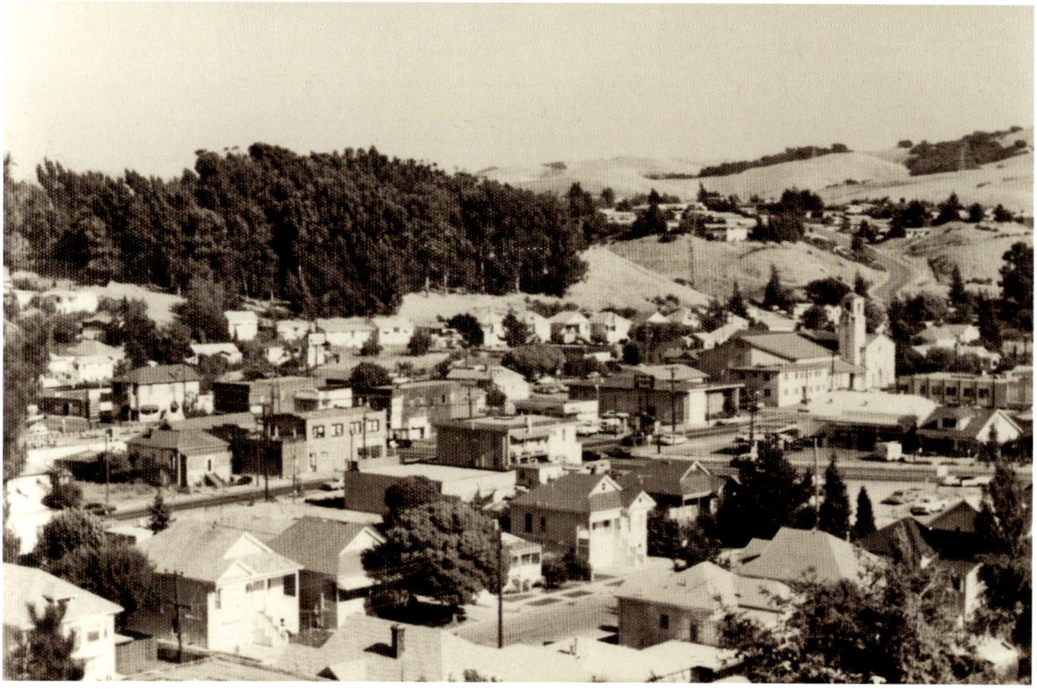

Downtown from Summit Drive: A 1970s photo taken from approximately the same location shows a grove of eucalyptus trees protecting the site of the beloved Pinole-Hercules School #1, which was demolished in 1968, and a modern downtown with a thriving business district. Quinan Street is one of the few areas in the city that has been preserved; sadly, many historic structures were torn down in the name of progress. The once-barren hills in the background are dotted with homes.

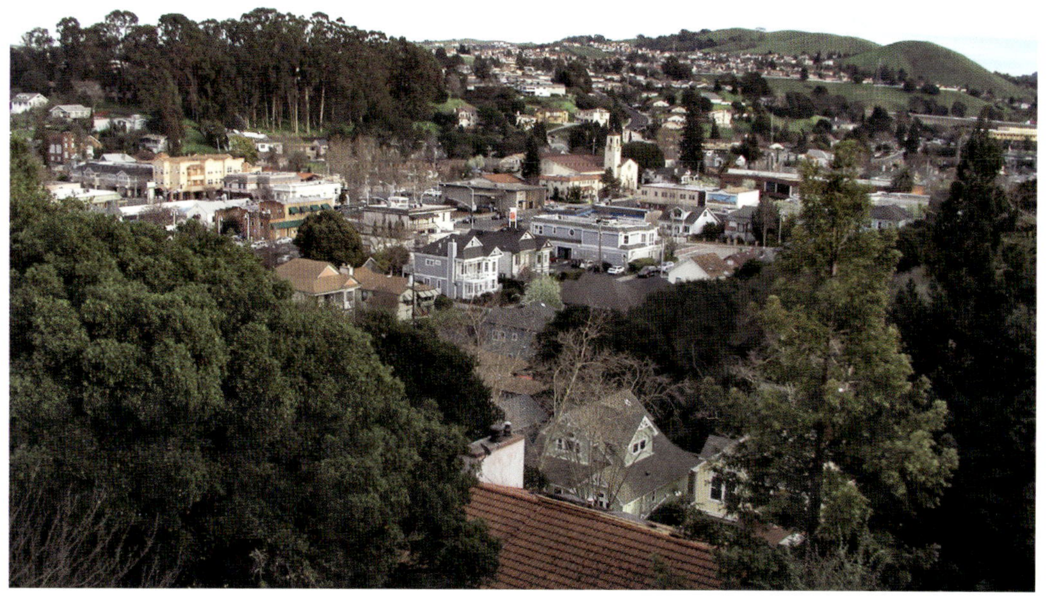

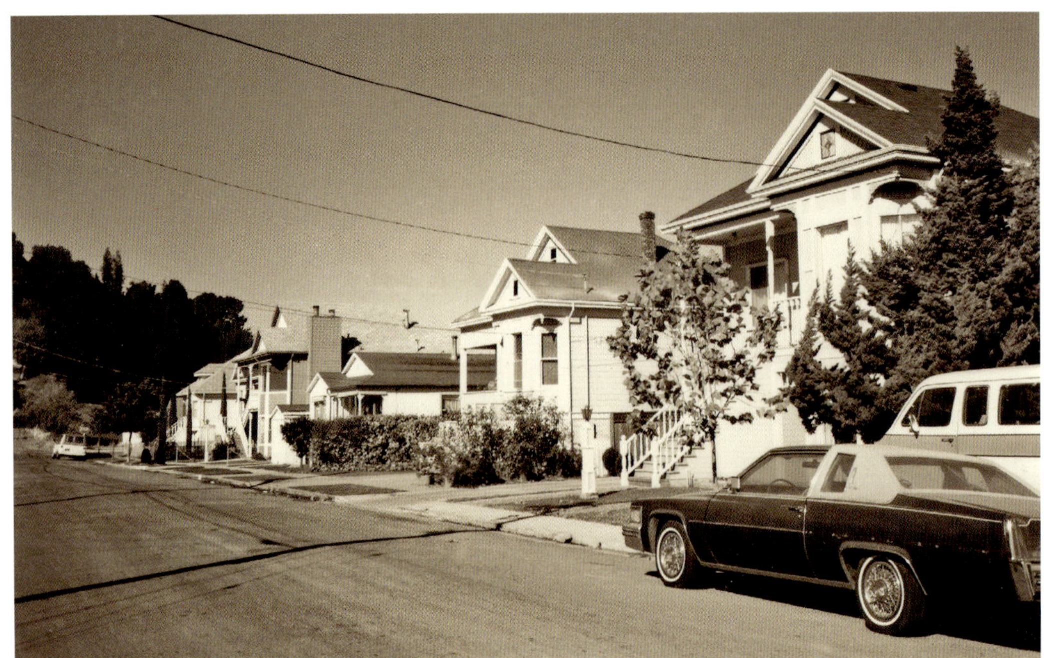

QUINAN STREET: One of the few preserved areas from the late 1800s in the city, nearly all of the homes were built for individuals who either worked at the California Powder Works or in other Pinole businesses. They are great examples of Queen Anne, Italianate, and Neoclassic architecture. Several prominent people and families in the city's history lived on this street, including Theresa Curran Baldwin, Antone Lopes Sr., his son, Tony Lopes Jr., and his family, and Armand Marieiro and his family. Armand owned Arm's Grocery, later Blackie's. Quinan Street was named after Capt. William Russell Quinan, a West Point graduate who was superintendent of the California Powder Works from 1883–1899.

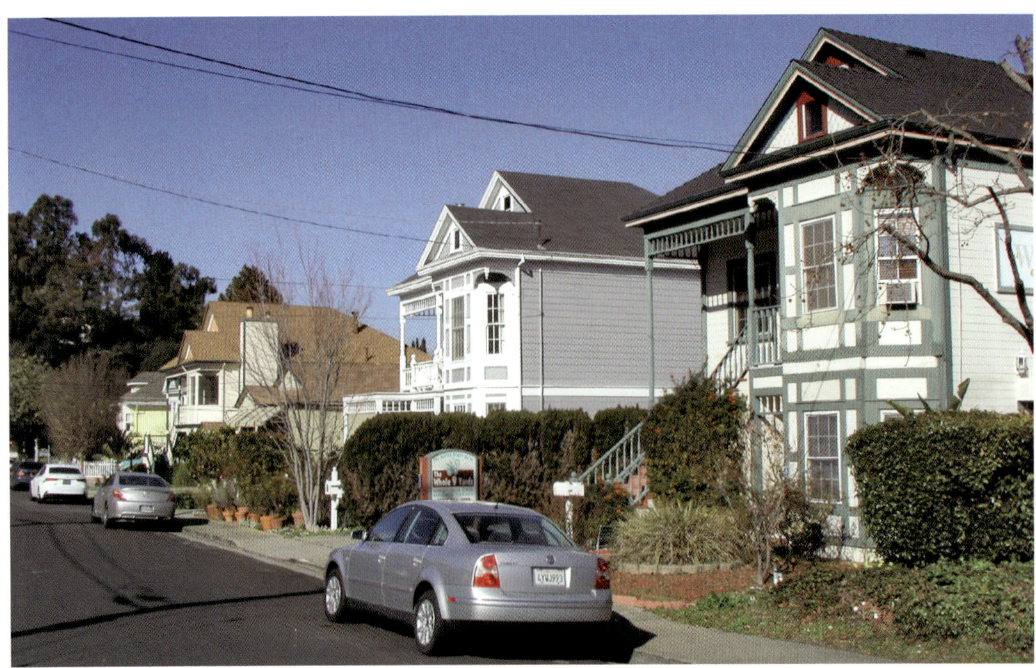

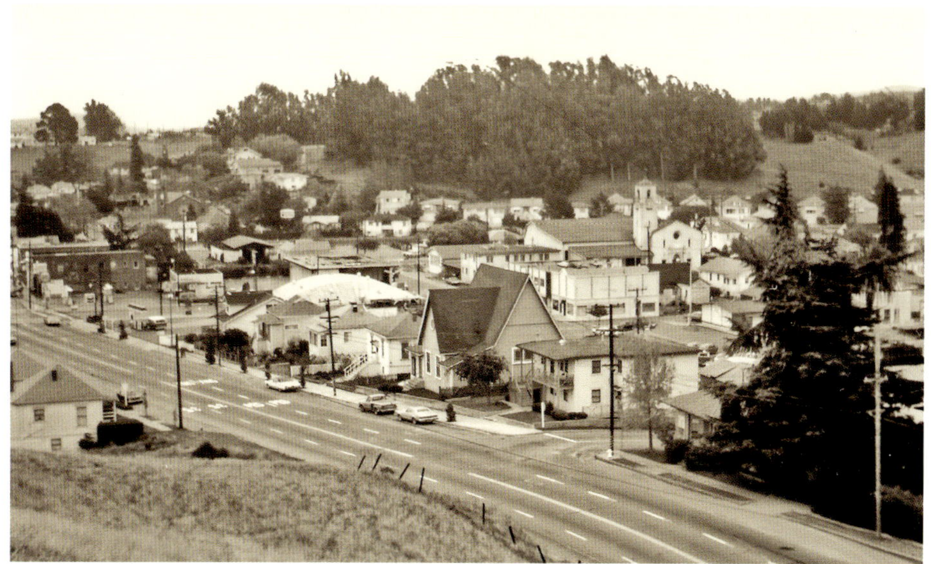

DOWNTOWN FROM SHALE HILL: The 1970s view of the south side of downtown Pinole's San Pablo Avenue is remarkably similar to the 2015 photo, both taken from Shale Hill, behind the Pinole United Methodist Church. The Second Fiddle, a thrift store in the two-story building at 2101 San Pablo Avenue bordering School Street, next to the Pythian Castle (the A-frame building in the middle of the photo), was destroyed on February 17, 1998, when an East Bay Municipal Utilities District crew accidentally cut through a shallow PG&E gas line with a backhoe and blew up the building. The explosion shook surrounding buildings and was felt for miles. Four people suffered minor injuries. No one was killed.

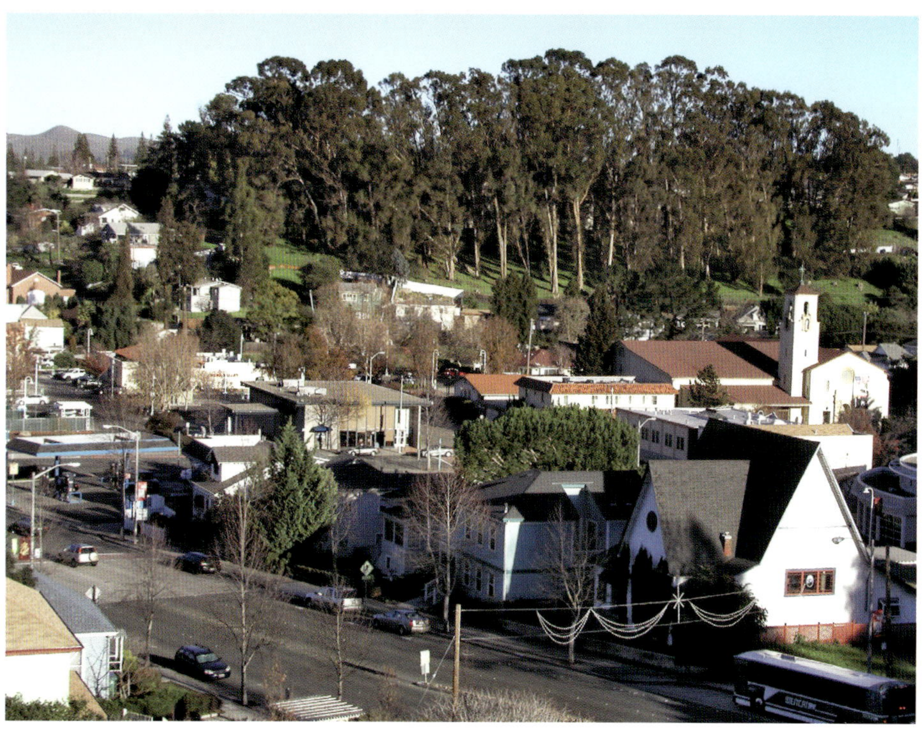

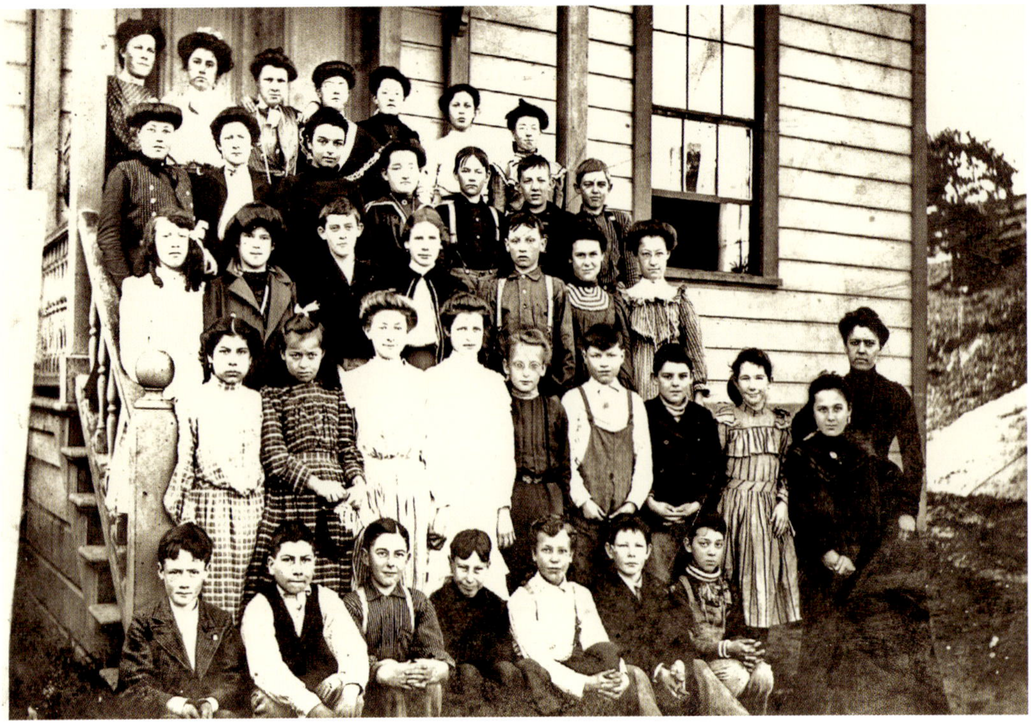

PLAZA SCHOOL/POST OFFICE: The 1904 Plaza School class, taught by Frances Ellerhorst (far right), attended a small schoolhouse on Pear Street. Samuel and Raphaela Tennent donated the land for the school. The school was demolished in 1933. Ellerhorst spent her entire adult life as a teacher and principal in Pinole. Ellerhorst School in Pinole Valley is named after her. The United States Post Office, built on the site of the Plaza School, opened in 1960. Previously, the post office was a short walk away on Tennent Avenue, near the Golden West Hotel.

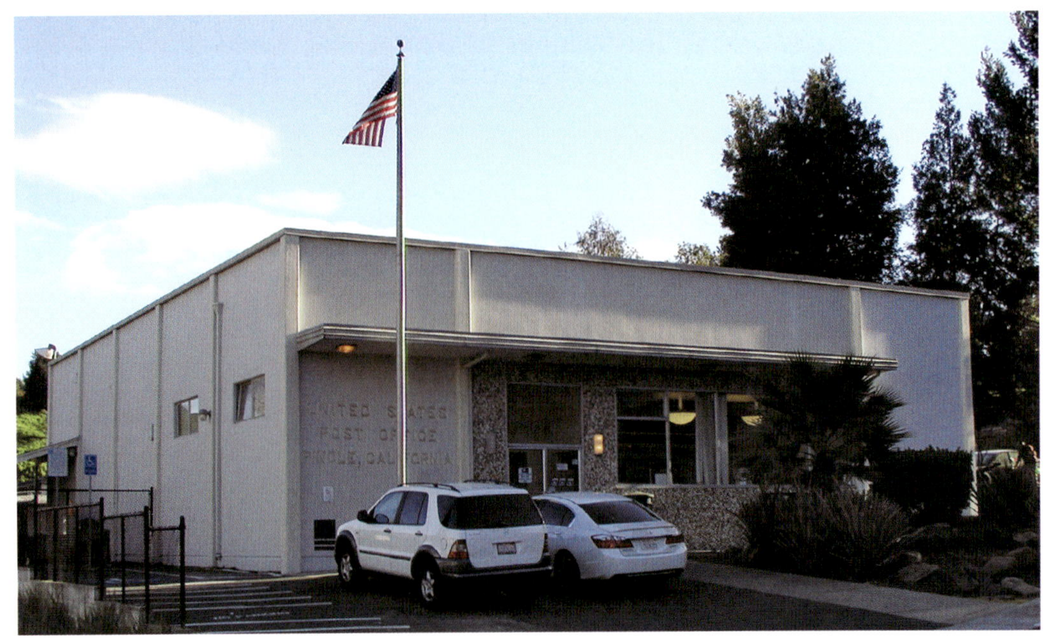

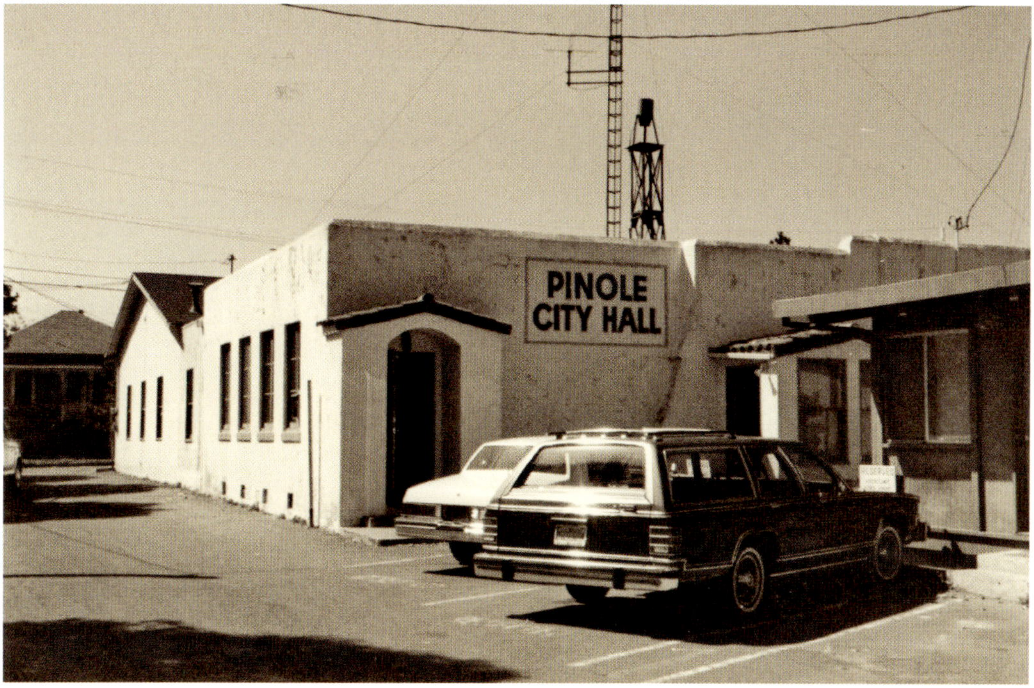

PINOLE CITY HALL: Pinole outgrew its old, single-story city hall on Pear Street in the late 1980s as the population exceeded 19,000. Plans were drawn for a seismically safe facility after the 1989 Loma Prieta earthquake severely damaged the Ruff and Downer buildings on San Pablo Avenue, which were subsequently demolished. A modern Pinole City Hall opened to the public on June 2, 1998. In addition to housing all city departments, it also hosts city council and various committee and commission meetings.

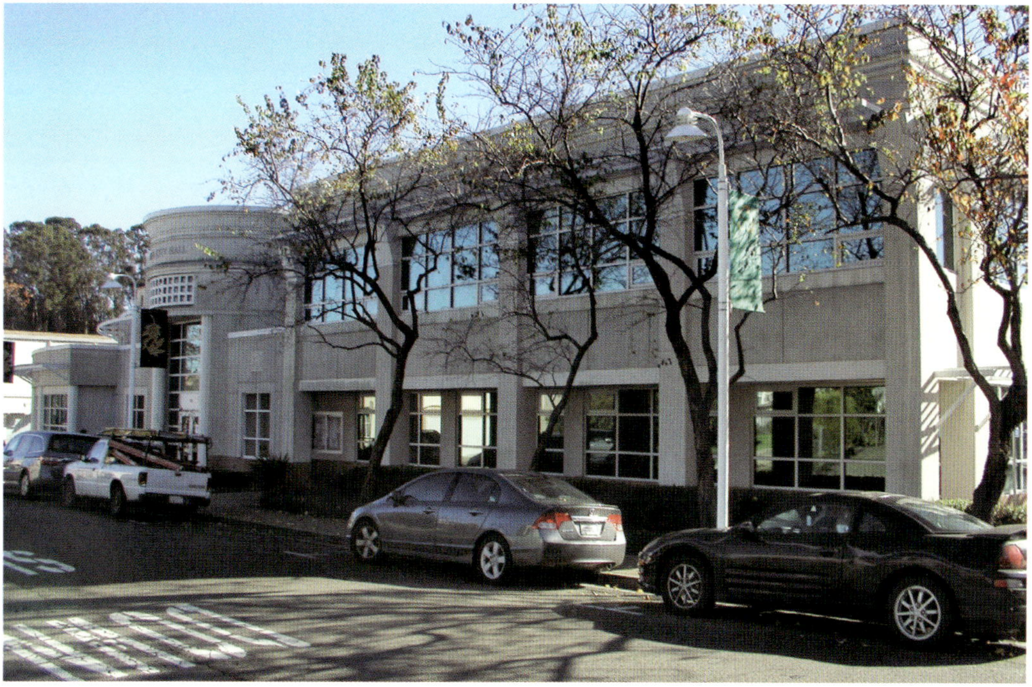

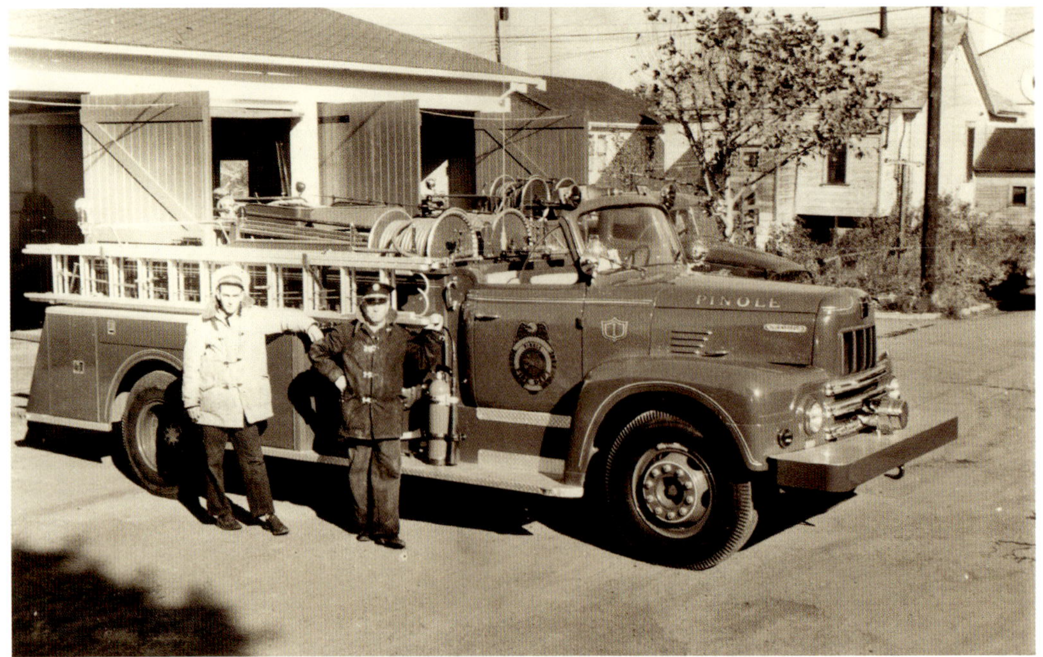

Pinole Fire Department: Pinole grew from a bucket-brigade fire department in 1900 to a staff of full time professional firefighters. The old fire station on Plum Street, built by volunteers with lumber from a torn-down school, gave way to the Pinole Public Safety Facility, which houses the fire and police departments. The Hercules Powder Company put in a well and pumping station in Pinole in 1904. Fire protection in the newly incorporated city consisted of six fire hydrants, two hose carts, and 500 feet of hose. The carts were pushed to a fire, where volunteers connected the hose to a hydrant. In 1959, Chief Wallace "Pepper" Martin (Pinole's sixth chief) became the city's first full time paid fireman.

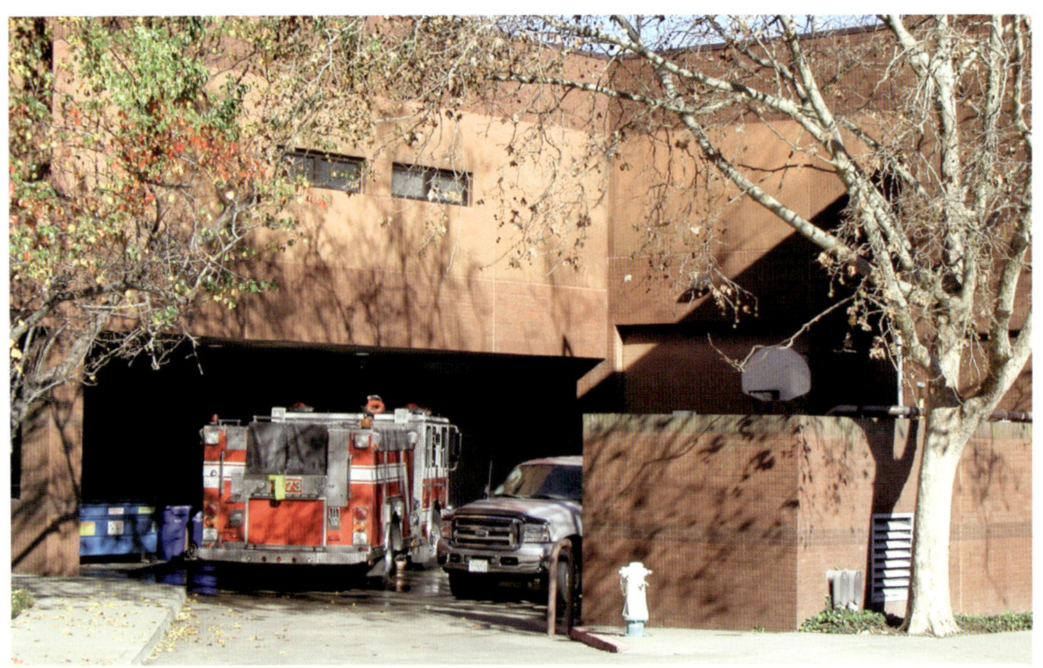

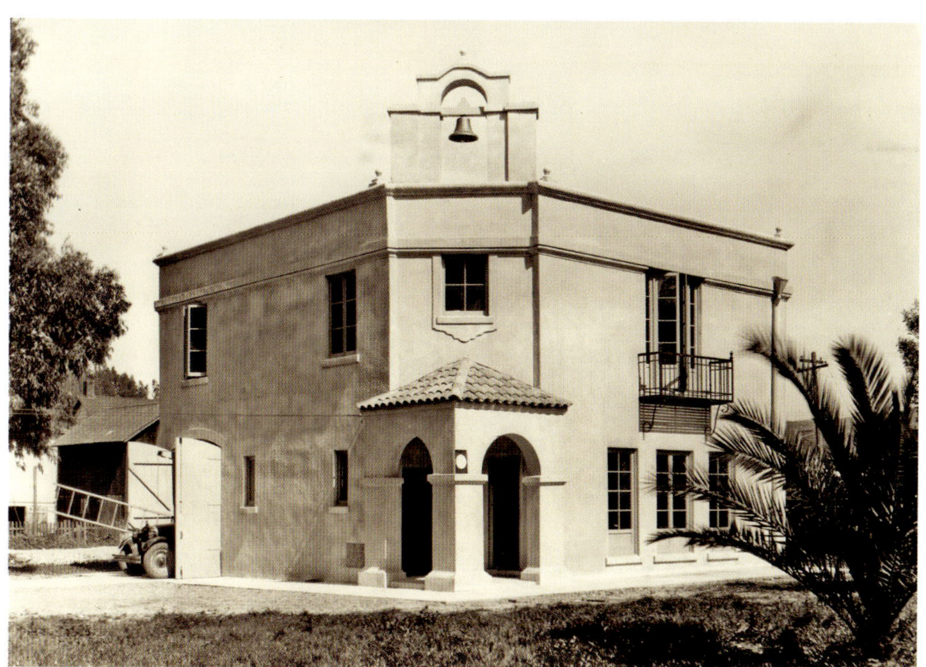

PINOLE LIBRARY/FIRE STATION/JAIL: The Pinole Chamber of Commerce financed the first municipal building in 1926 to house the firehouse, library, jail, and council chambers. A subsequent fire station was built on Plum Street, behind city hall; the police moved to a station next to the old city hall. As the city grew, modern police and fire services required a modern facility for both departments. In 1983, construction started on the Pinole Public Safety Facility, which houses the police and fire departments, and the Alex Clark Community Room, named for the city's former fire chief.

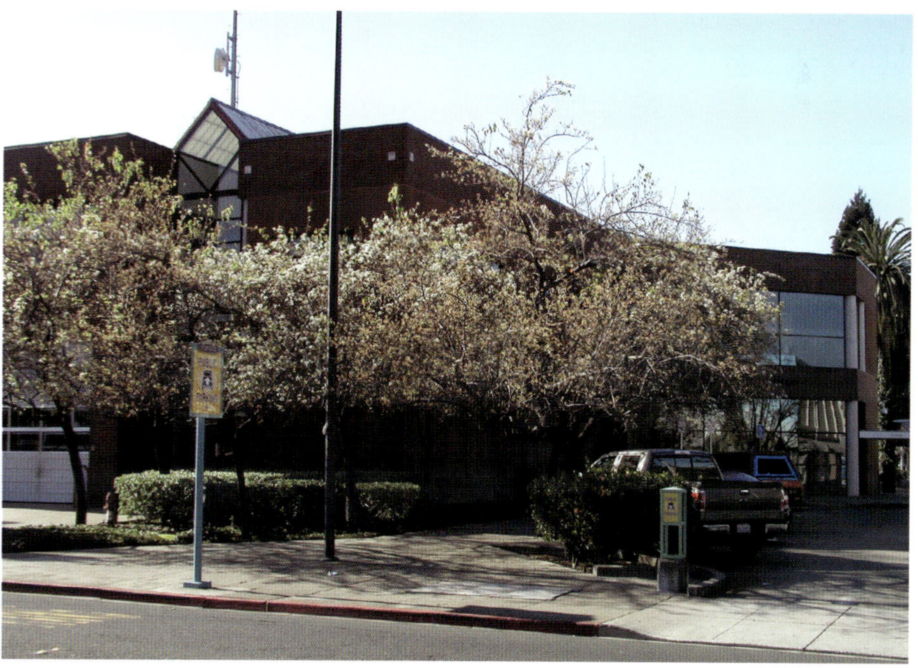

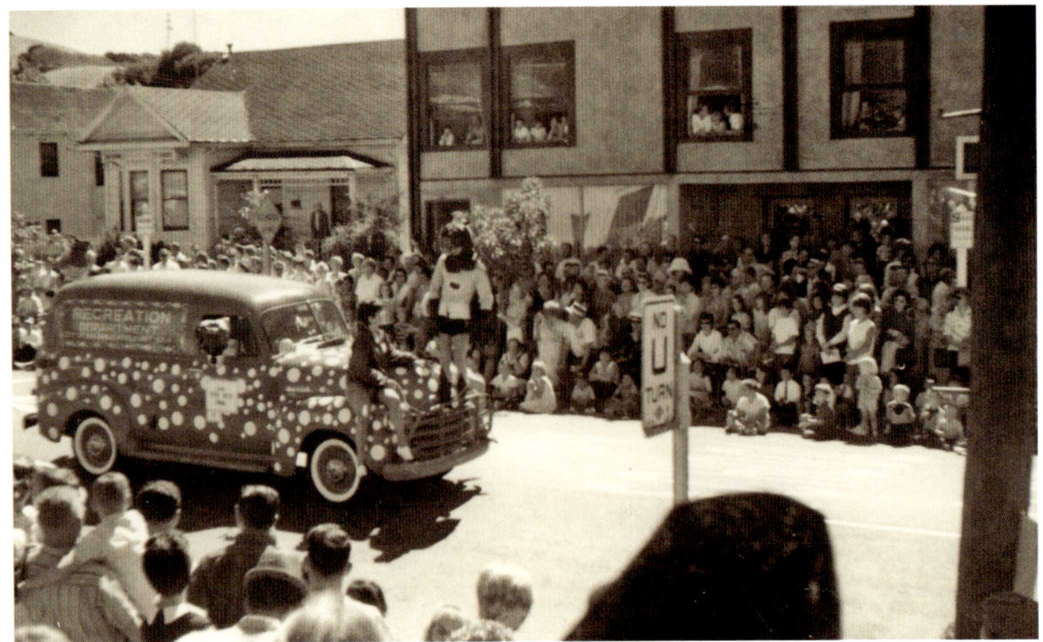

GREENFIELD'S DEPARTMENT STORE: In 1905, Pinole merchant Abraham Greenfield built a large, three-story building with a cupola and a skylight on Pear Street, across from St. Joseph's Church, and called it the "Big Department Store." Greenfield sold everything one would need without having to go out of town—hardware, furniture, groceries, notions, liquor, tobaccos, kerosene, farming tools, clothing, shoes and candies. The Greenfield building and business was a downtown landmark for many years. In the 1930s, Mr. and Mrs. Greenfield and daughter, Rosalie, moved to San Francisco. New owners removed the third story of the building. In the 1950s, the building was purchased and remodeled by locals Alex Clark and Bob Dutra. Many Fiesta del Pinole parades passed by it.

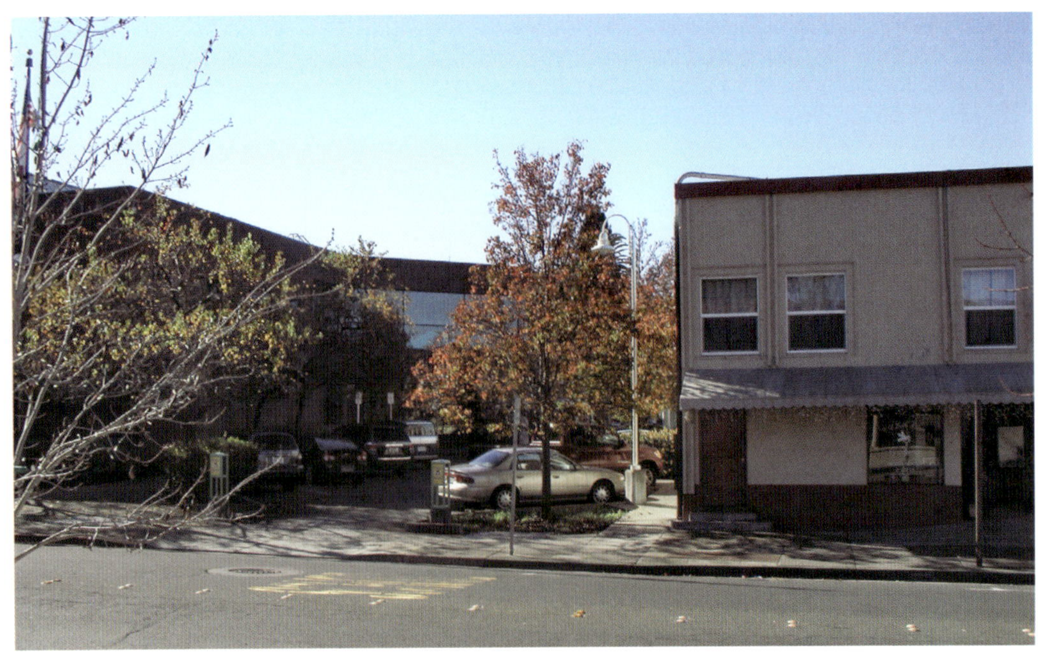

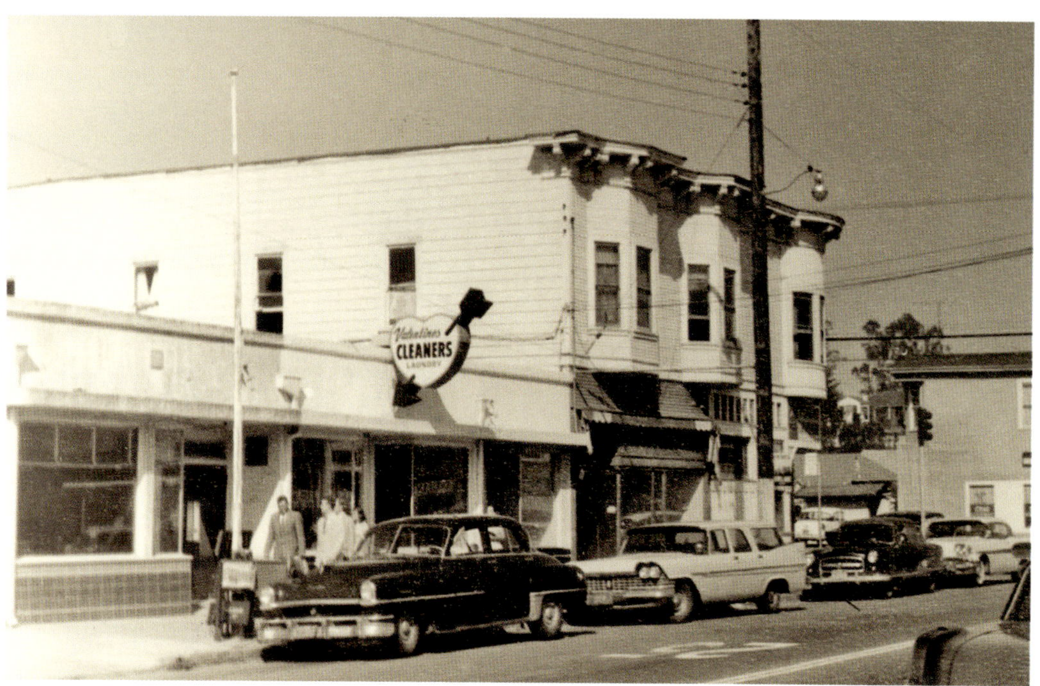

TENNENT AVENUE BUSINESSES: In 1958, some cars had fins and the west side of Tennent Avenue between San Pablo Avenue and Pear Street was fully occupied, with the Pinole Shopping Center/Pinole Food Center grocery store and meat market (inset), the post office (before it moved to a new building on Pear Street), Valentine's Cleaners, and the Town Tavern. These buildings are gone and all the land is vacant, save for the Pump House gas station and convenience store on the southwest corner of San Pablo and Tennent.

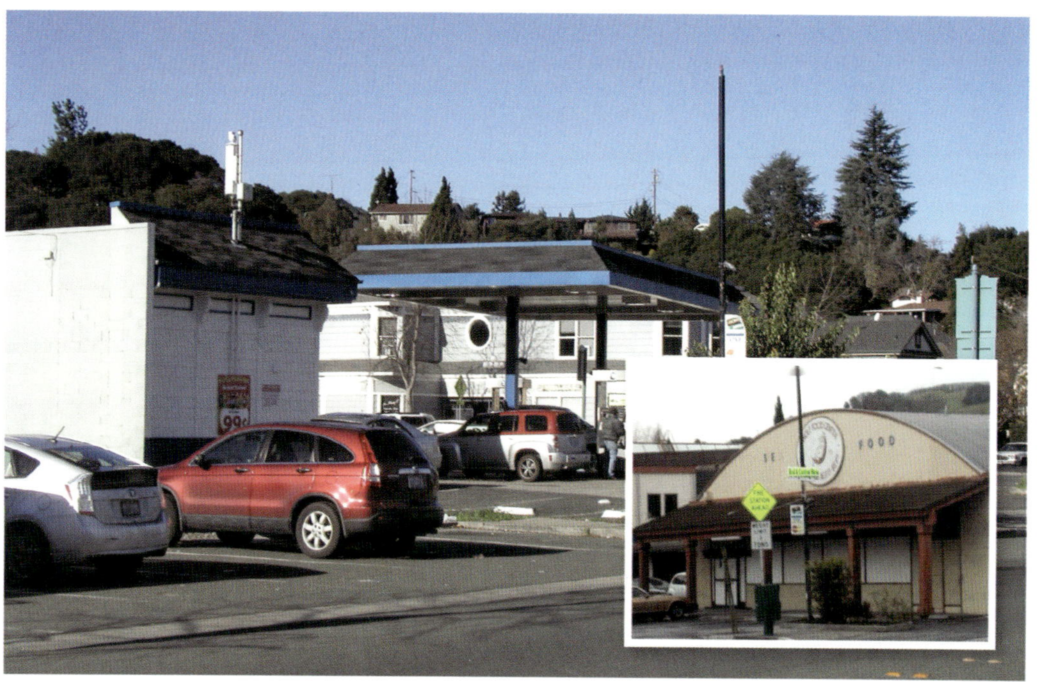

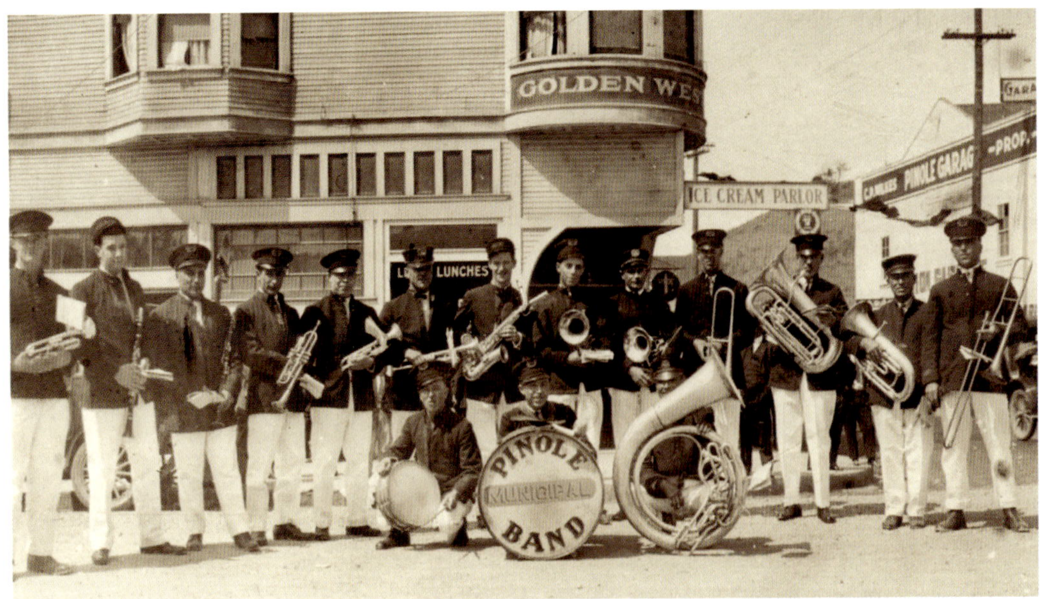

GOLDEN WEST HOTEL: Cipriano Silvas and his wife, Maria Rosario Alvarado Silvas, built the hotel in the early 1900s on the southwest corner of Tennent and San Pablo avenues, one of Pinole's Four Corners, known as such for the bars on each corner. Cipriano's brother, Jimmy, ran the bar on the first floor. The building later housed the Joe Lunghi Trovatore Café, which served Italian food and had a bar, and the Town Tavern. The Pump House convenience store and gas station is there now.

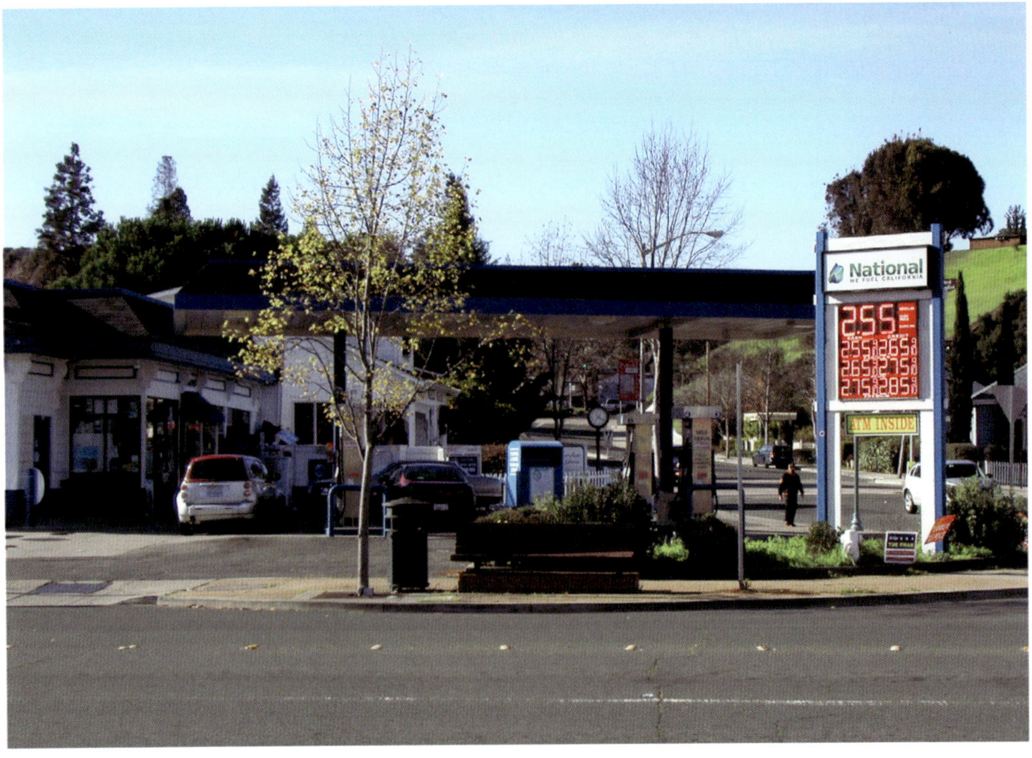

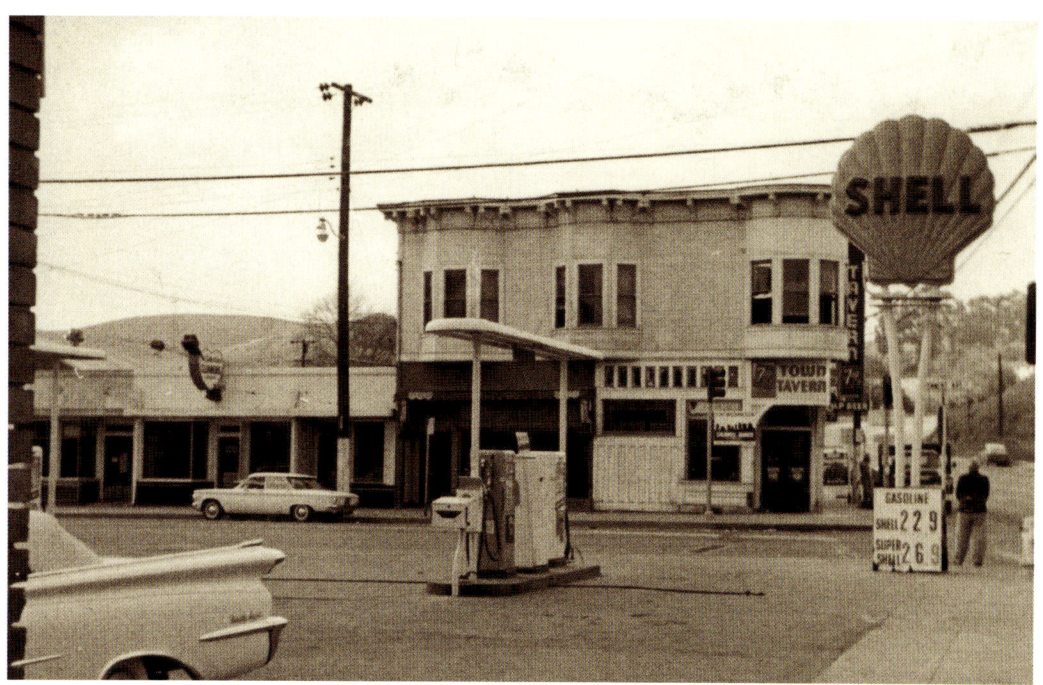

TOWN TAVERN/COMMUNITY CORNER: Pinole was about to undergo another major facelift shortly after this photo was taken in the 1960s when the Town Tavern and adjacent buildings were torn down. The tavern, formerly the Golden West Hotel and Jimmy Silvas's bar at the turn of the twentieth century, was replaced by a gas station and convenience store, called the Pump House. The Shell station is gone, too; a landscaped community corner with a "Welcome to Pinole" sign was built on the station's vacant lot. Note the price of a gallon of gas. Those were the days!

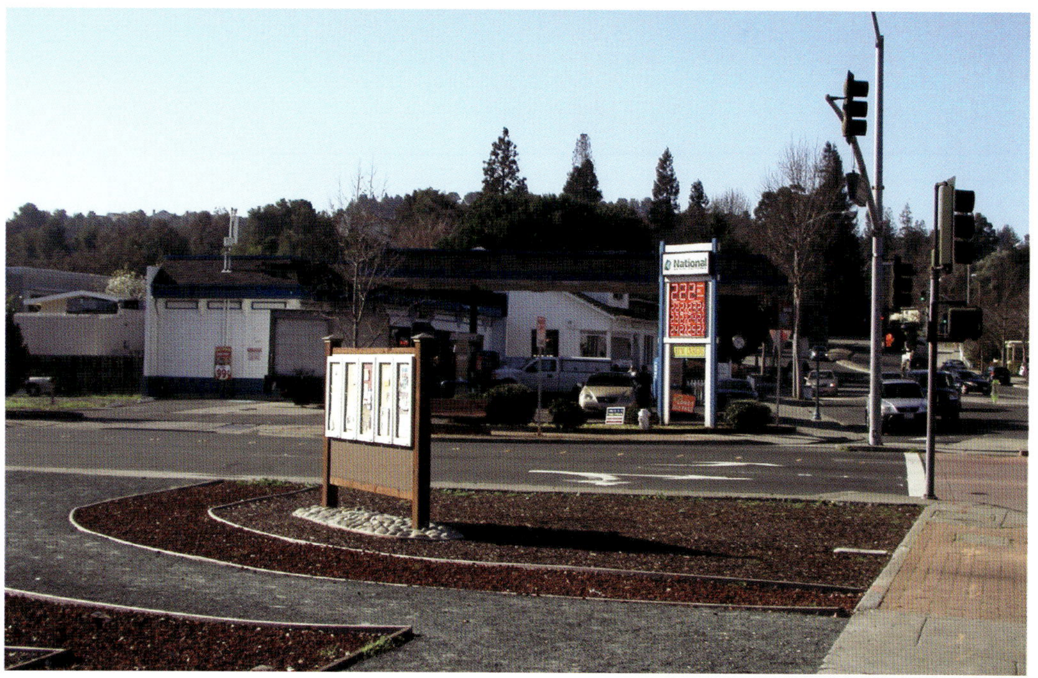

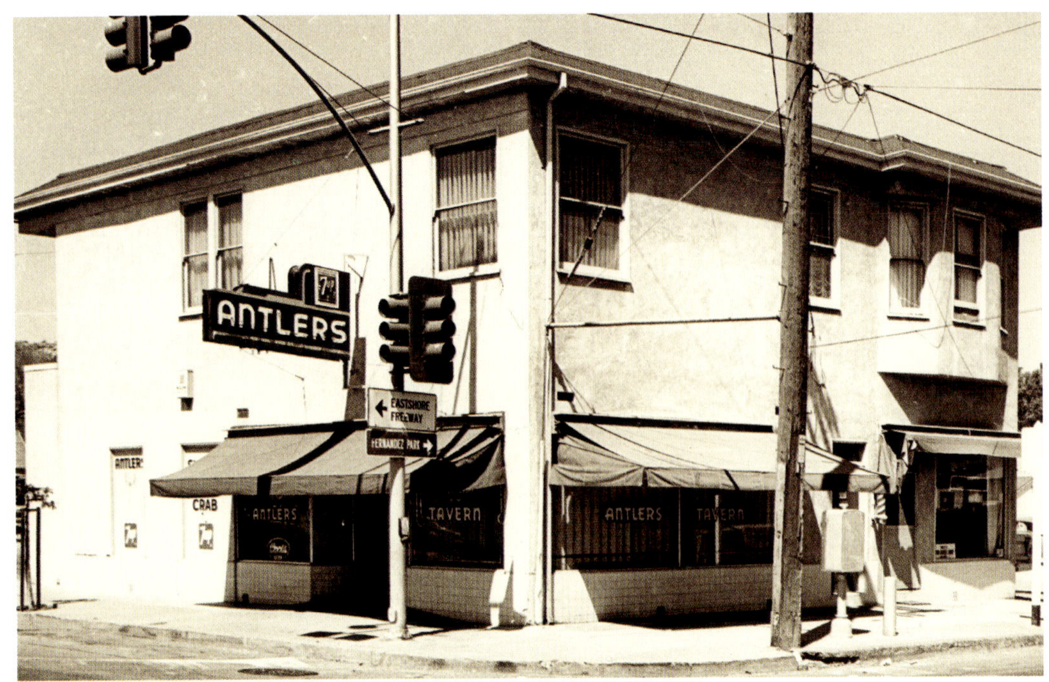

ANTLERS TAVERN: This building on the northwest corner of San Pablo and Tennent avenues was Lehman's, a small department store, in 1900. It became the Swenson and Lewis Saloon, owned by Jack "Squeaker" Silva. Jack was nicknamed "squeaker" because that's how his voice sounded when he talked. Antlers was owned by Frank Lunghi from 1950–1976. Lunghi took over the Trovatore Café, across the street, from his parents, Joe and Maria, but closed it when he bought Antlers. The Torretta family has owned Antlers since the late Al Torretta bought it from Lunghi.

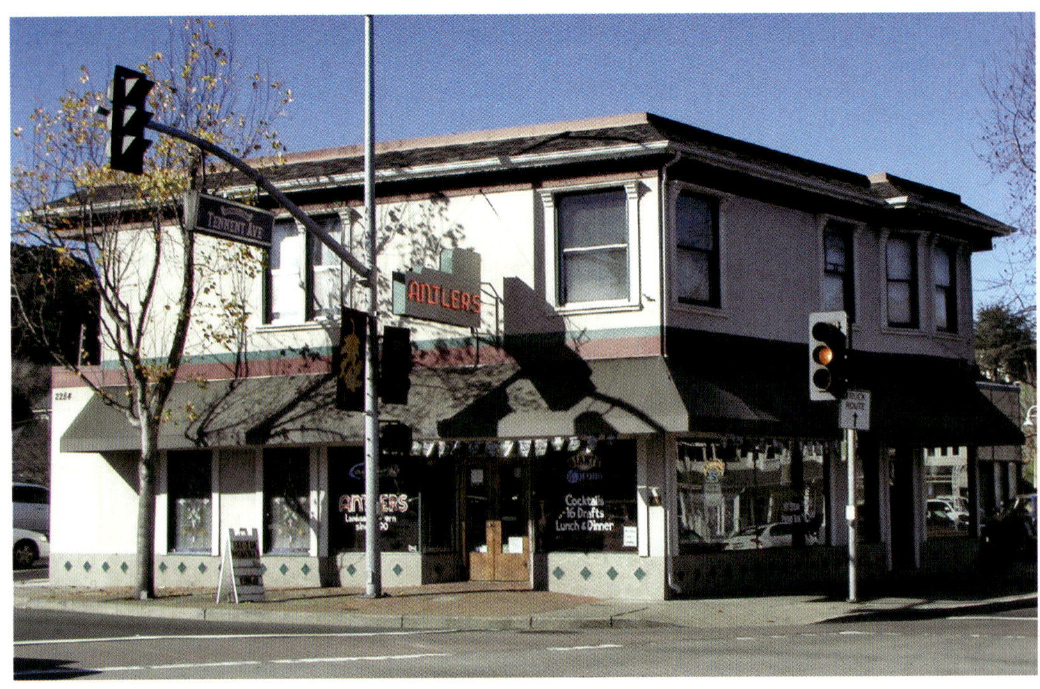

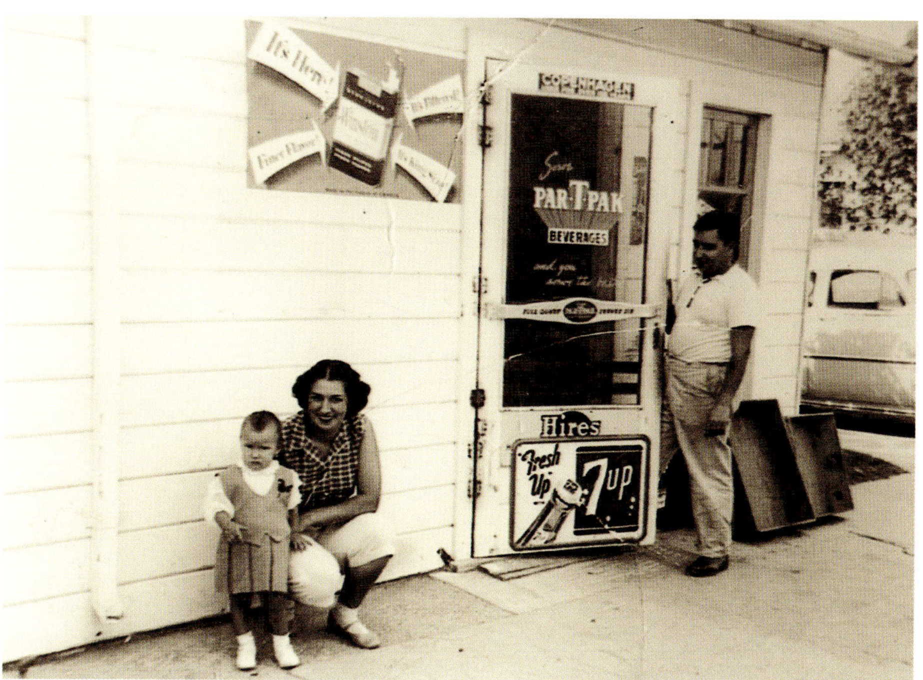

ARMS'S GROCERY/BLACKIES: Ann, Mamie, and Armand (left to right) in front of their grocery. Armand worked at Mare Island Shipyards during World War II. Afterward, he opened this store at the intersection of Tennent Avenue and Park Street. The family operated the store for 18 years. Armand died in 1967. The site became Blackie's, a restaurant well-known for its Maryland Fried Chicken and burgers. It was a favorite spot for Fernandez Park patrons and fans watching baseball games across the street.

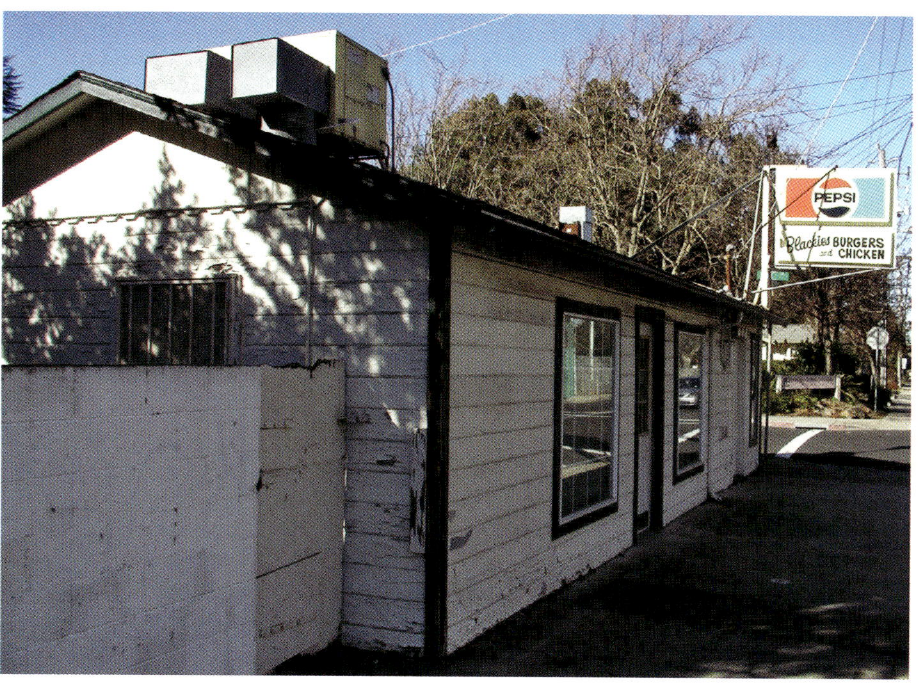

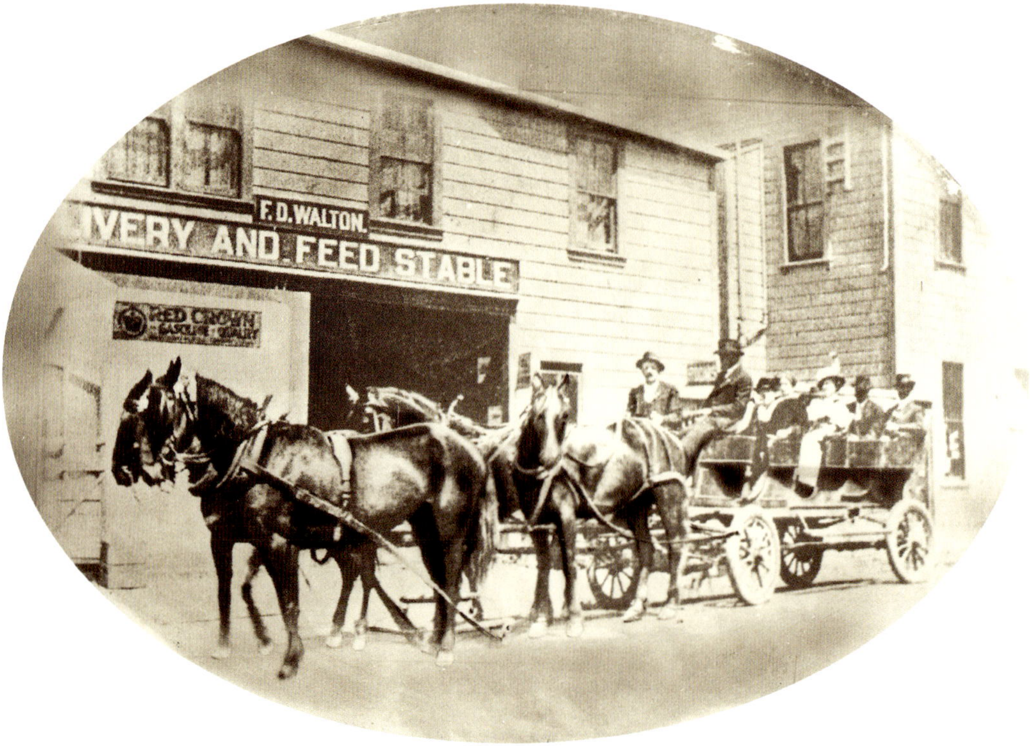

WALTON LIVERY/PARK PLACE: The Walton Livery and Feed Stable on Tennent Avenue between San Pablo Avenue and Park Street provided the first taxi service in Pinole. A major part of its business involved picking up travelers from the Pinole Southern Pacific depot in a horse-and-buggy and delivering them to their destinations. The livery also supplied carriages for funerals. Park Place, a commercial/residential complex next to the Pinole Youth Center, is on this site now.

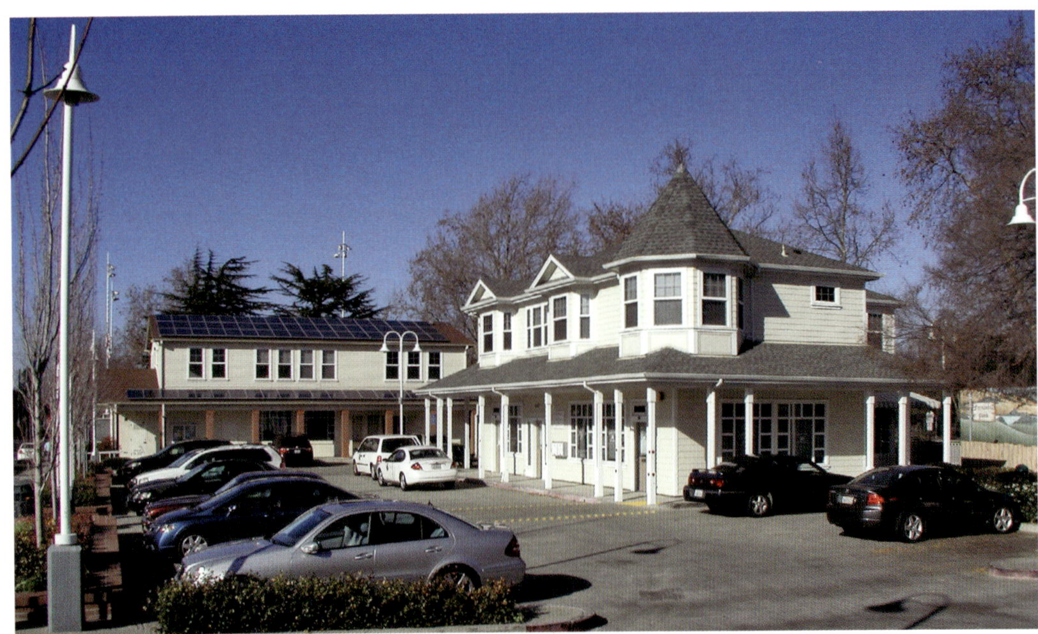

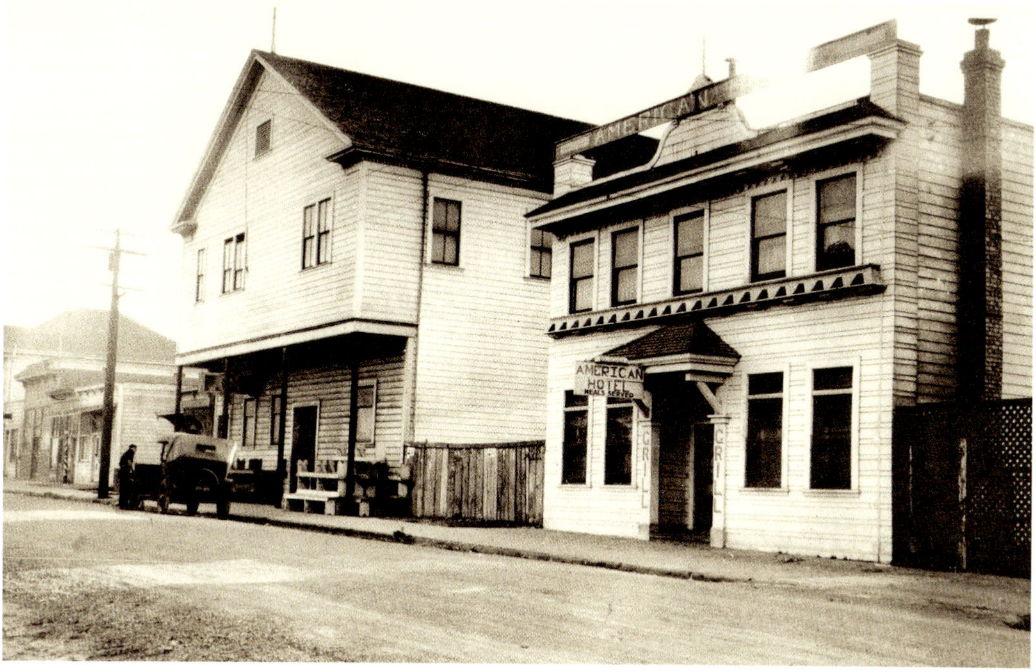

Forester's Hall/American Hotel: In 1903, Pinole citizens met at Forester's Hall and voted 150 to 6 to incorporate. The hamlet of Pinole was now a city, population 665. Forester's Hall (left) and the American Hotel were on Tennent Avenue between San Pablo Avenue and Park Street. Both were destroyed in a massive fire in 1908. The Pinole Opera House was built there soon after, but it burned down in 1931. Forester's Hall was the social center of Pinole, with lodge meetings, dances, and stage plays. Anjee's Dance, Etc., and a public parking lot occupy this space today. The Collins house is at the far right.

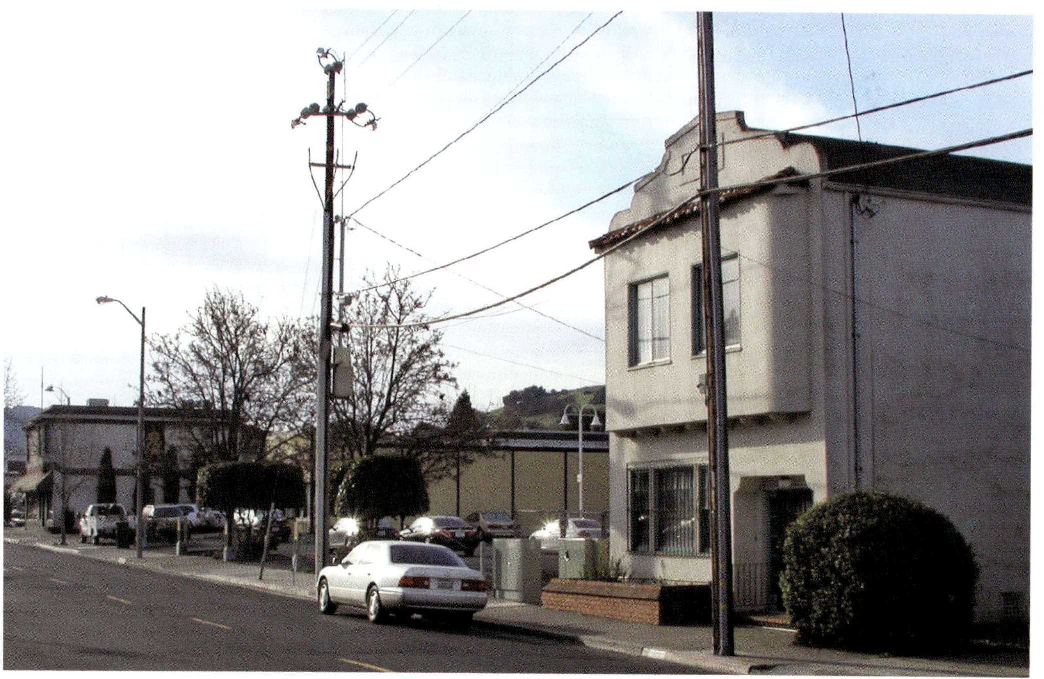

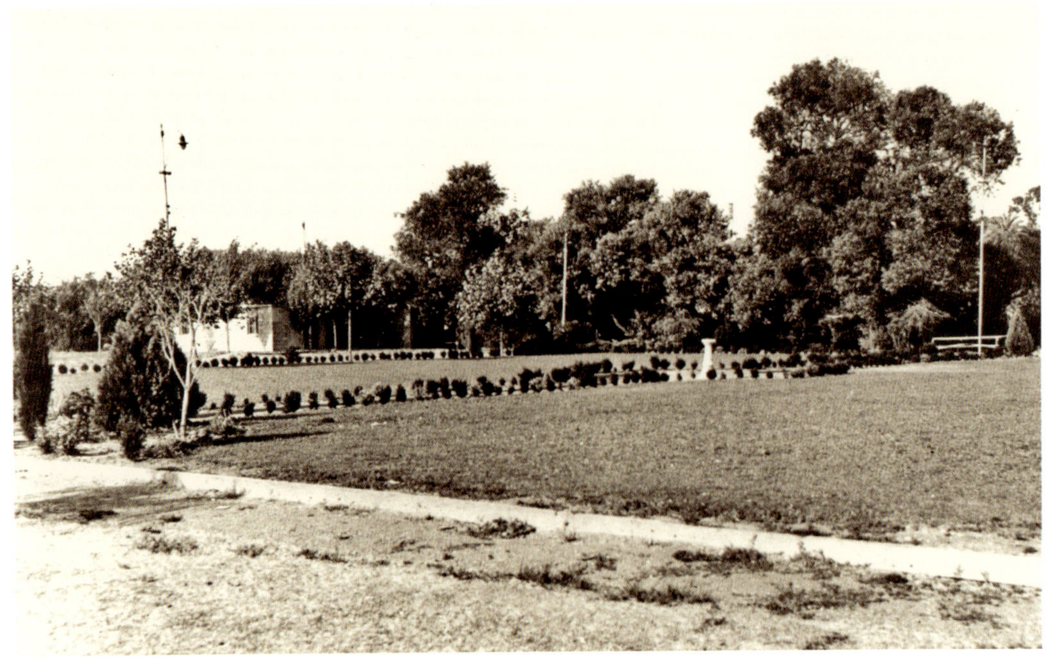

FERNANDEZ PARK: Before the 1930s, the site of Fernandez Park was occupied by the two-story Commercial Hotel, owned and operated by Manuel Marcos of Pinole, who also ran the saloon where The Bear Claw is today. Dr. Manuel Fernandez, son of Bernardo Fernandez and long-time doctor for the Hercules Powder Works, gifted the land for a city park in the 1930s. Fernandez Park has long been a gathering place for children and adults, with recreation activities such as concerts, barbecues, picnics, horseshoes, children's play areas, and basketball. The baseball field has hosted everything from Little League to the Pinole Merchants semi-pro baseball team. On May 30, 1961, the city dedicated a memorial to servicemen in the park.

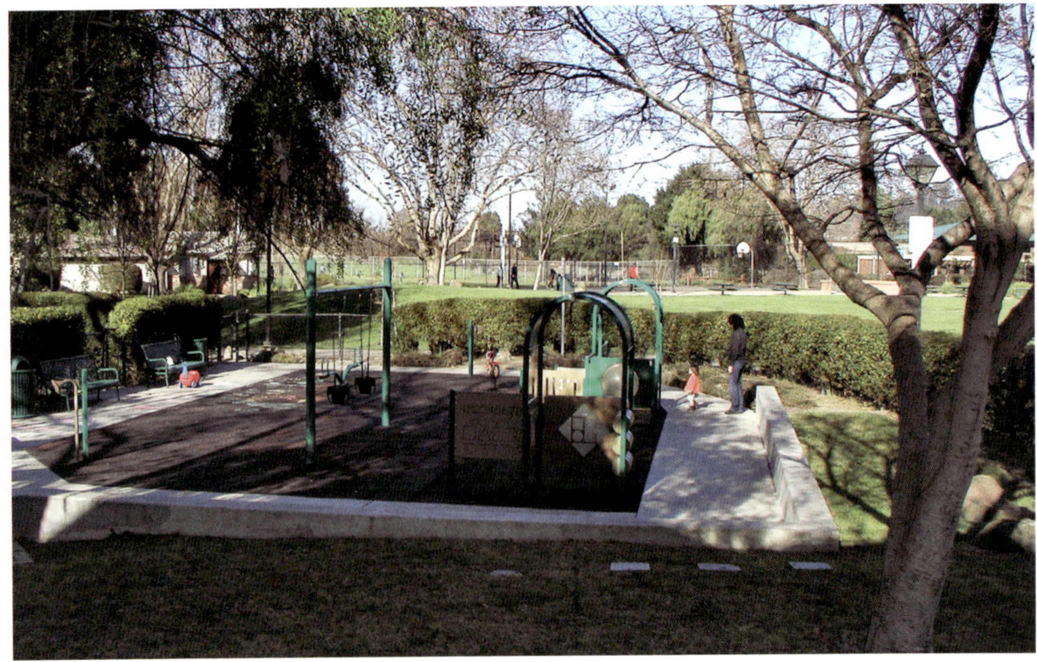

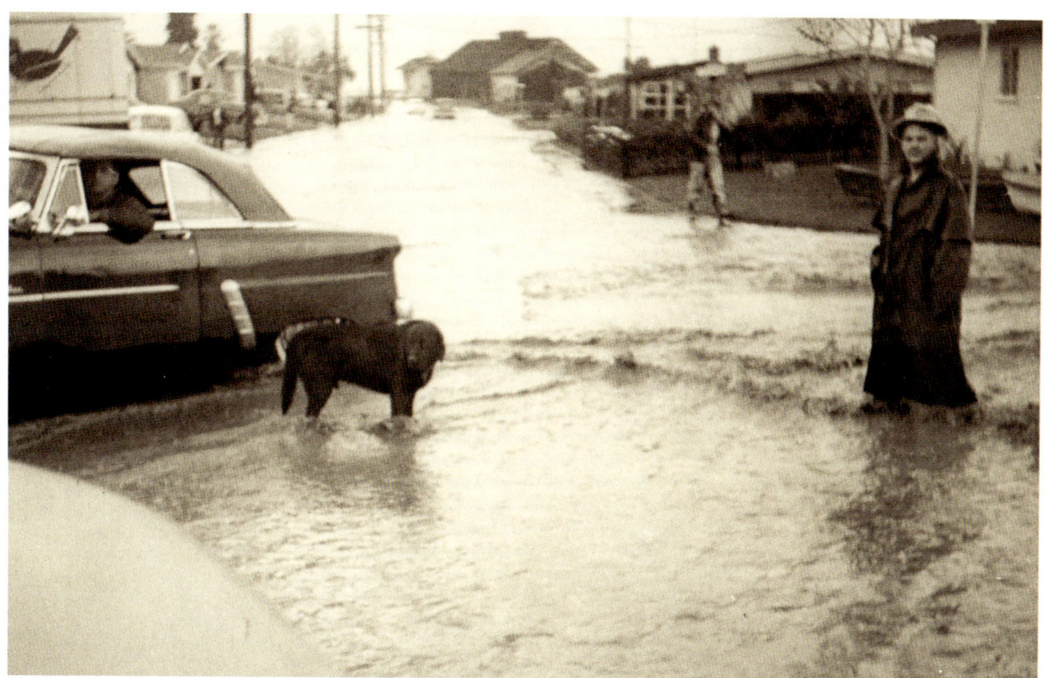

1958 FLOOD FROM TENNENT AND LA SALLE: Pinole Creek took a circuitous route on the way from its Alhambra Valley watershed to San Pablo Bay. Its hairpin turns and shallow depth created havoc for the city's residents throughout the first 60 years of the twentieth century. The 1916 Pinole Creek flood floated wooden sidewalks into the bay, and the 1940 flood left three feet of water downtown. The last of the Bernardo Fernandez warehouses are seen at the end of Tennent Avenue from the intersection of Tennent Avenue and LaSalle Drive during the 1958 flood. A motor home storage yard occupies that space today.

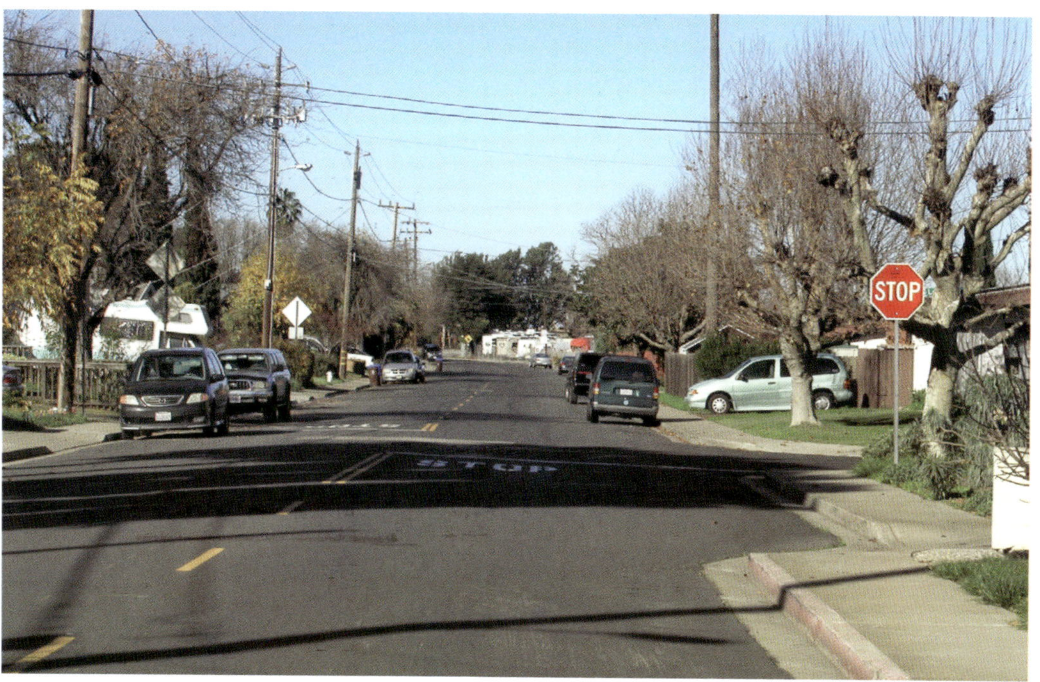

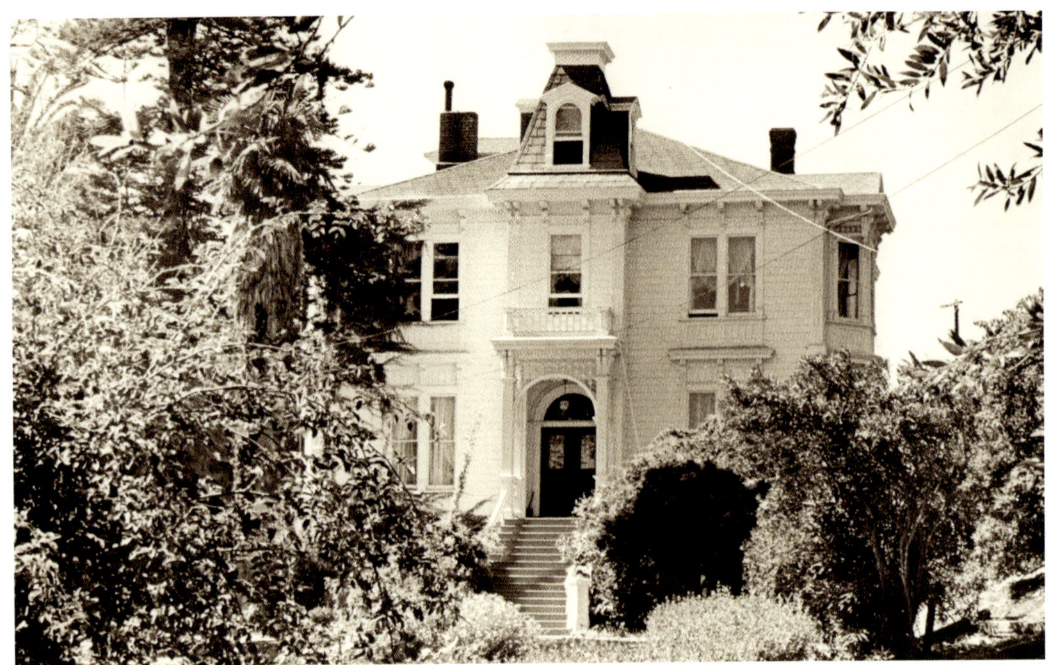

FERNANDEZ MANSION: The home Bernardo Fernandez built in 1894 is the most well-known building in Pinole. The 22-room mansion was built along the waterfront on land purchased from Dr. Samuel J. Tennent. Fernandez had a thriving shipping business, with schooners, wharves, warehouses, and a store. He owned most of the Pinole Valley lands and ranches. His family gifted the land for Fernandez Park and for a waterfront sewage-treatment plant. Dr. Joseph Mariotti, and his wife, Gretchen, bought the mansion (photographed here by Larry Neptune), lived there for decades, reared a family there, and saved it from destruction. It's on the National Register of Historic Places.

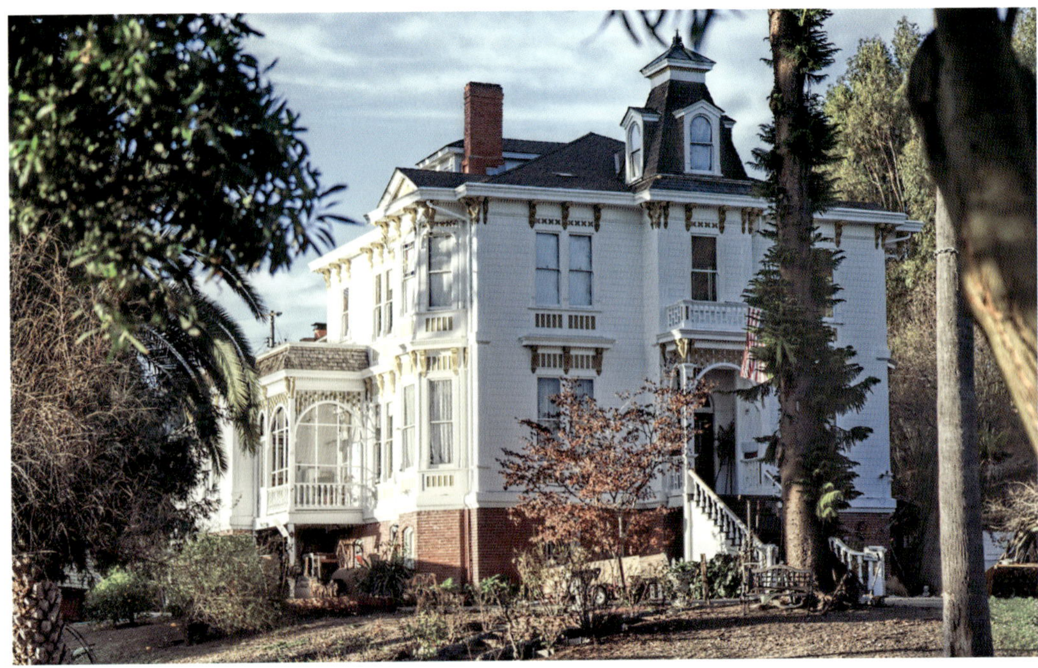

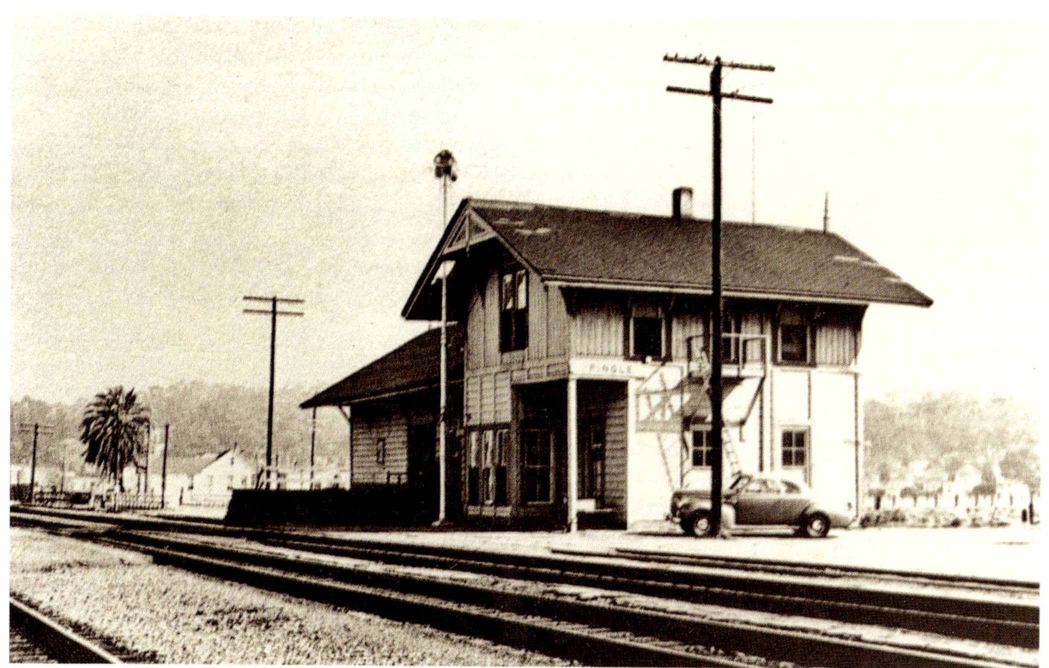

SOUTHERN PACIFIC DEPOT: The Southern Pacific Railroad (formerly the Northern Railway and now Union Pacific) came to the Pinole waterfront in the late 1870s. With the railroad came a Pinole depot at the end of Tennent Avenue, across from the Bernardo Fernandez home. Until 1910, the depot served as Pinole's post office. In 1889, Edward M. Downer came to Pinole at age 19 and served as the first official postmaster and the Southern Pacific's transfer agent and telegrapher. Southern Pacific depots were always painted yellow and had a palm tree planted beside them. This depot, by the shores of San Pablo Bay, was demolished in 1958.

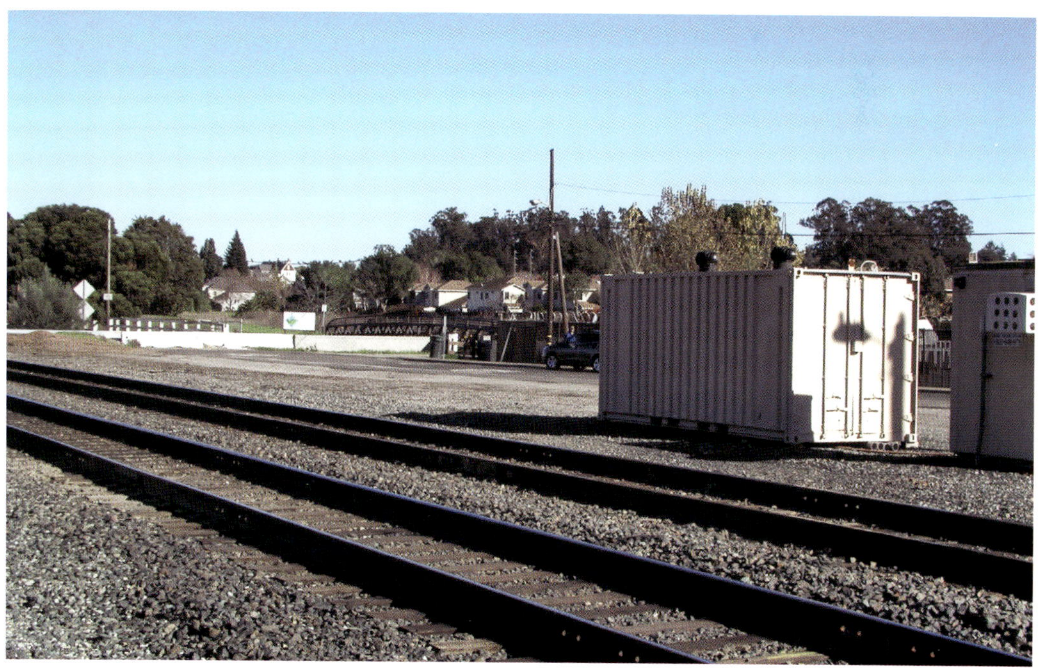

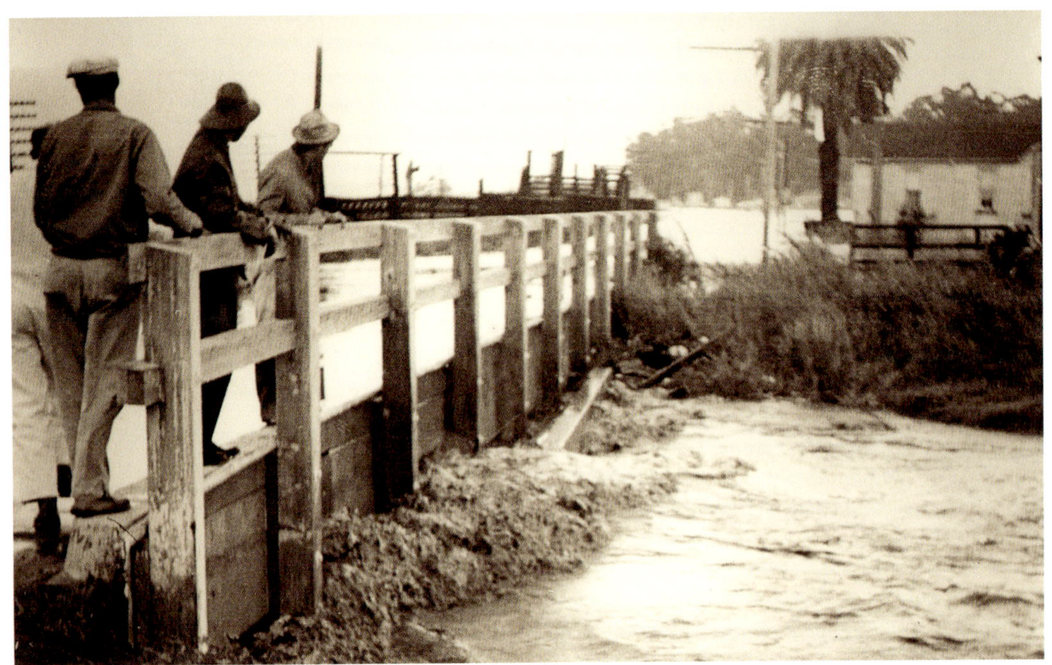

Flood of 1958, mouth of Pinole Creek: On April 2, 1958, after several days of hard rain, high tides contributed to the overflow of Pinole Creek, which flooded the downtown area. Boats tied up along Tennent Avenue so the fire department could rescue people from their flooded homes. Boats went up and down Tennent Avenue, which was like a river. Fernandez Park was under three feet of water. Children got on the bridge connecting Valley Avenue with Prune Street in makeshift rafts and "surfed" down the creek. The flood almost wiped out the Railroad Avenue Bridge. In the 1960s, the U.S. Army Corps of Engineers widened, straightened, and deepened the creek. Downtown Pinole has not flooded since.

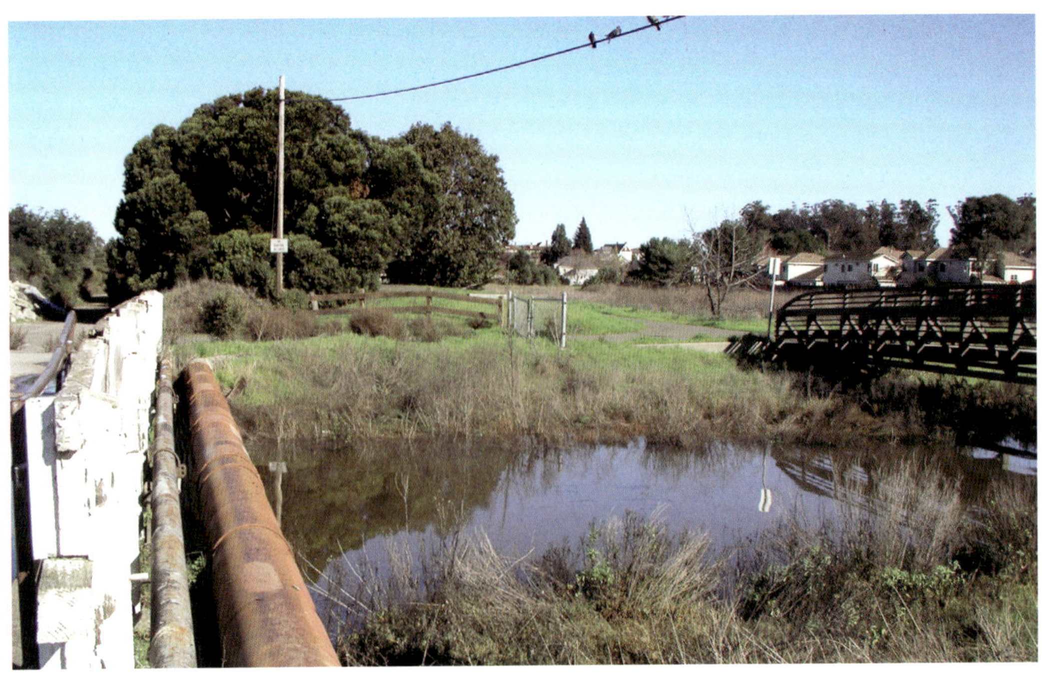

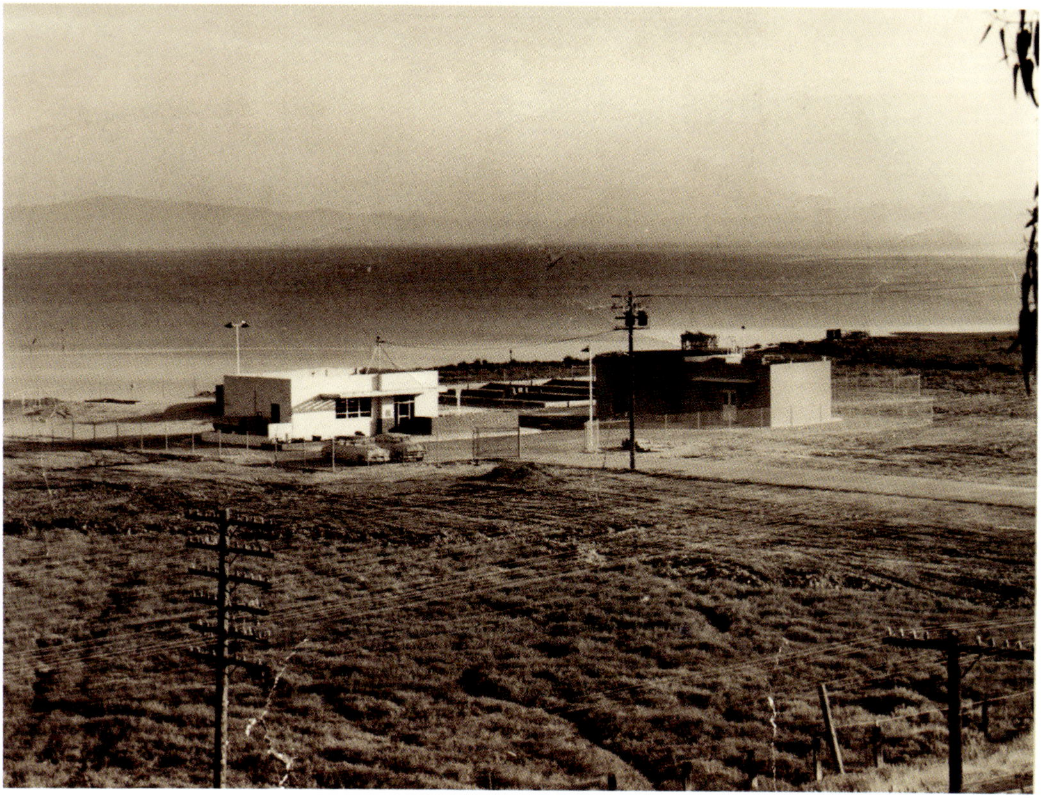

PINOLE-HERCULES WATER POLLUTION CONTROL PLANT: Commissioned in 1955, the plant at the foot of Tennent Avenue sits on land that was gifted to the city by the Fernandez family. The land grant also includes Bayfront Park, a popular waterfront refuge for dog-walkers and strollers walking to the mouth of Pinole Creek, where it meets San Pablo Bay. The plant has had two major expansions and several modifications (as seen in this Google Earth photo) and is about to begin another state-mandated upgrade. It serves a combined population of approximately 40,000, with an average daily flow of 3.5 million gallons.

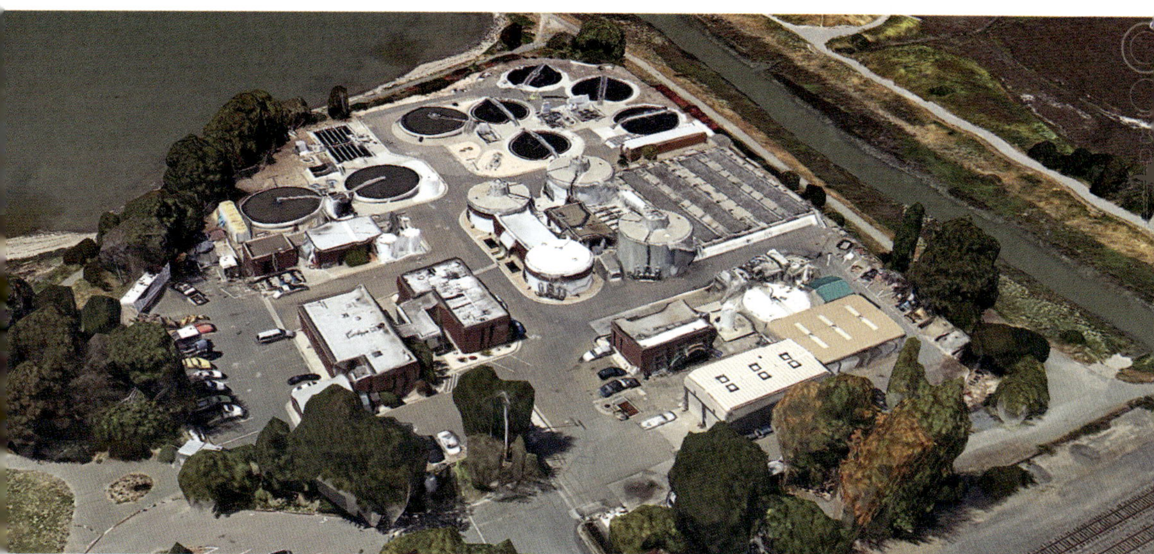

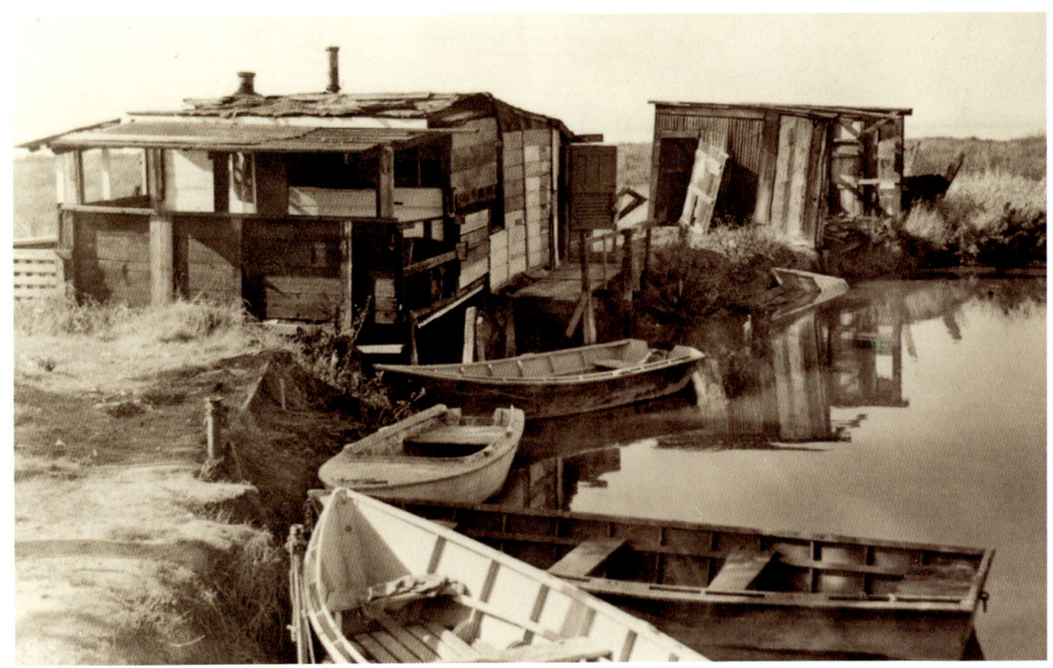

Bill Sexton home: The William Sexton home lay across the Southern Pacific Railroad tracks, northwest of the mouth of Pinole Creek. Sexton rented from the Fernandez family. William Sexton was born in Ireland in 1861. He immigrated to the U.S. in 1868 and became a naturalized citizen. His son, Bill, was born in 1898. In 1930, father and son were living in this bay-front home. Bill attended Pinole-Hercules School #1 and worked as a carpenter and truck driver for the Selby Smelting Company. By 1940, Bill and his wife, Vera, had moved to a home on San Pablo Avenue. The 1958 Pinole flood washed away what was left of the Sexton home, seen here in 1955.

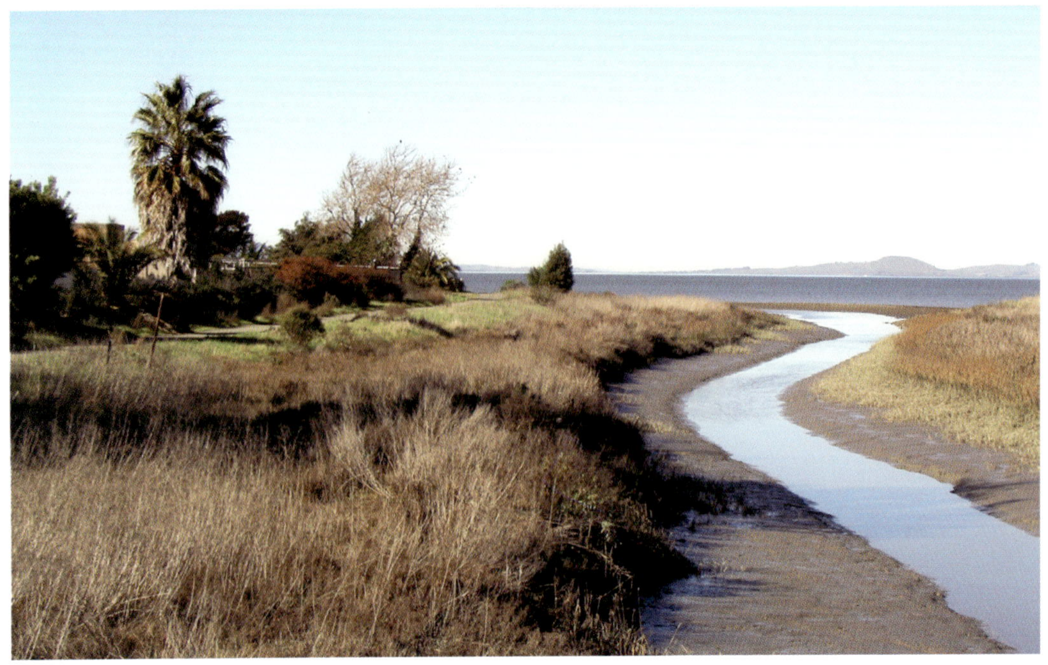

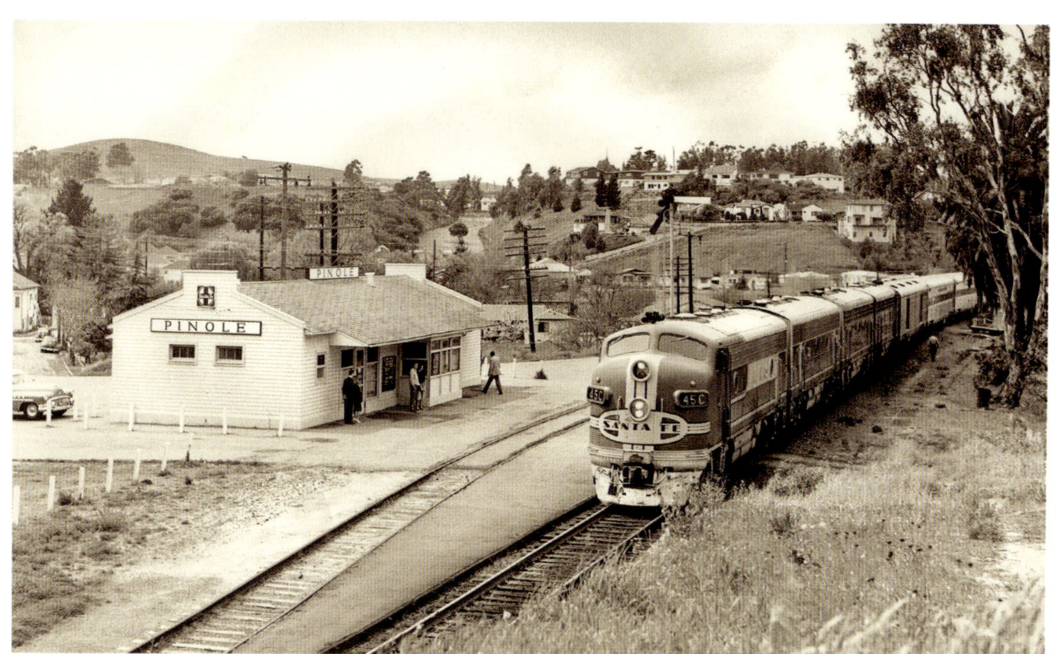

Santa Fe Depot: In March 1881, the Atchison, Topeka and Santa Fe Railroad reached Southern California, turned northward, crossed the Tehachapi Mountains, and went into the great San Joaquin Valley. At Stockton, it veered west toward Oakland and San Francisco, dealing with swampland, Delta waterways, and the hills and valleys from Martinez to Pinole on its way to Point Richmond. It provided freight and passenger service, connecting to San Francisco by barge. In 1901, the railroad known today as BNSF (Burlington Northern Santa Fe) built a red train depot at the northeast corner of Charles Street. It burned down in 1944 while a new depot (in this Robert Morris photo) adjacent was being built. That depot was demolished by the railroad in 1998.

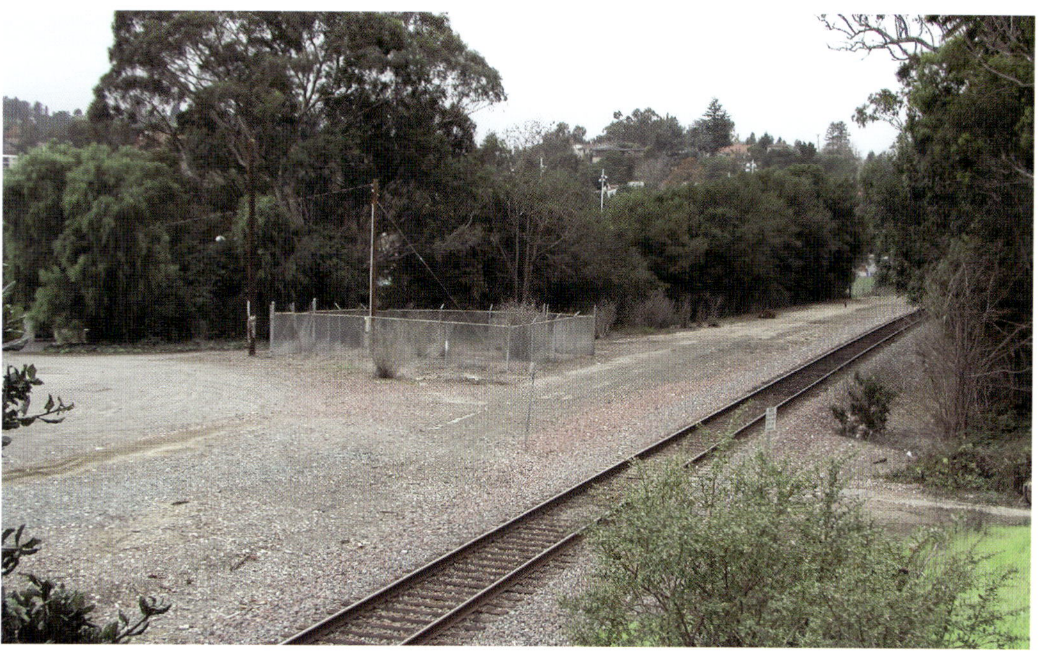

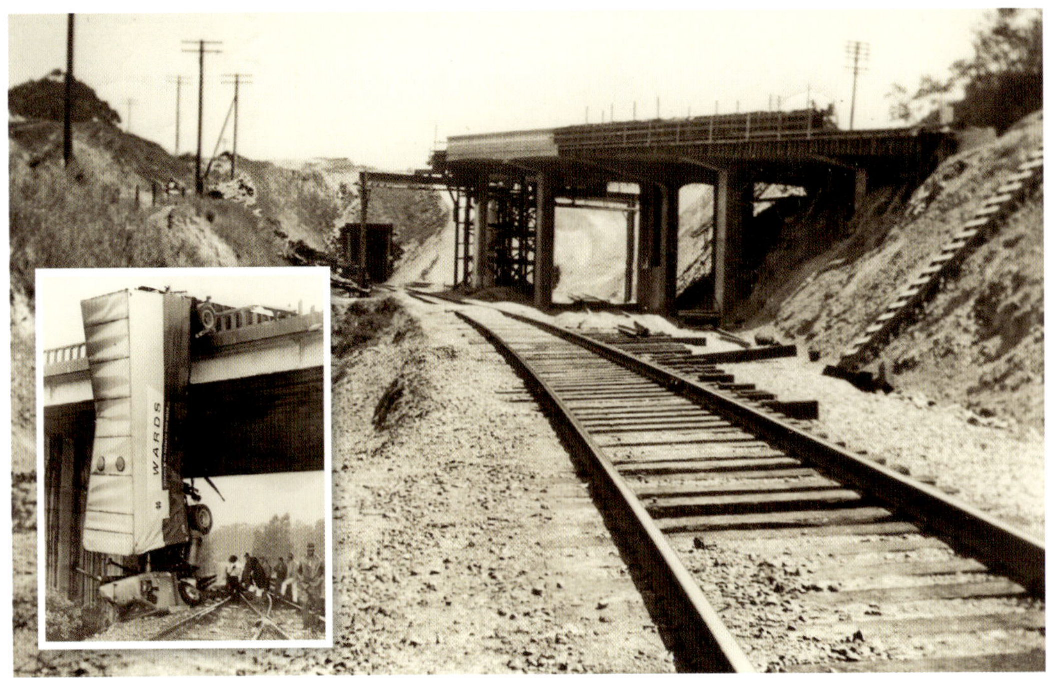

SANTA FE CUT: In 1933, The Santa Fe Railroad decided to "daylight" a tunnel just east of Pinole, making it a "cut" instead, leaving a railway-style timber overcrossing into Hercules. This required a highway bridge over the "cut" (formerly the county road, later U.S. Highway 40, and now San Pablo Avenue). The early photo shows the bridge under construction. In 1963, a Wards tractor-trailer crashed through the highway bridge railing (inset). The BNSF is strictly a freight service now through Pinole—no more passenger service here.

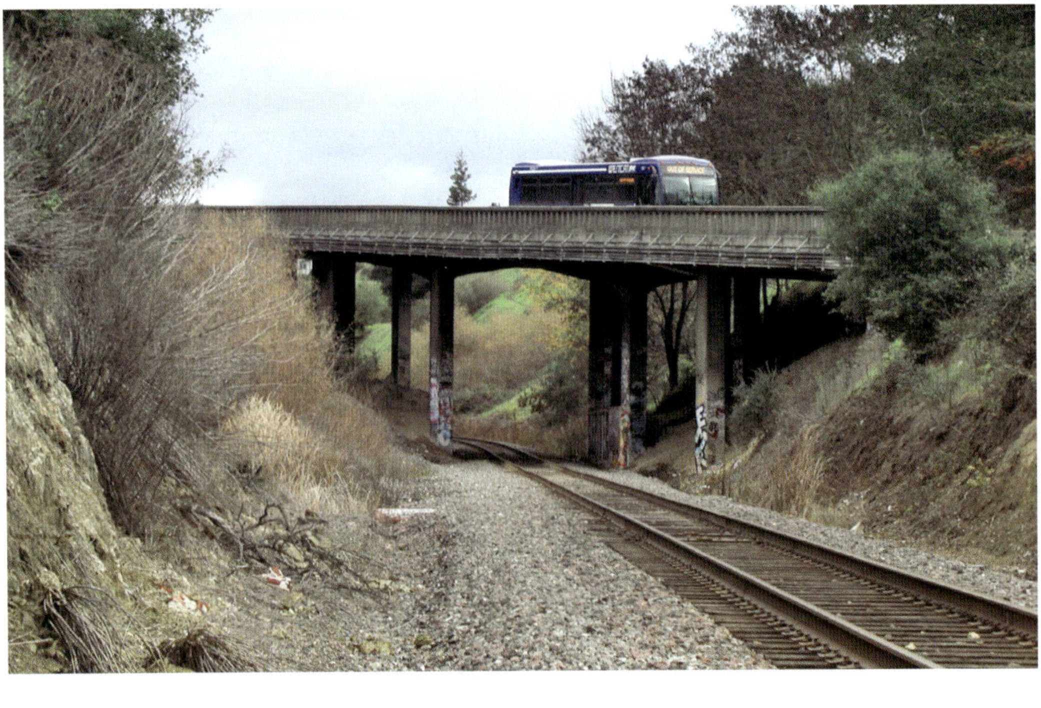

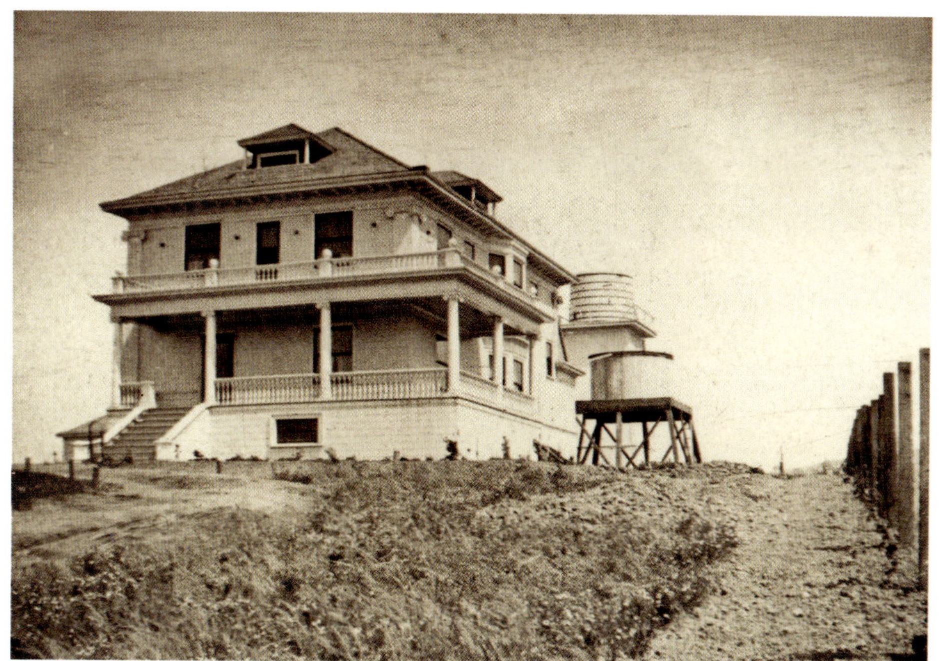

DOWNER MANSION: Edward M. Downer, one of the most influential and prominent business figures in the history of Pinole and its surrounding communities, built his home at 2711 San Pablo Avenue in 1900. He was Pinole's first official postmaster, was transfer agent and telegrapher of the Southern Pacific's Pinole depot, and co-publisher of the *Pinole Weekly Times*, the town's first newspaper. He was city clerk when Pinole incorporated in 1903. He was elected to the city council in 1910, and was mayor from 1913 until his death in 1938. He founded the Bank of Pinole in 1905. Don and Lynda Bartels, Realtors® and philanthropists, own and live in the home today.

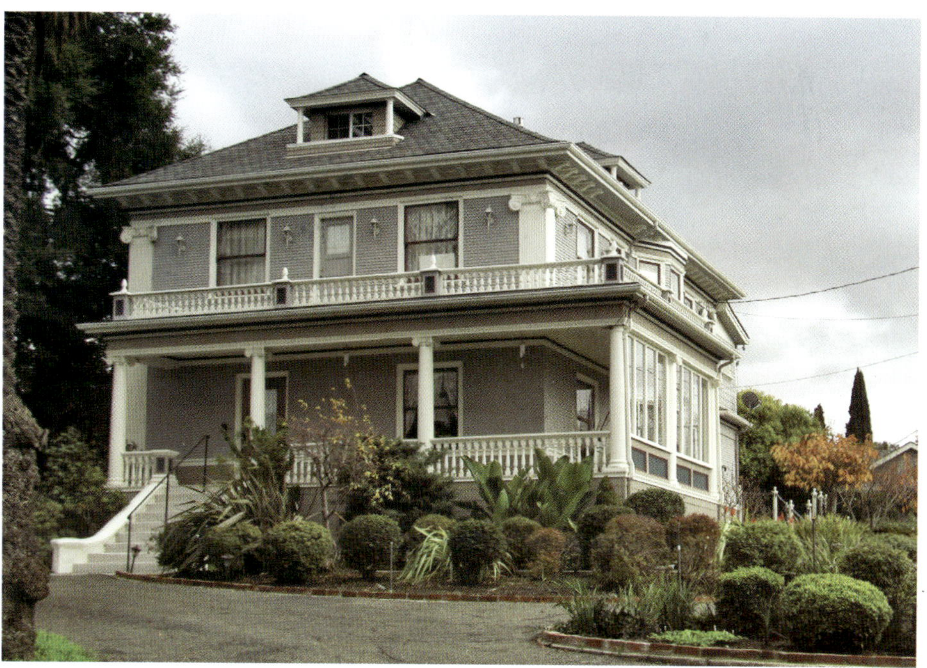

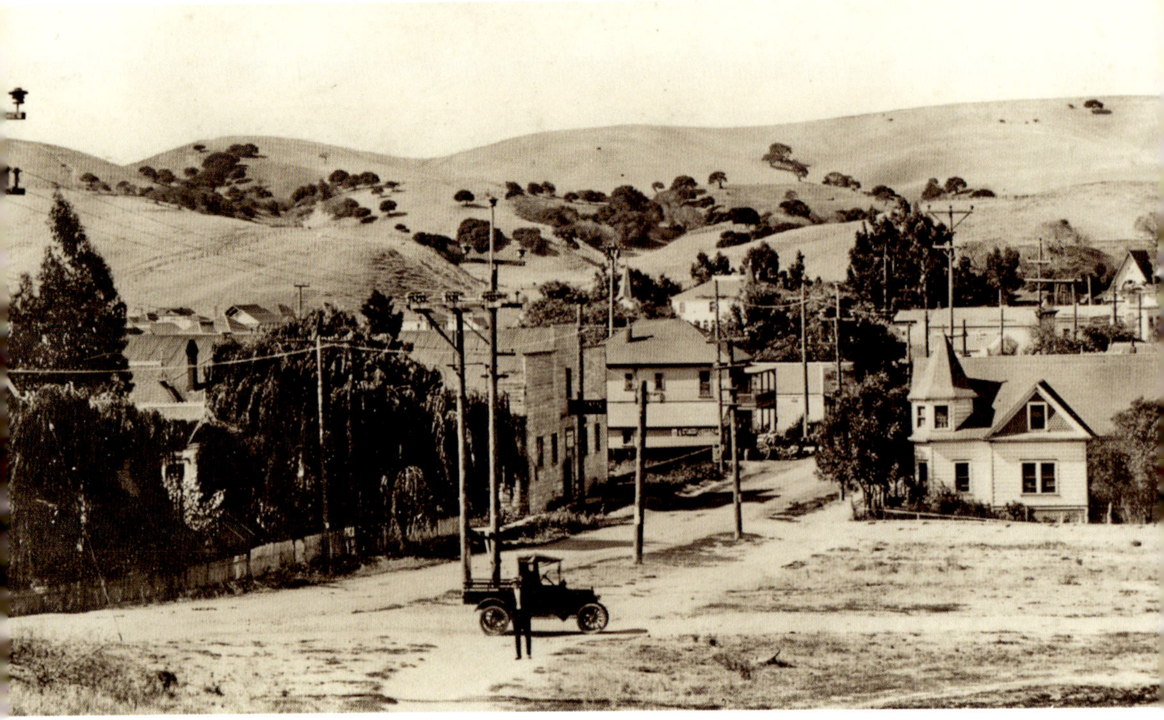

LOOKING WEST ON SAN PABLO AVENUE: Looking west on San Pablo Avenue: This 1910 photo was taken on San Pablo Avenue just east of the entrance to the Santa Fe train depot. San Pablo Avenue was narrow then, one lane in each direction for horse carts and the occasional automobile. The home with the steeple-like cupola, built in 1895, belonged to William W. Mann and his wife, Elizabeth. William was a foreman at the California Powder Works. The now-developed hills in the background were unspoiled, save for a reservoir that diverted water from Pinole Creek to serve the water needs of Pinole and Hercules residents and the powder works.

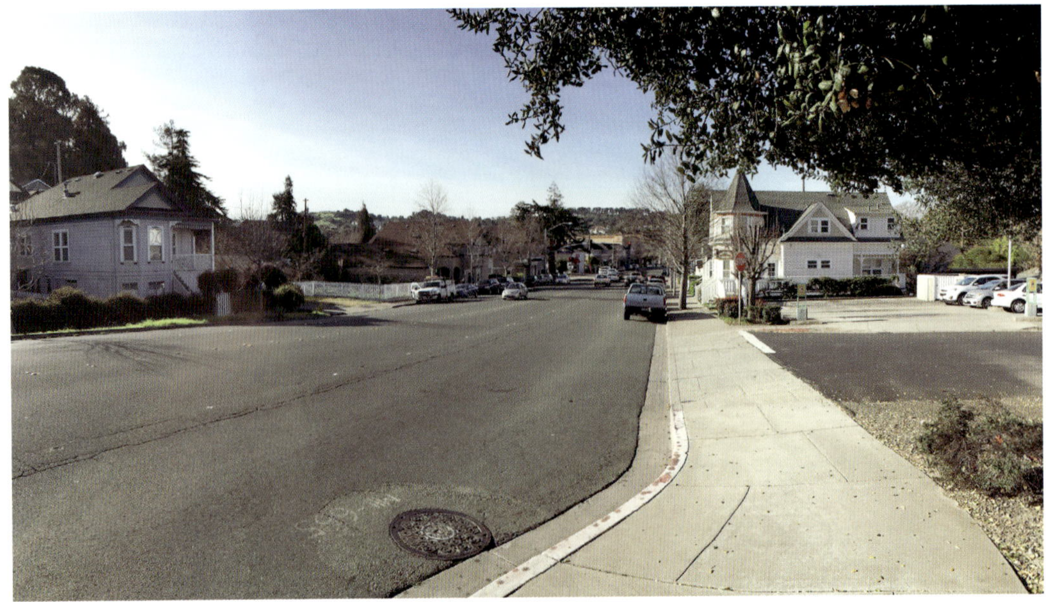

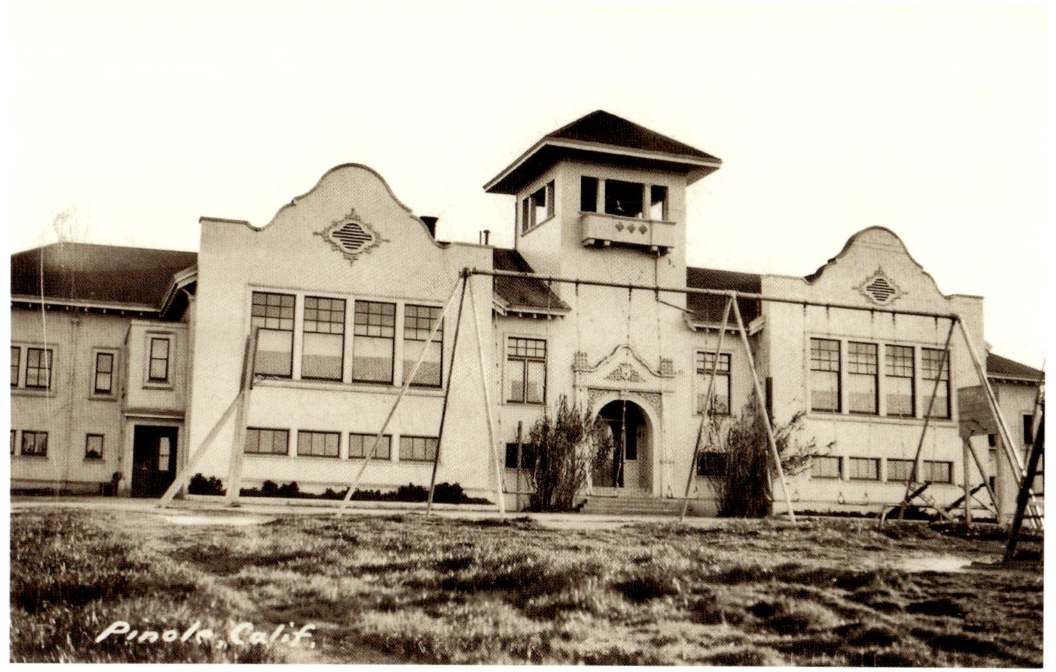

PINOLE-HERCULES SCHOOL #1: Class reunions are still held for graduates of this school, the "School on the Hill" or the "Old School," which served the Pinole and Hercules communities for 60 years, beginning in 1906. Several of Pinole's most-beloved teachers taught at this school, including Frances Ellerhorst, Elizabeth Stewart, and Margaret Collins, all of whom have schools named after them in the city. It was razed in 1968 to make way for the Pinole Grove Senior Housing, a residence for senior citizens, which incorporated some of the architectural elements of the school in its facade.

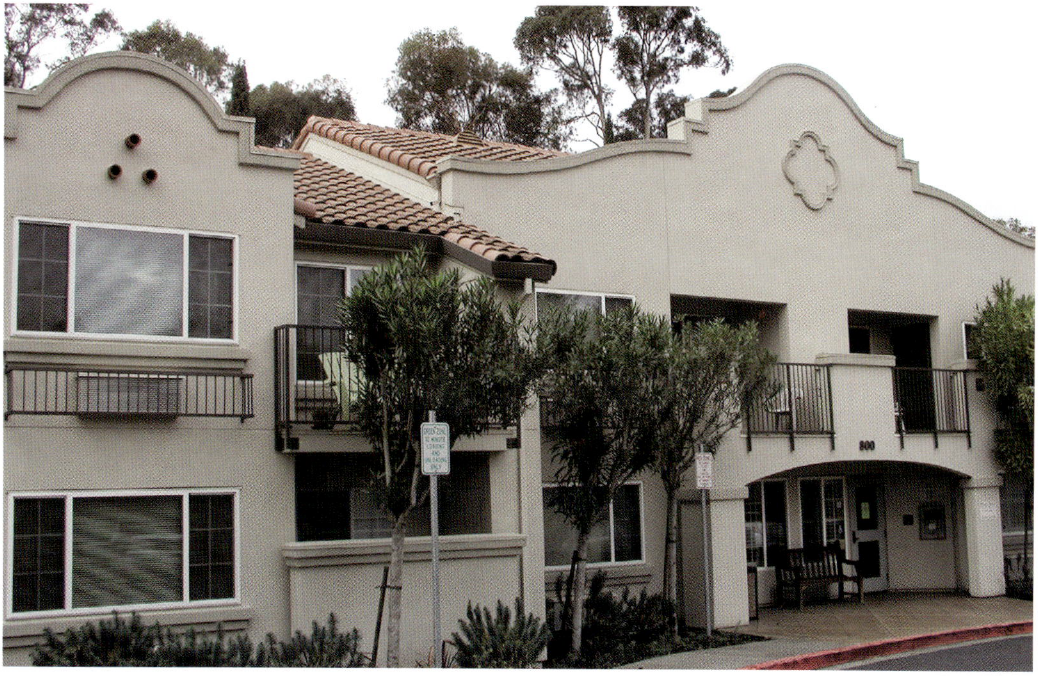

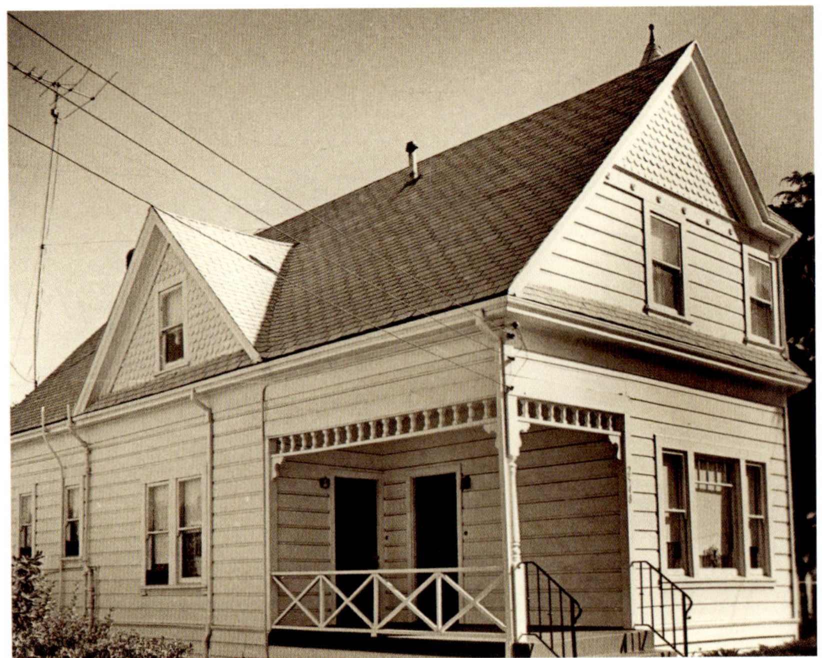

MANN HOME: William W. Mann and his wife, Elizabeth, were born in England in 1861. They married in 1882 and immigrated to Pinole in 1886. William was a foreman at the nearby California Powder Works. Their imposing 1895 Victorian home at 2458 San Pablo Avenue, the northeast end of the city, stood out with its high steeple-like cupola. Here they raised their three children — sons Joseph and Robert were born in England, daughter Georgina was born here in 1887. More recently, the home was the Captain's Cottage, a Victorian-style tea house, and the offices of Old Time Realtors, owned by the late former Pinole mayor Tom Gozzano, who also owned the building.

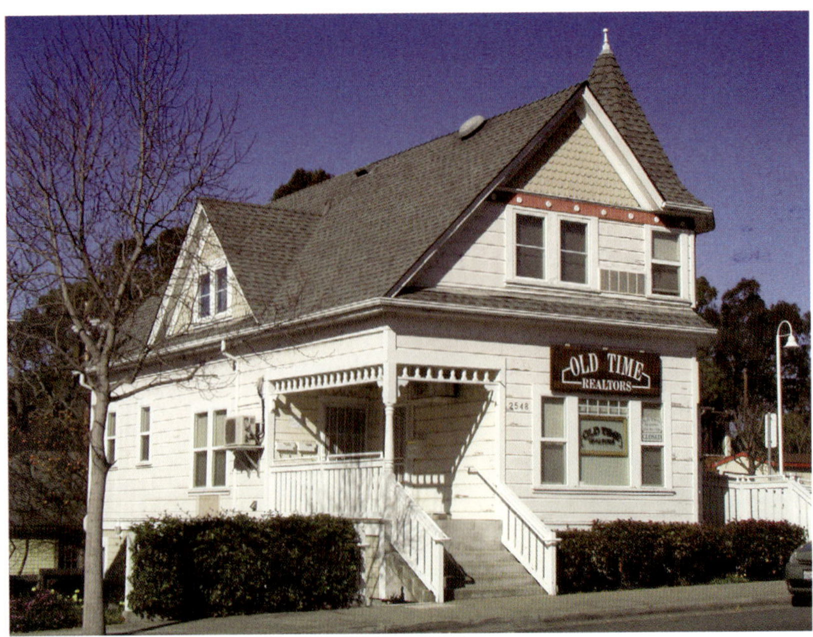

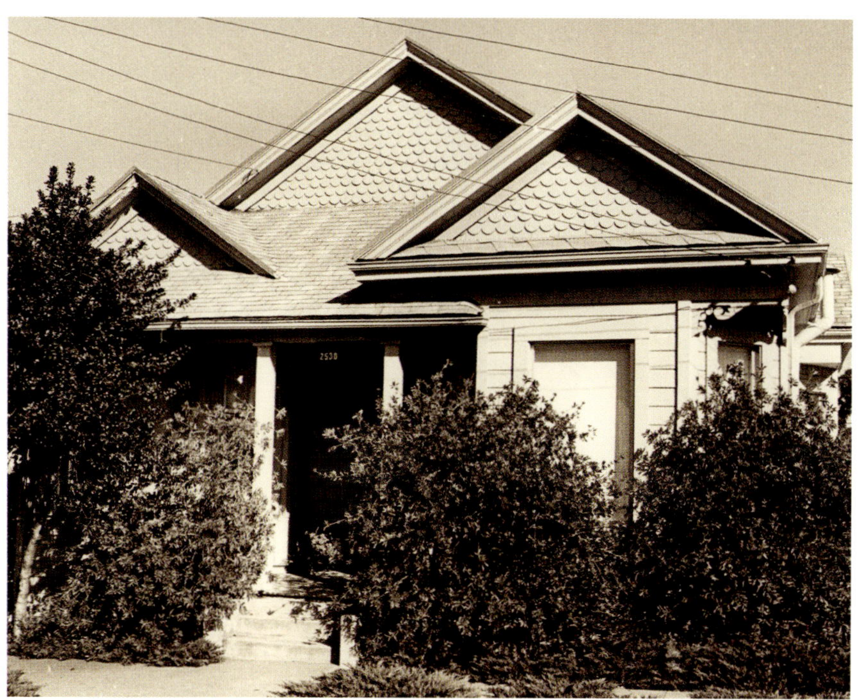

McDONALD HOME: Township 11 Constable Arthur (Jerry) McDonald gained his fame in death. He died in a hail of machine-gun bullets in 1929, shot by members of the Fleagle Gang, who were robbing the Rodeo branch of the Bank of Pinole. He and his brother, Fred, owned a men's clothing store on Tennent Avenue. Later in 1929, the Fleagle Gang robbed the First National Bank in Lamar, Colorado. By 1930, all members of the Fleagle Gang had either been killed in shootouts or executed after being found guilty in Colorado trials. Today, McDonald's Queen Anne-style home at 2350 San Pablo Avenue, built in 1898, remains a private residence.

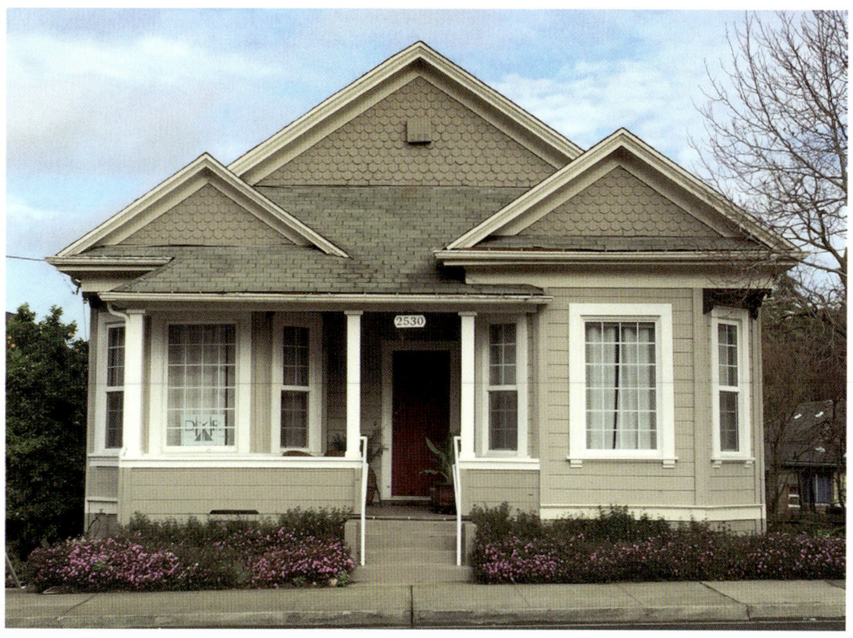

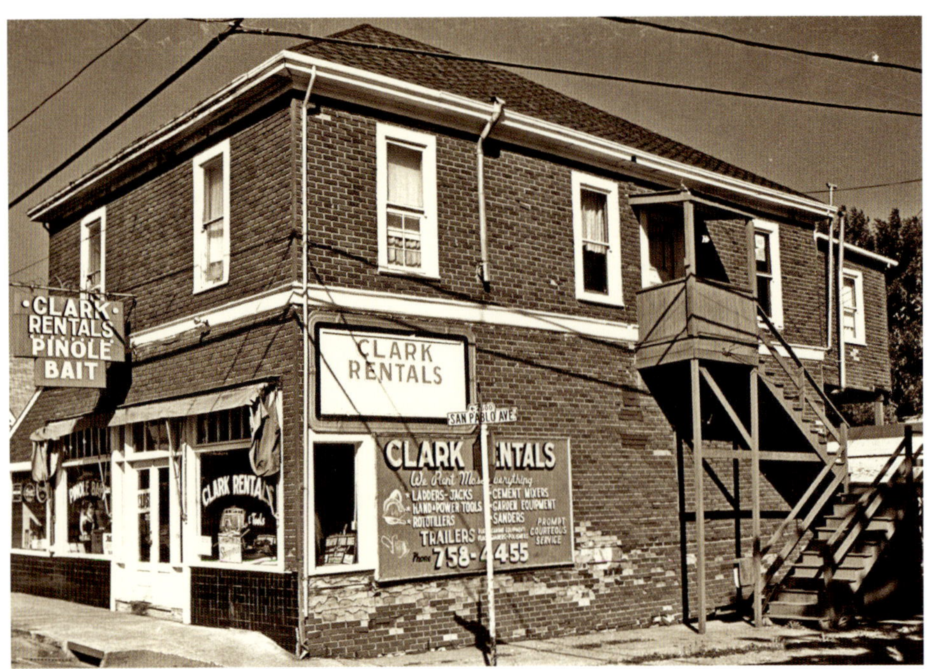

CLARK'S GROCERY: In 1901, Mr. and Mrs. Charles Clark opened a grocery store at 2511 San Pablo Avenue, at the southeast intersection with Pinole Valley Road. The Charles Clarks, his parents, and later brother William Clark and his family lived above the store. The Clark brothers eventually went to work at the Hercules Powder Company. William Clark moved his family across San Pablo Avenue into the Queen-Anne style home adjacent to the northern half of the Pinole Creek Bridge at 2494 San Pablo Avenue. Charles Clark lived in a large Victorian home behind his brother's house, adjacent to today's Pinole Senior Center on Charles Street, named after Charles Clark.

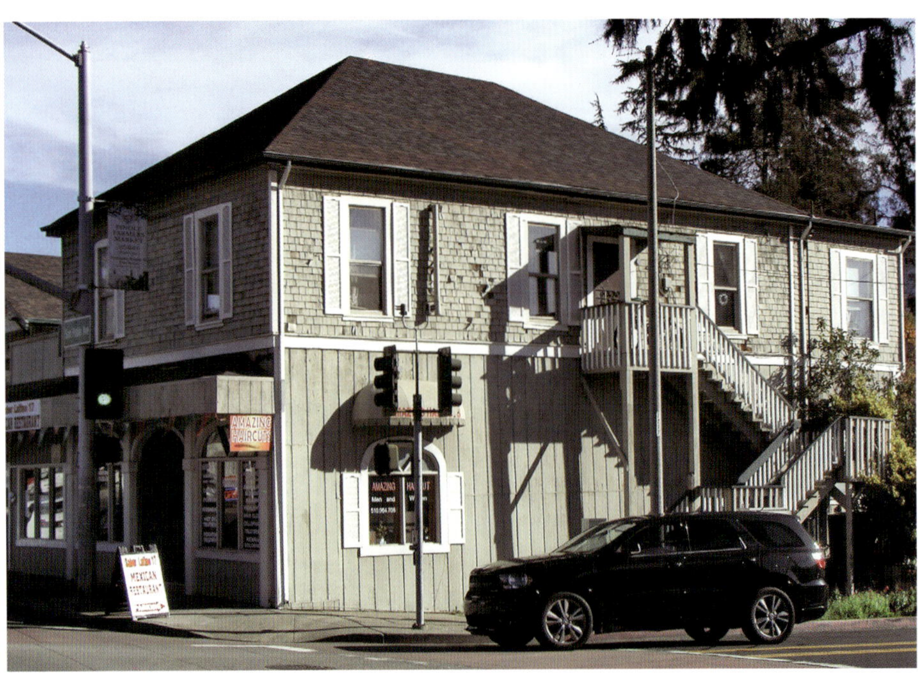

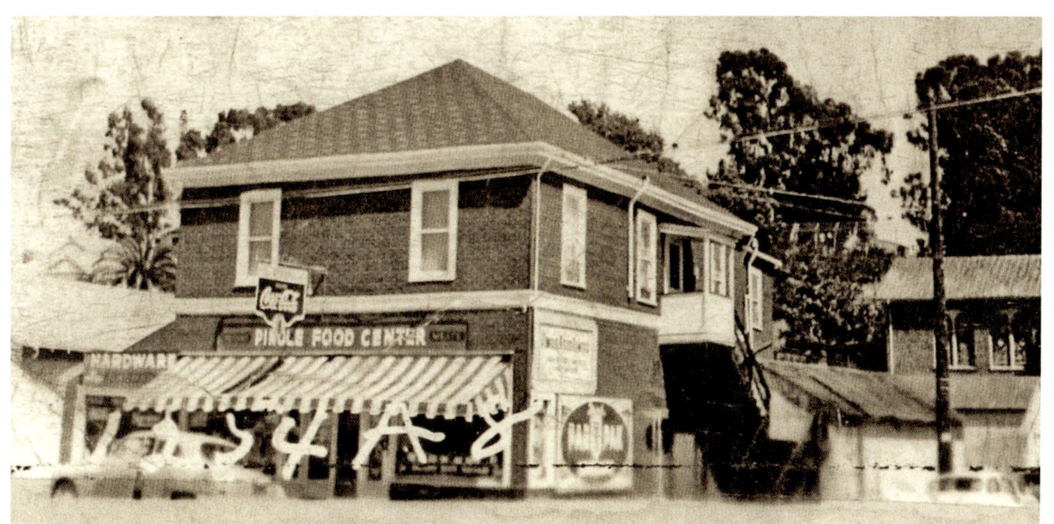

Joseph Lewis Store: Charles Clark sold his grocery store to Joseph Lewis in 1912 and went to work for Hercules Powder Company. Lewis delivered groceries in a horse cart, accompanied by his dog, Star. Every year he gave commemorative china plates to his customers. The Pinole Historical Society has several of them, donated by Marilyn Ponting. In 1920, Joseph Lewis sold the grocery store to his brother, Bill. In the 1940s it was sold to Glen Ellis and remained the only grocery store at the east end of the city. Then came Mickey's Bait Shop and Clark Rentals. Sabor Latino 17, a Mexican restaurant, and Amazing Haircuts, are in this building now.

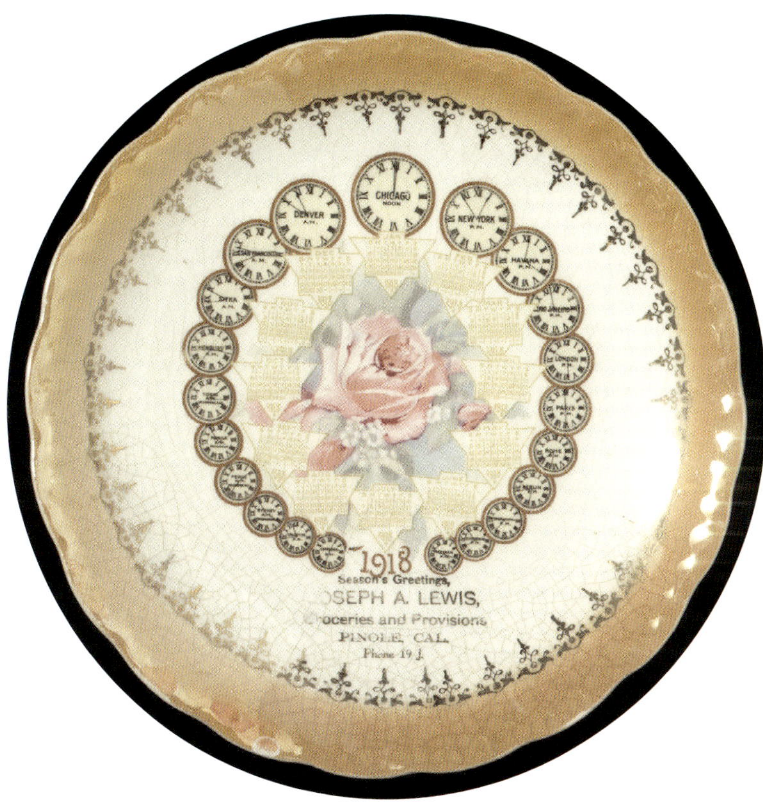

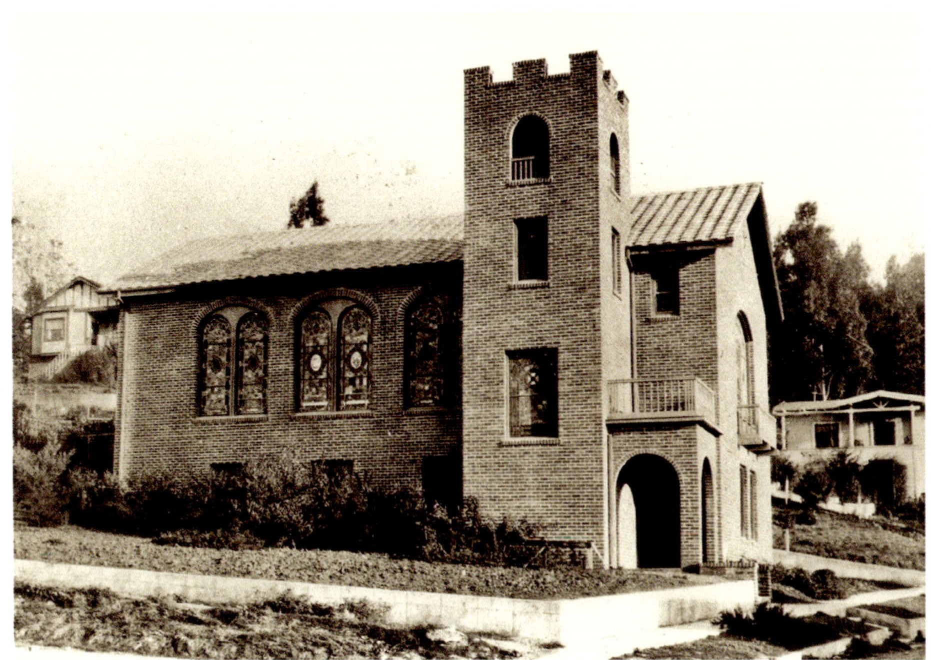

METHODIST EPISCOPAL CHURCH/CHURCH OF CHRIST: Meetings of the Pinole-Hercules Methodist Episcopal Church were held in Pinole's schoolhouse on the city plaza when it was organized in 1890. The church built its own building on San Pablo Avenue, near School Street, in 1898, an A-frame structure that is still in use. The second Methodist Episcopal Church on Valley Avenue, a modern brick building, was built in 1925, and dedicated to the memory of Elizabeth Downer, an impassioned volunteer in the church for many years and the wife of Bank of Pinole founder E. M. Downer Sr. This Valley Avenue church is now the home of the Church of Christ.

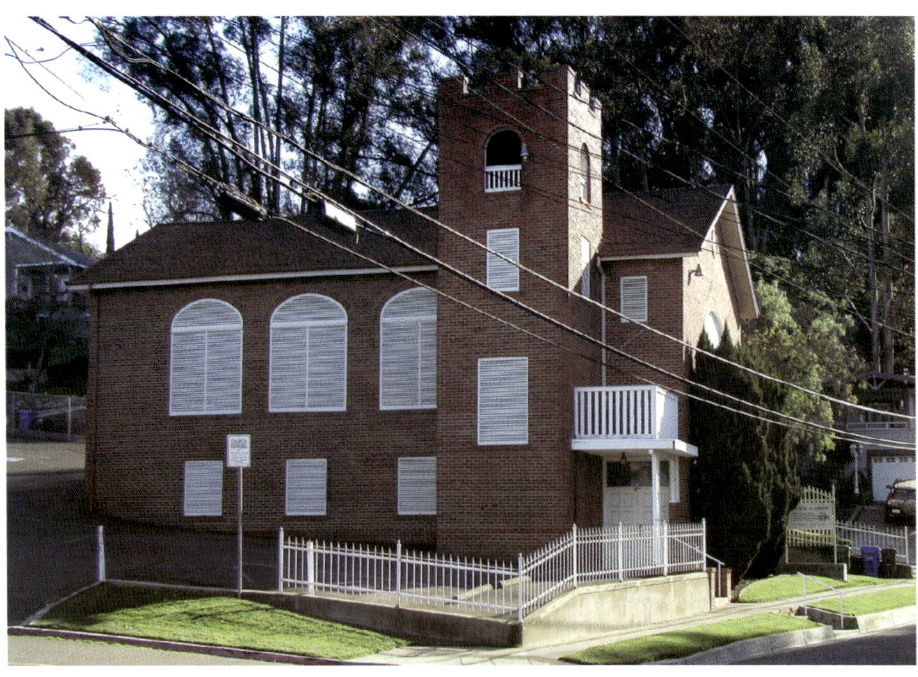

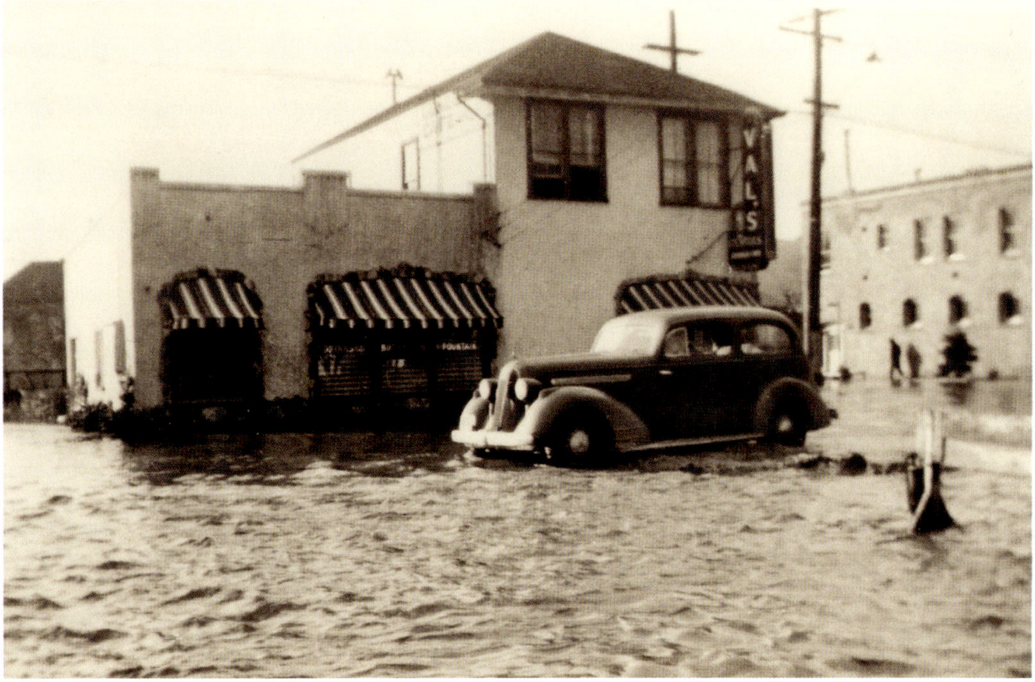

VAL PERA'S GONDOLA RESTAURANT: Val Pera and his wife, Nina, operated the Gondola Restaurant, on the southeast corner of San Pablo and Fernandez avenues, where Italian food and drinks were served in the 1930s and 1940s. As with many buildings downtown, several businesses were their occupants over the years. Many years before the Gondola, this had been the site of Charlie Vincent's Saloon. After the Gondola, it became the Club Alibi. Cole Vocational Services and apartment dwellers occupy the site now.

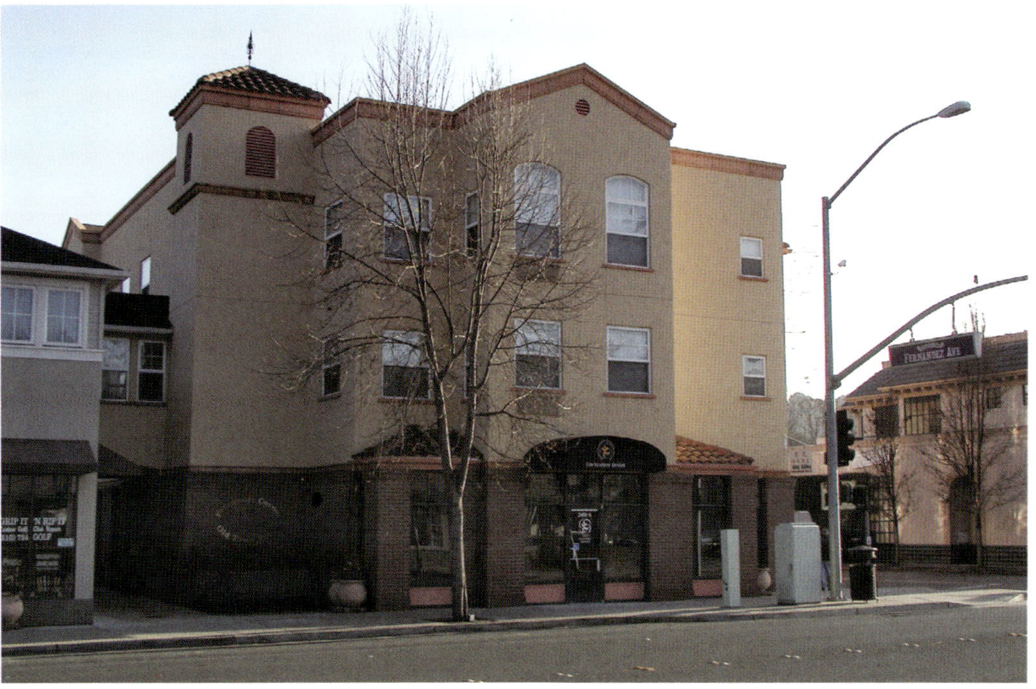

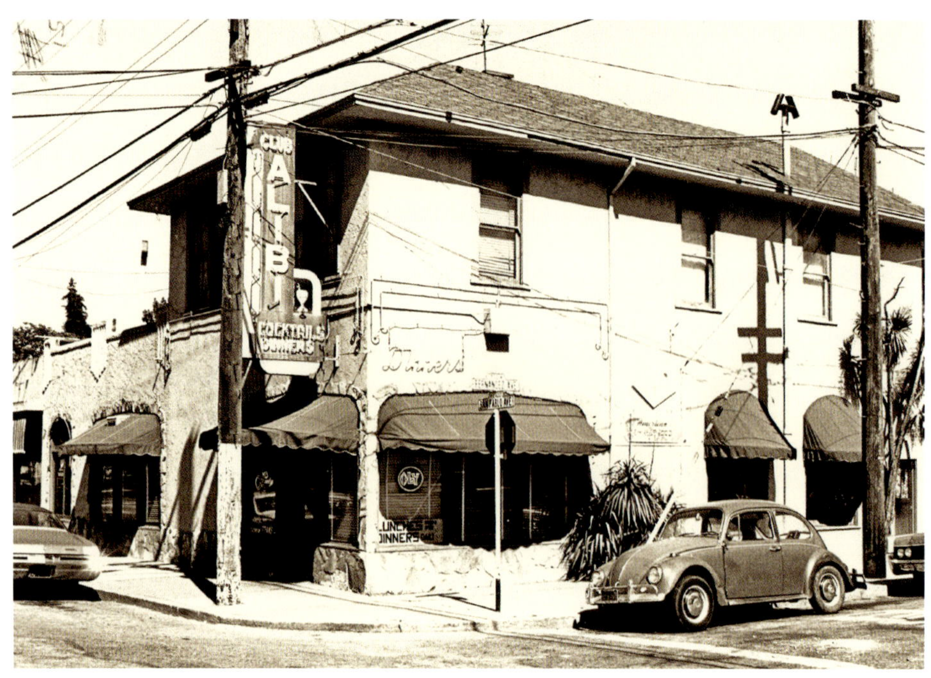

Gondola Restaurant/Club Alibi: In the early 1900s, this site on the southeast corner of San Pablo and Fernandez avenues was the Charles Vincent Saloon. It was Val and Nina Pera's Gondola Restaurant from the 1930s to the 1940s, serving drinks and Italian food. From the 1940s through the 1970s, it was the Club Alibi, run by Mike Lewis and Joe Costa; it had a bar and served Chinese and American food. The club was known for a female mannequin dressed in a blue formal seated on a toilet in the men's room. When the door to the men's room opened, her arm raised up with toilet paper in her hand; astonished men thought they were in the wrong restroom.

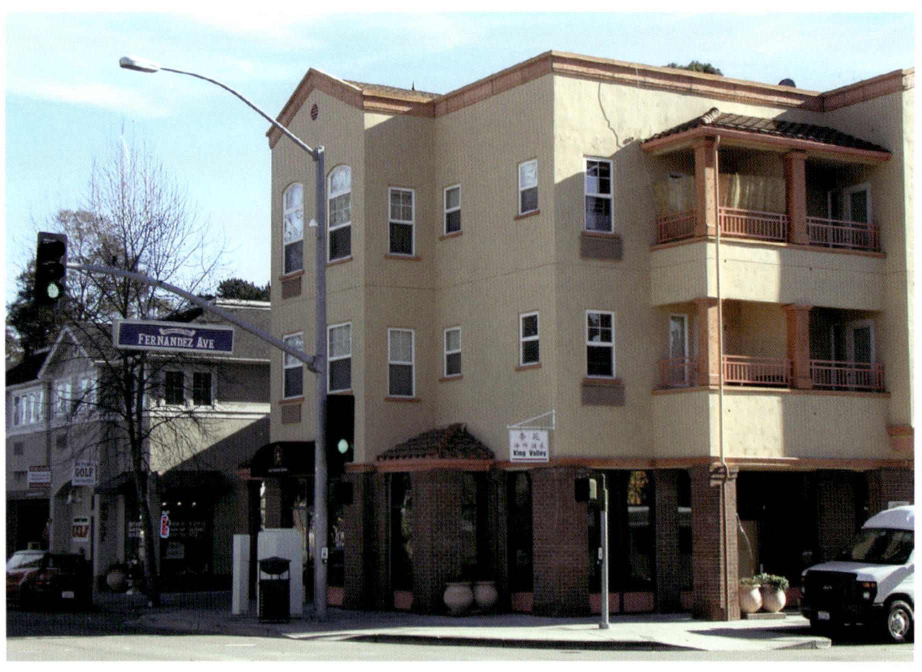

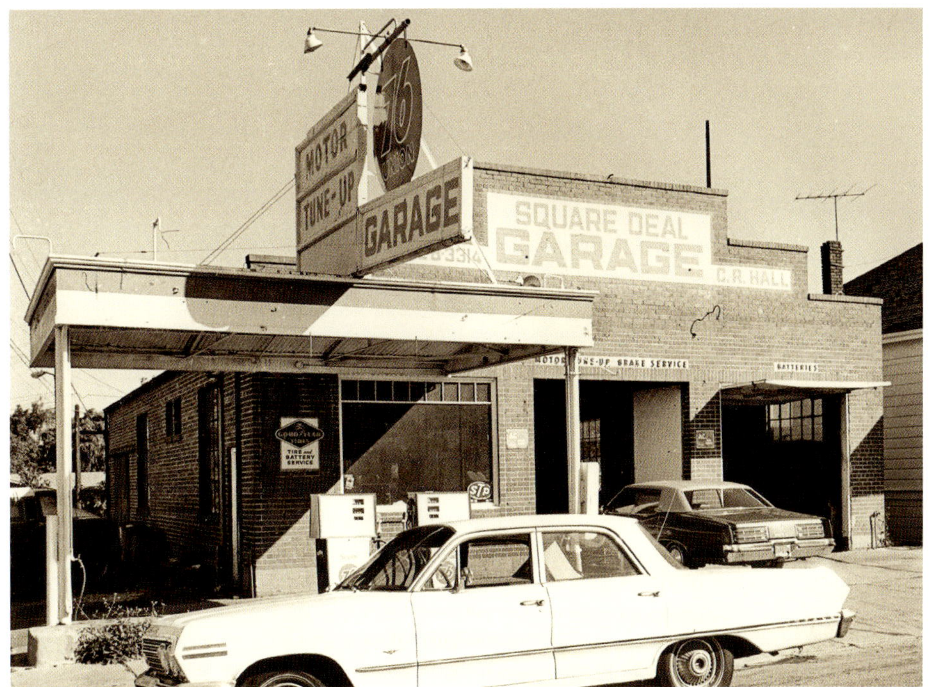

SQUARE DEAL GARAGE: This is one of Pinole's most recognized landmark businesses. In 1913, Will Gerrish's butcher shop was on this site. Gerrish, Hokie Silva, and Molly Rose ran the shop. Later, the Smith and Hemleb meat market was here. Bert Hall first opened his garage in the Fraser blacksmith shop on San Pablo Avenue, across the street from Val Pera's Gondola restaurant (later the Club Alibi). Bert opened the Square Deal Garage in 1928 in the former butcher shop on the northeast corner of San Pablo and Valley avenues. Bert's son, Chet, ran it for many years. Kevin Osman, a local businessman, bought the garage in 1981. Kevin's sons, Brian (service manager) and Brandon (shop manager) run the business.

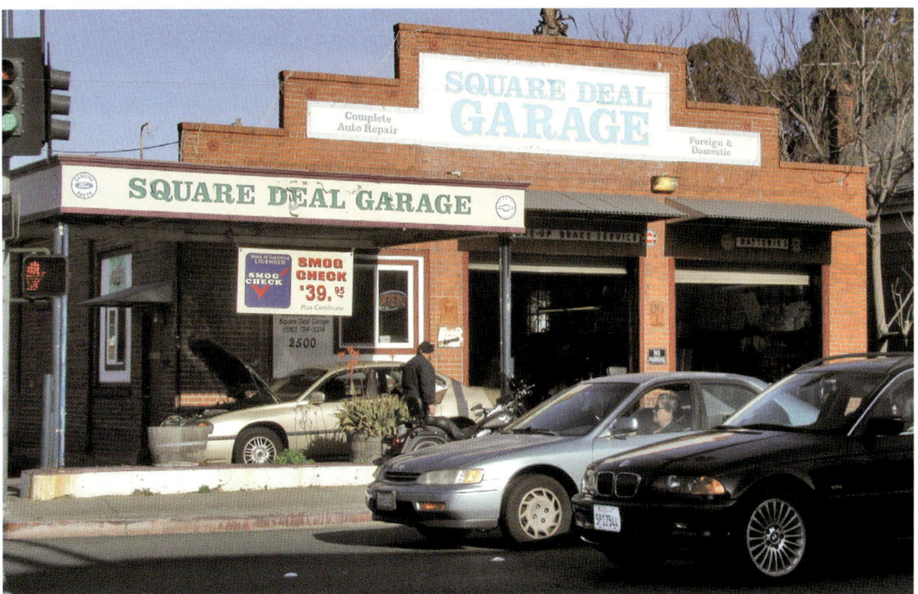

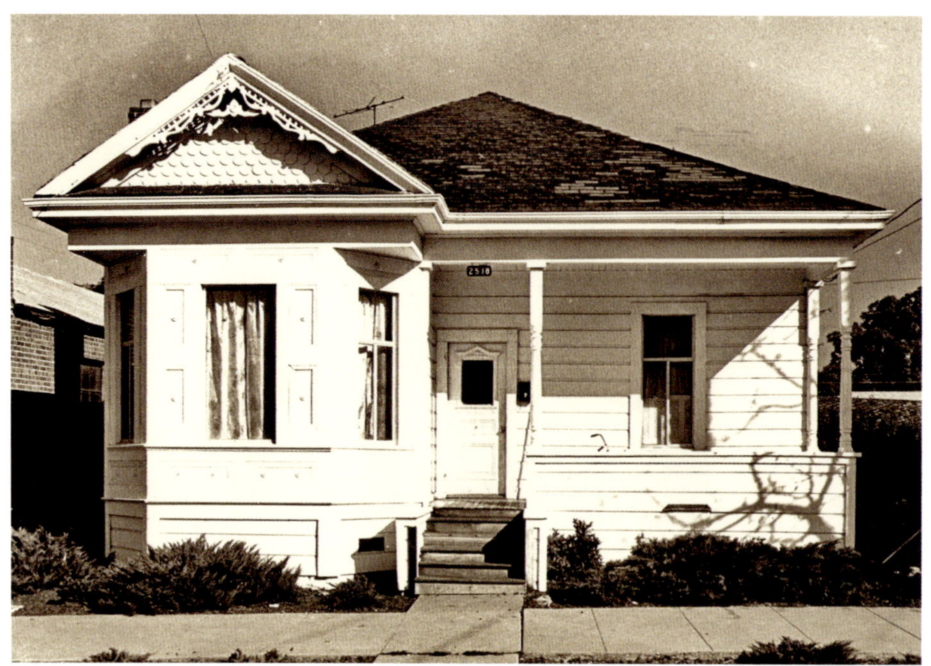

THOMAS J. STATS HOME: This was a turn-of-the-twentieth-century Queen Anne-style home with a large front porch at 2518 San Pablo Avenue, at the northeast end of the city, next to the Square Deal Garage. In the 1920s, San Pablo Avenue was widened, taking away much of the home's front yard. The Stats brothers (Thomas and Harry) were early Pinole saloonkeepers. The large Stats Saloon stood on the northeast corner of Tennent Avenue and Main Street. Thomas Stats at one time ran the local barbershop and, after incorporation in 1903, was one of the original members of the city's board of trustees. Today this building is a law office.

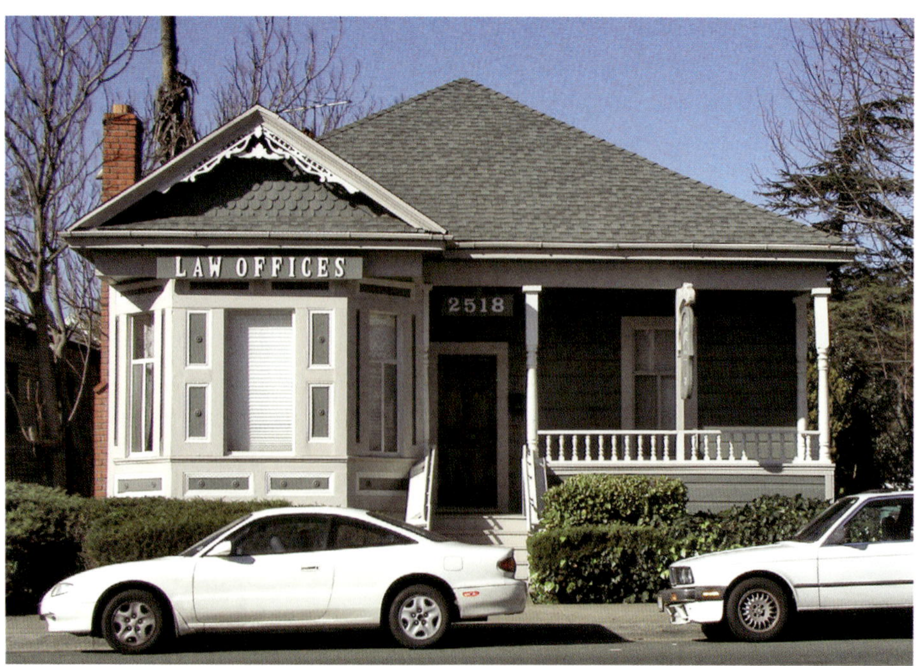

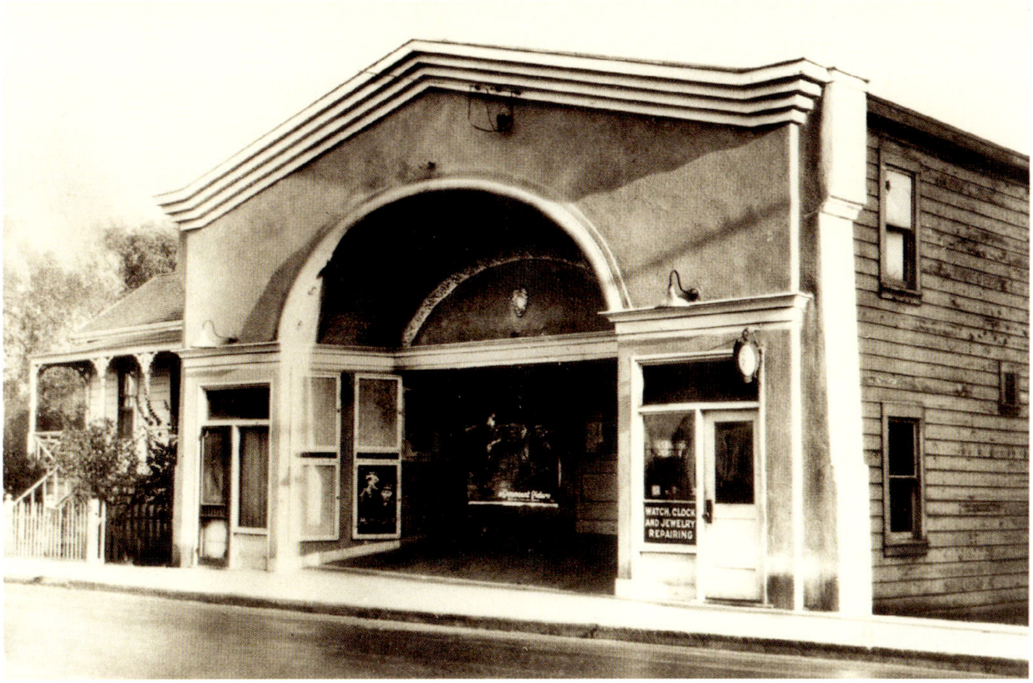

RINKS THEATER: Pinole's movie palace was centrally located on San Pablo Avenue between Fernandez and Valley avenues. It showed all the first-run movies of the early years of Hollywood, from silent films to talkies. It was owned and operated by David Herscher, brother of Mrs. Abraham (Bella) Greenfield, wife of the owner of the Pinole Department Store, on the southwest corner of Pear Street and Tennent Avenue. A commercial/residential complex is on the theater site today.

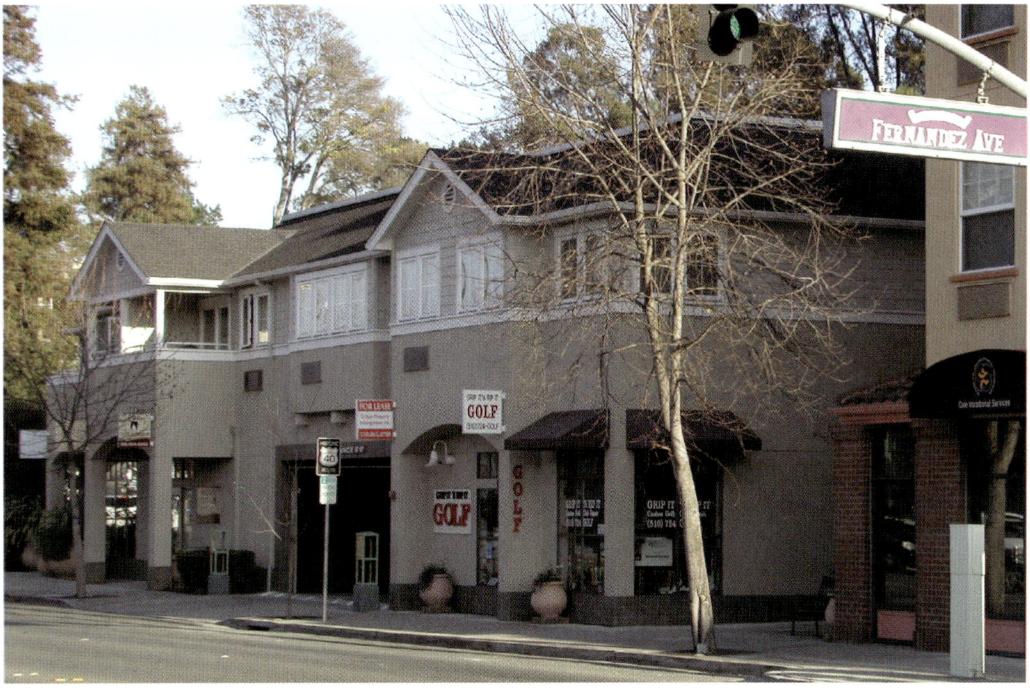

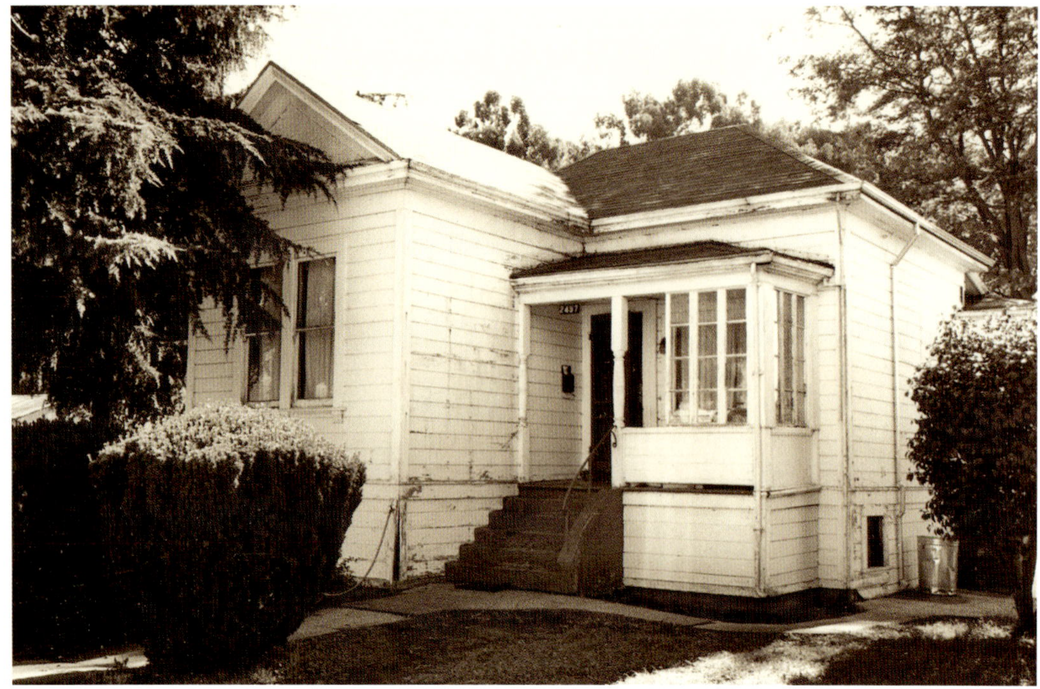

WOY HOME: Theodore and Mary Woy, and their daughter, Blanche, lived in this home at 2497 San Pablo Avenue in the early twentieth century. The Woys owned the Pinole Bakery next door, which featured the city's first auto delivery service. After Mary Woy died, Clarence and Ruth Hall (Ruth was the daughter of William and Nell Clark and grew up across the street at 2494 San Pablo Avenue) bought the home. The Halls's children, Don and Janet, inherited the home, which they still own. It remains a private residence.

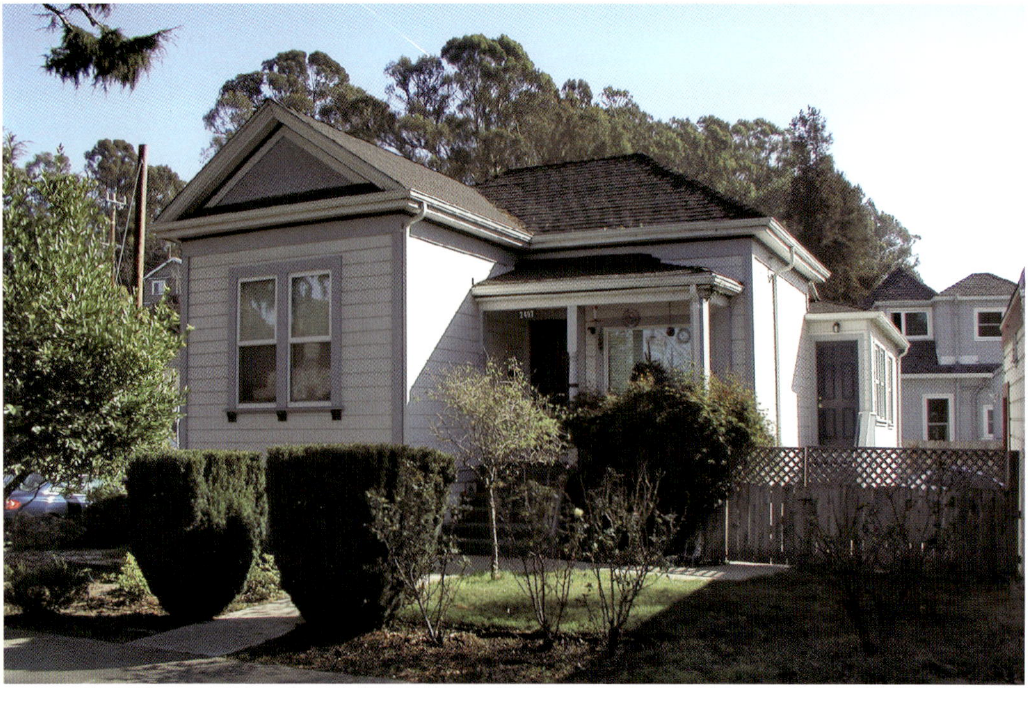

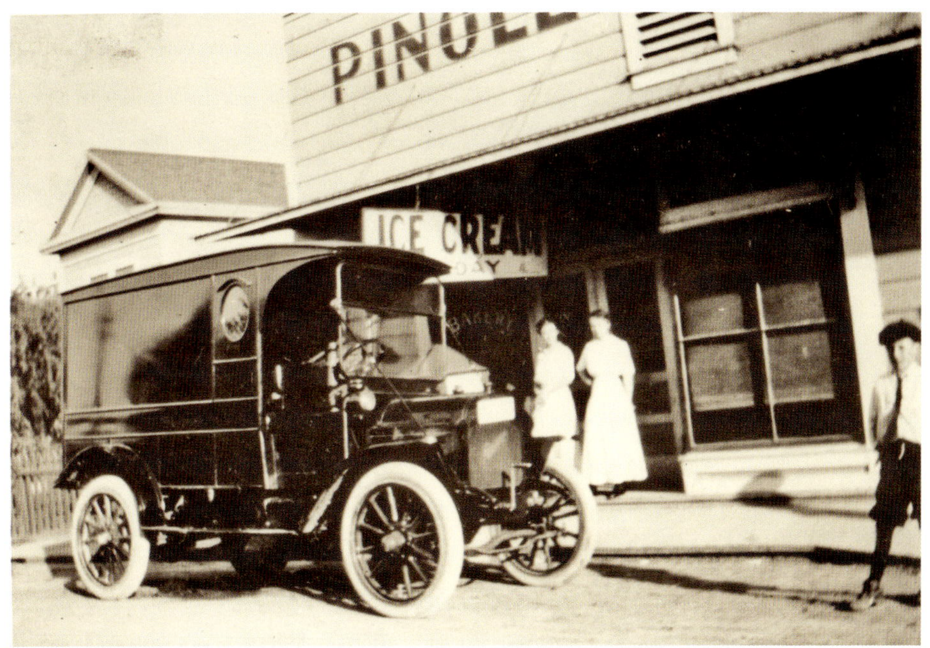

PINOLE BAKERY: A State Farm insurance agency (below) resides in one of Pinole's oldest buildings, which looks much the same today as it did 100 years ago. Theodore and Mary Woy bought the Pinole Bakery from J. B. Downer, brother of E. M. Downer Sr., founder of the Bank of Pinole. Newcomers from Pennsylvania, the Woys expanded into the grocery business in 1906 and had the only gas-powered delivery truck in the city. Children and adults loved the ice cream sold there. The Woys' home at 2497 San Pablo Avenue, on the southwest corner of San Pablo and Valley avenues, was next to the bakery. In later years this building housed the Top Café, Shepp's Leather Boutique, and other businesses.

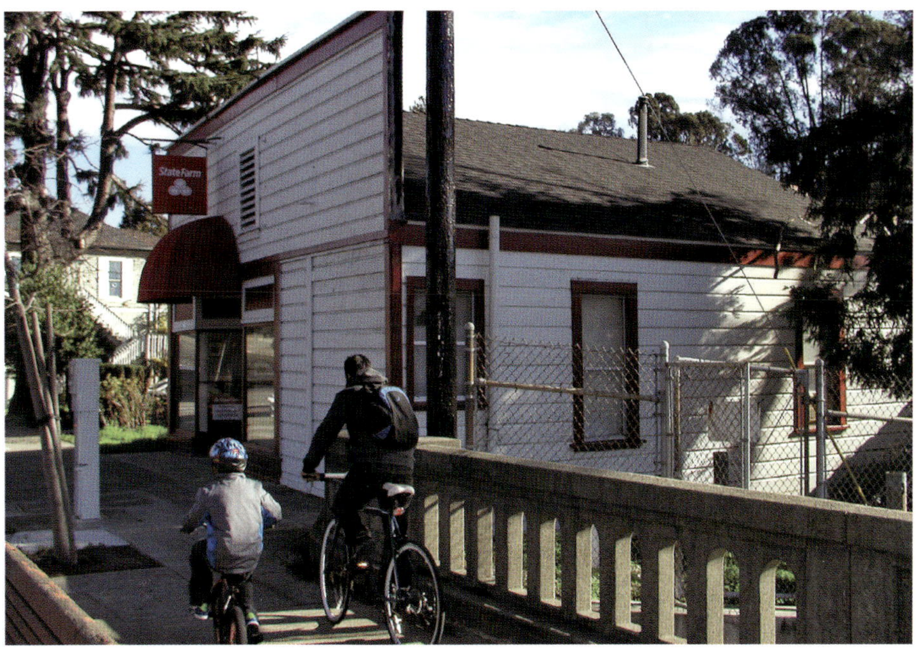

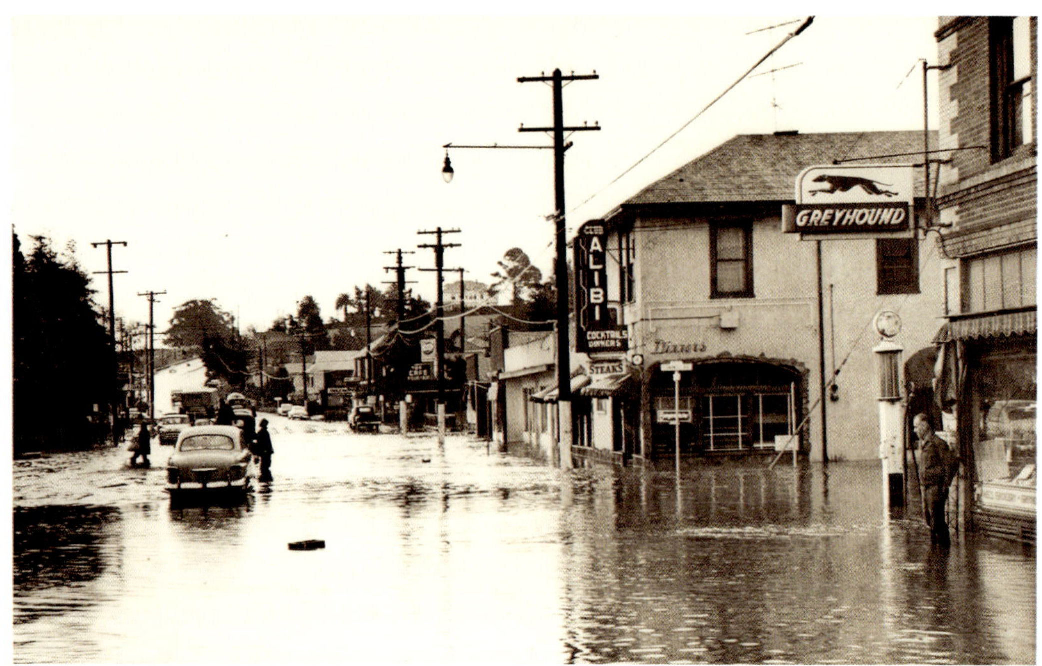

SAN PABLO AVENUE LOOKING EAST: When Pinole Creek overflowed its banks during the flood of 1958, San Pablo Avenue and most of the downtown businesses and adjoining residences became a waterway rather than a thoroughfare. All kinds of objects floated down the streets, including people in rowboats. Water engulfed Mel Marcos's grocery store (formerly Louis Ruffs's), which housed a Greyhound Bus terminal, and the Club Alibi, whose floorshow, had they had one, could have featured mermaids. The Army Corps of Engineers redesigned the creek and ended the flooding, and progress brought new buildings to replace the old.

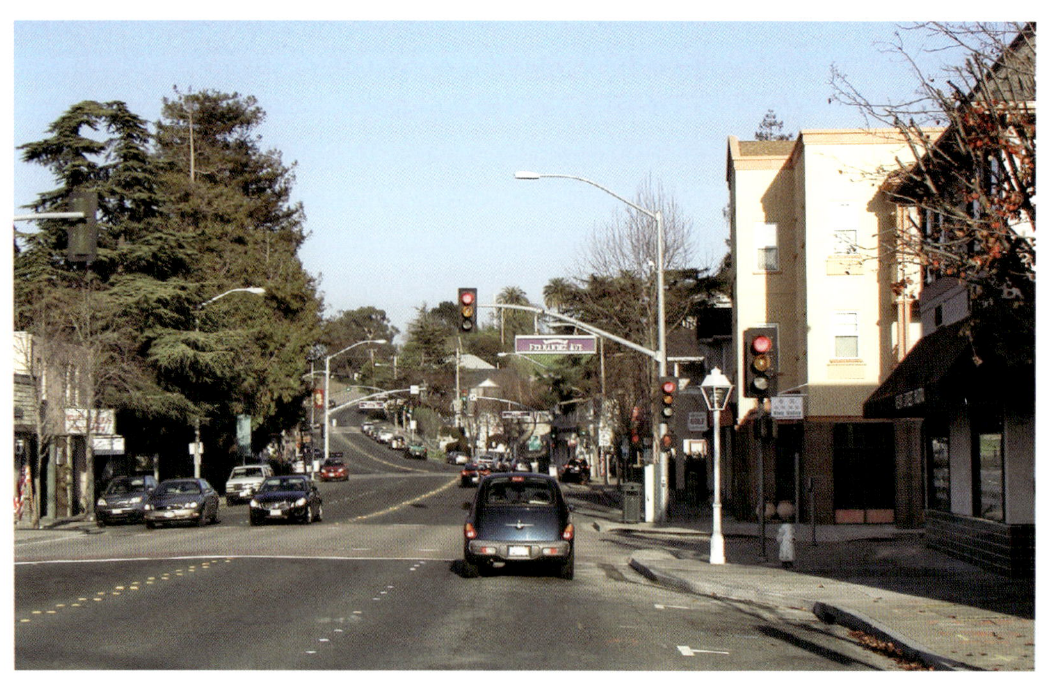

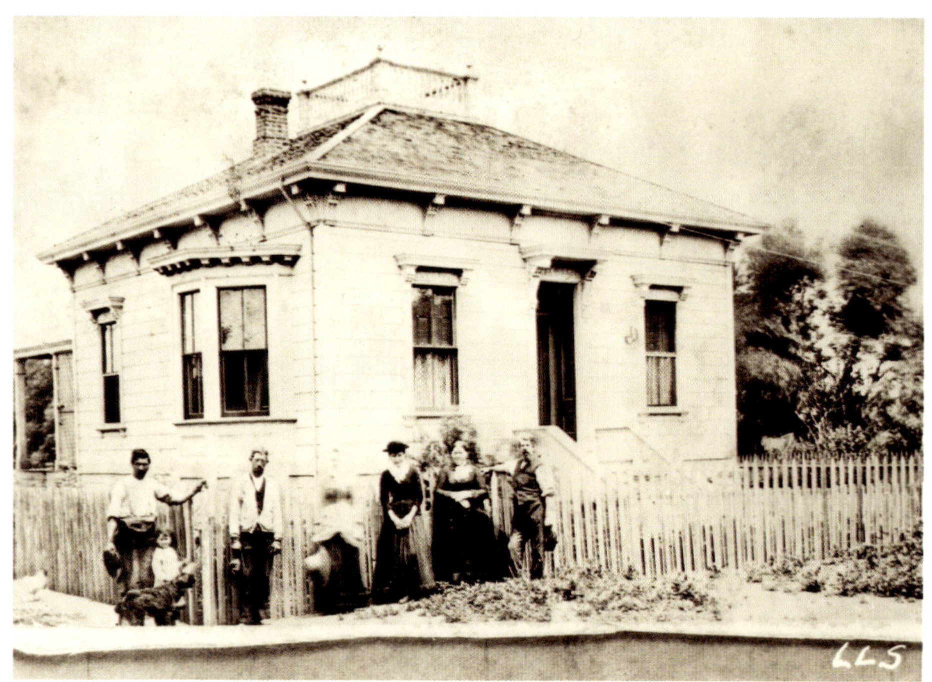

Boyd home/Pinole Creek Café: This home was built in 1874 at the edge of Pinole Creek and San Pablo Avenue. John Boyd, a blacksmith, lived there with his first wife, Katherine, and their daughter, Susie, then with his second wife, Lucy, and Lucy's daughter. Lottie Race and her husband, George Pfeiffer, a Hercules carpenter, bought the house in the early 1900s. Pfeiffer remodeled the house into a Victorian home. Lottie Race moved to Pinole in 1898 at the age of 18 and lived in the home 73 years. It was sold in 1979 and today houses the Pinole Creek Café, a popular restaurant.

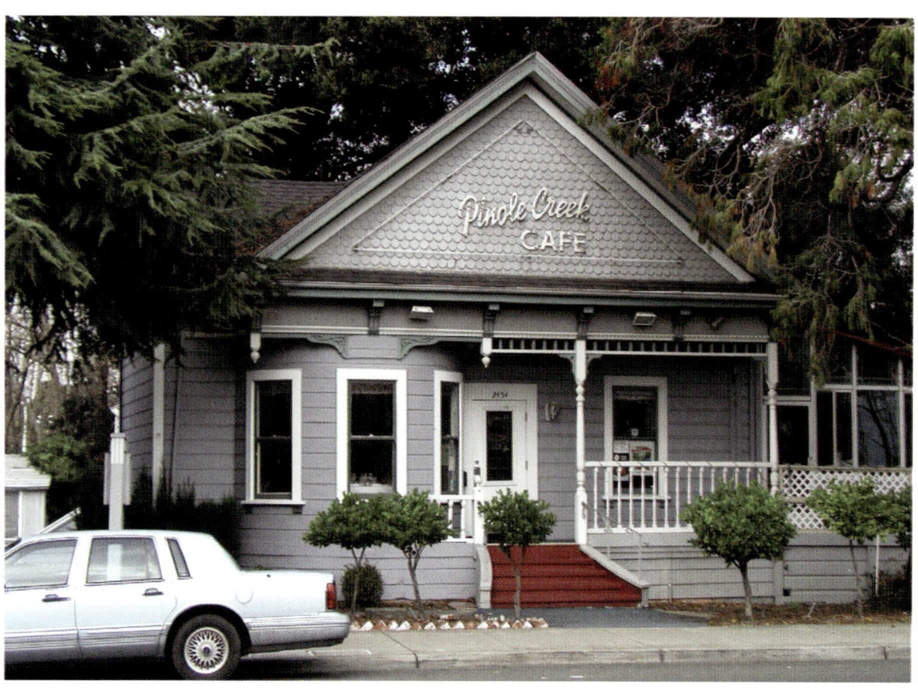

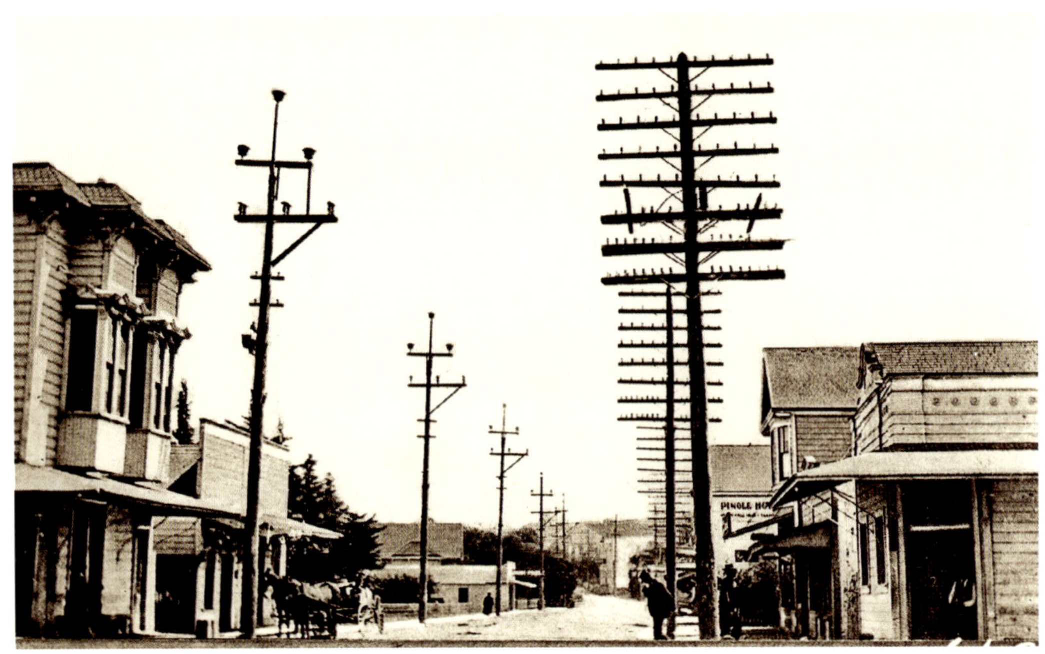

TRANQUIL DOWNTOWN PINOLE PRIOR TO WORLD WAR I, LOOKING EAST ON SAN PABLO AVENUE: Old Pinole is transitioning to the modernizations of the new century. Horses and cars now compete for curb space. Power poles bringing electricity and telephone lines dot both sides of unpaved San Pablo Avenue. Brick and stone buildings are replacing fire-prone wooden dwellings. A fireplug sits outside O'Brian's Corner Saloon in the right foreground. A manhole cover in the middle of the street is evidence of the town's first 1906 sewer line. A single auto is outnumbered by horse-drawn vehicles, including the grocery delivery cart of the Pinole Central Grocery. A hitching post and horse trough stand out as time-honored symbols of vintage Pinole's saloon culture.

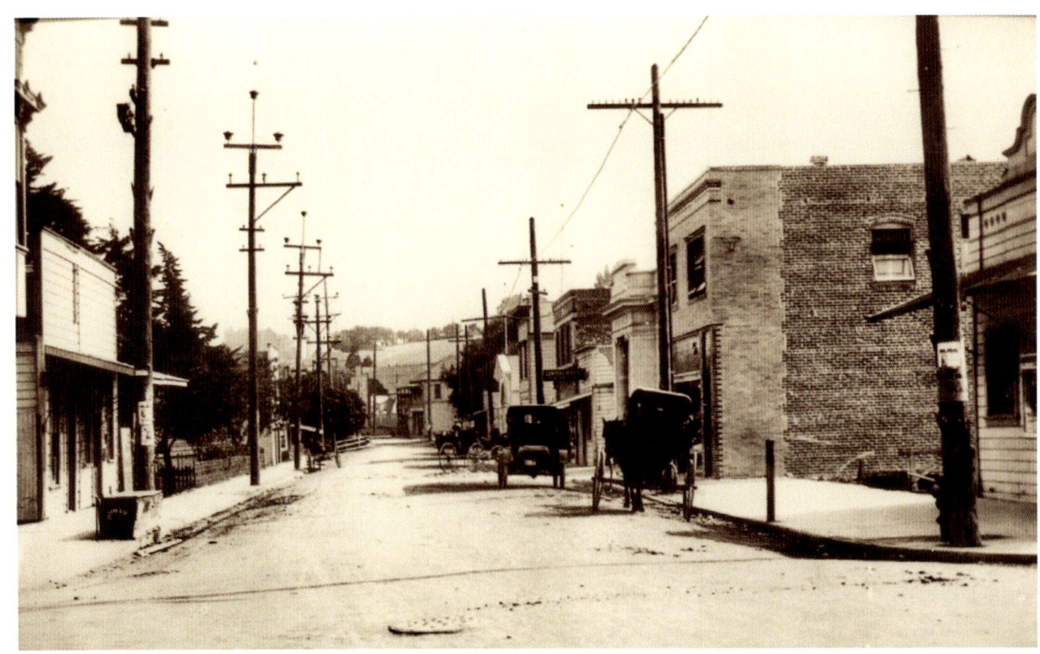

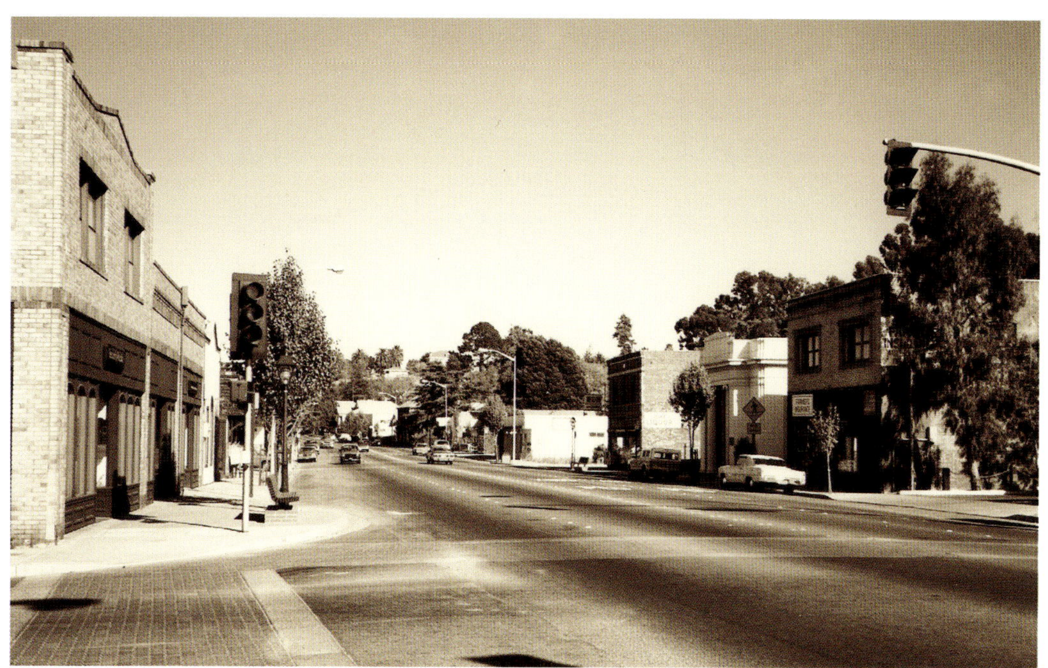

SAN PABLO AVENUE LOOKING EAST: By the middle of the twentieth century Pinole had a modern downtown business district. Wooden structures gave way to brick buildings that were less likely to burn down. San Pablo Avenue had been widened to allow for two traffic lanes in each direction, and many of the bars that had been a major part in much of the city's early history were gone, giving way to restaurants and retail stores. Louis Ruff's store (later Bill's Liquor), and the Downer Building that housed the offices of Dr. Manuel Fernandez and Greenstein's Pharmacy (later Snyder's Pharmacy) and a Farmer's insurance agency, were damaged in the 1989 Loma Prieta earthquake and later demolished.

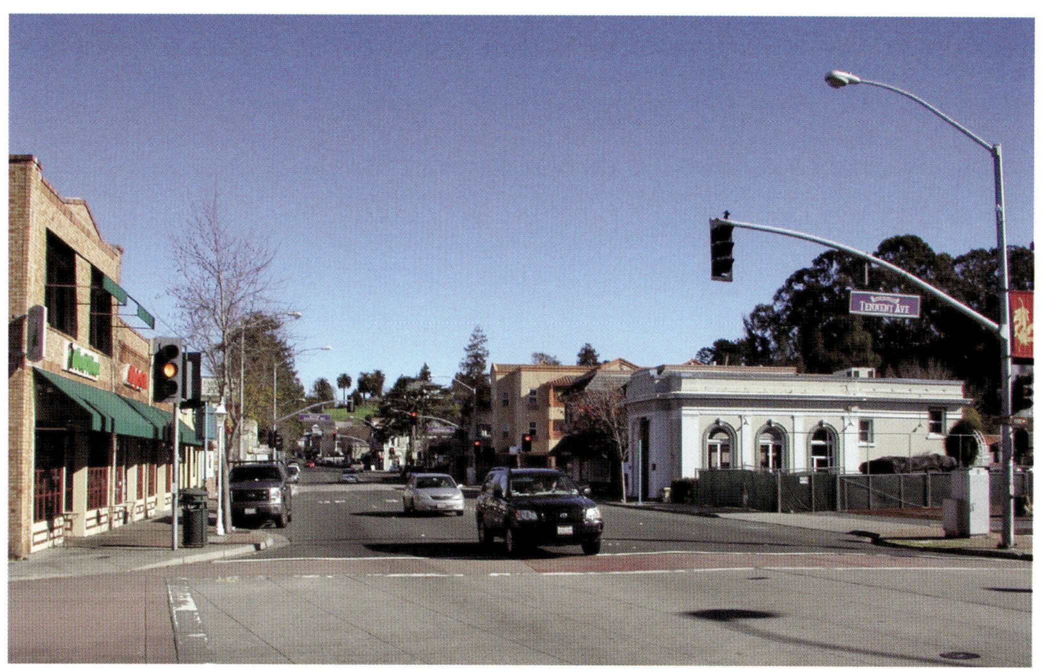

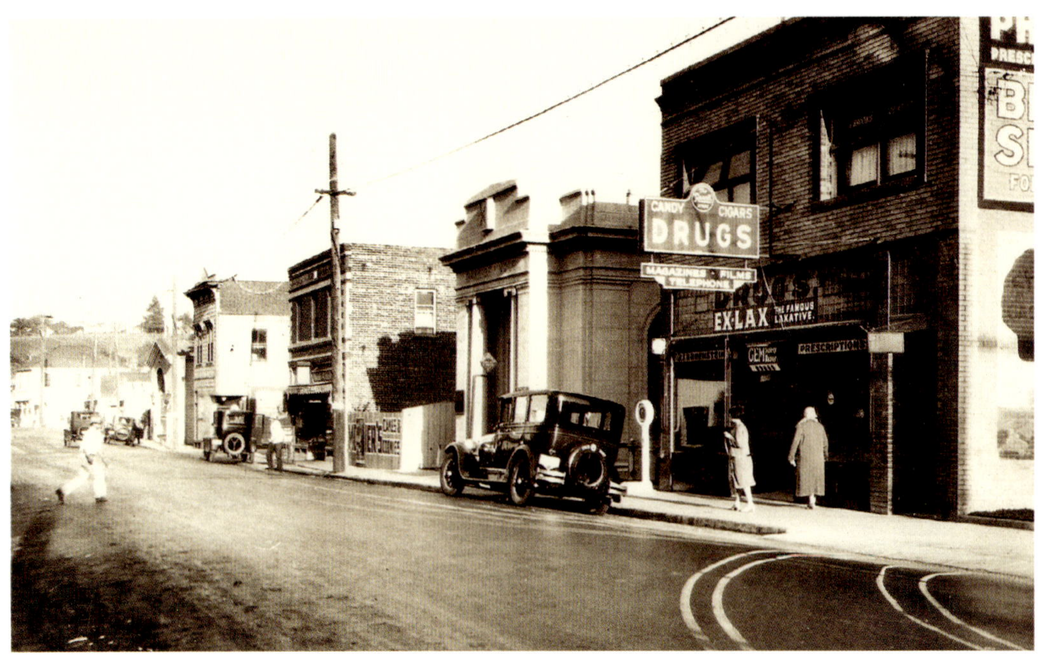

SOUTH SIDE OF SAN PABLO AVENUE LOOKING EAST: Downtown Pinole in the 1920s and 1930s was the place where people ventured to do their banking, shopping, and take care of their medical needs. All of these services existed in this one block between Tennent and Fernandez avenues, with Greenstein's Pharmacy and Dr. Manuel Fernandez sharing space in the Downer Building (far right), the Bank of Pinole (middle) and Louis Ruff's grocery store (the brick building on the left). On the west side of the brick Downer Building was a large mural featuring the city's slogan, "The Sun-Kissed Gem by the Bay," painted over a background of the bay. Residential and commercial buildings replaced many historic buildings of Old Pinole.

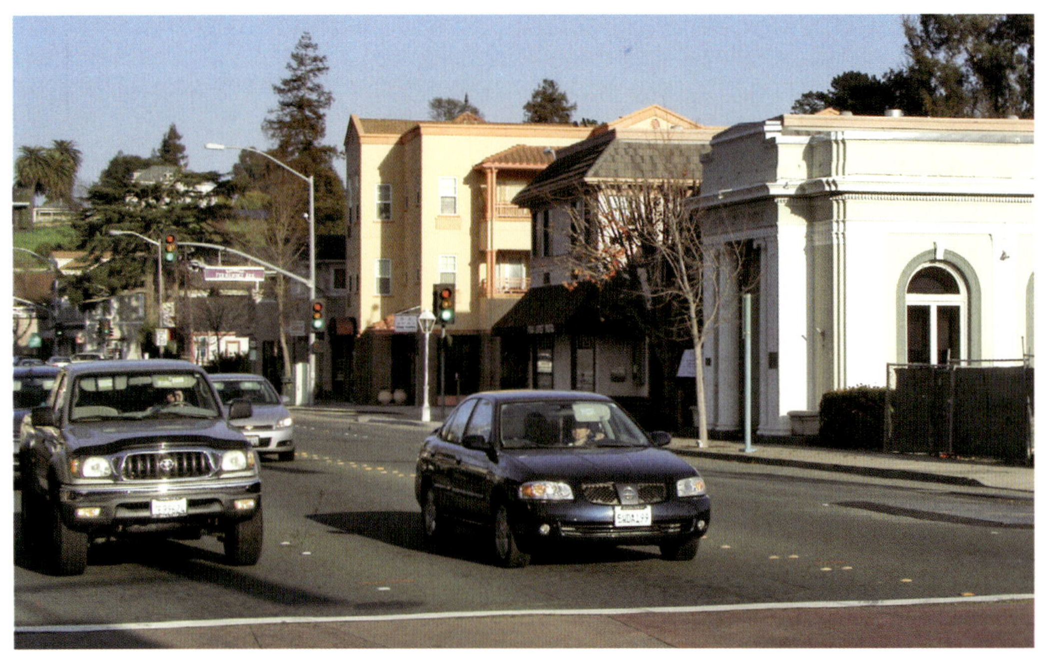

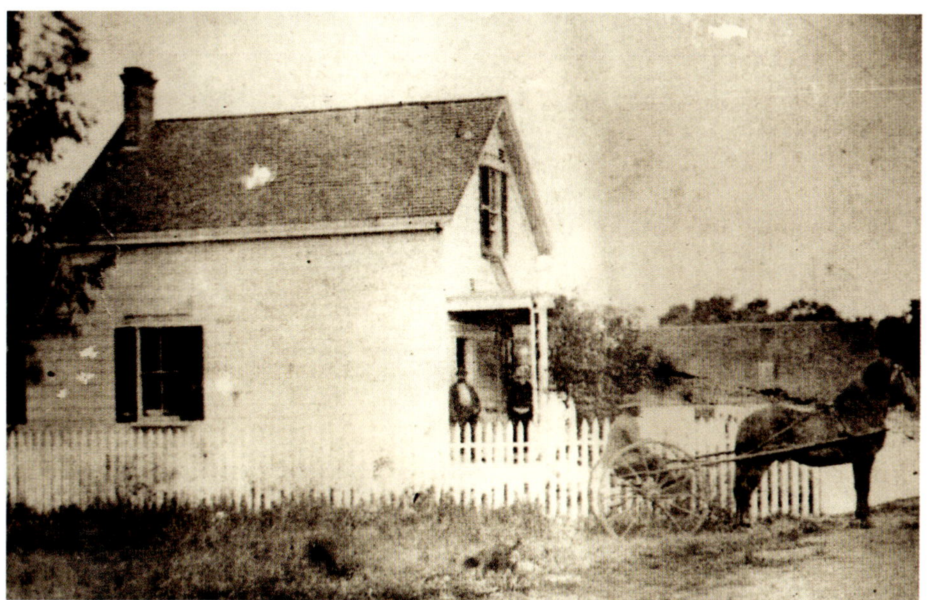

FRASER HOME: John Fraser built his home in the middle of town on San Pablo Avenue, next to Manuel Marcos's Saloon (now The Bear Claw). He built it for his bride, Susie, the daughter of neighbor John Boyd. Fraser and Boyd ran the local blacksmith shop in the early 1900s. Fraser had two sons, Harry and George, also blacksmiths. John Fraser was active in civic affairs and also served as town constable. In 1903, Fraser was one of the first members of the newly elected Board of Trustees of the now-incorporated City of Pinole. The home remained in Fraser hands until the 1950s, when it was torn down for the construction of Pinole Plaza, now Park View Plaza.

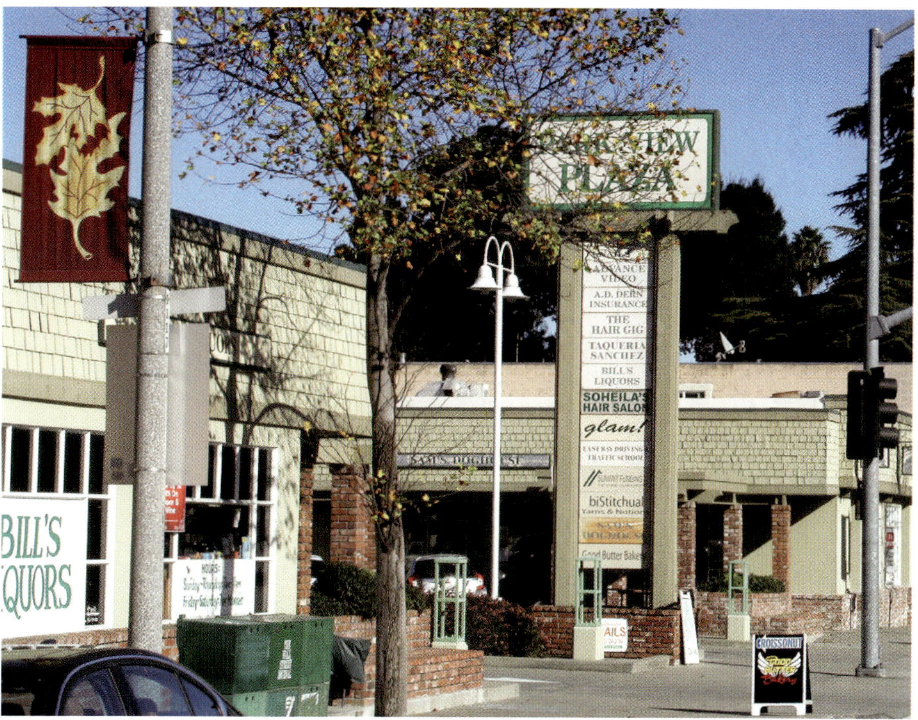

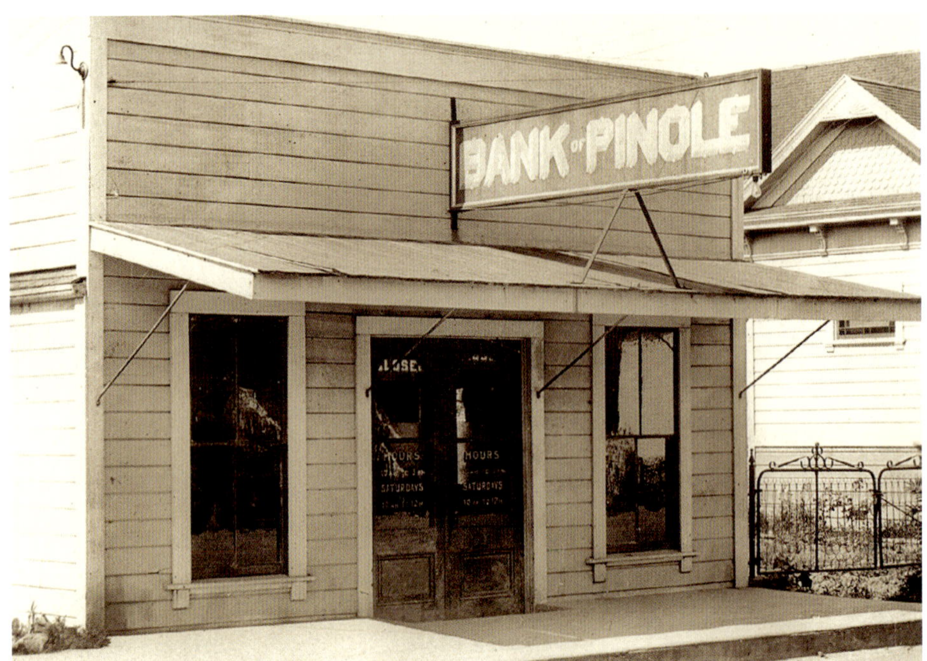

Original Bank of Pinole: From 1889 to 1938, Edward M. Downer Sr. was among the most influential and prominent business figures in the history of Pinole and its surrounding communities. When Pinole incorporated in 1903, he was its city clerk. He was elected to the city council in 1910. In 1913, he was elected mayor, a position he held until his death in 1938. In 1905, with a small floor safe in a one-room office, he opened the Bank of Pinole on San Pablo Avenue. There were no other banks in the area. Sam's Doghouse in Park View Plaza, a commercial/shopping center, now occupies the site of the original bank.

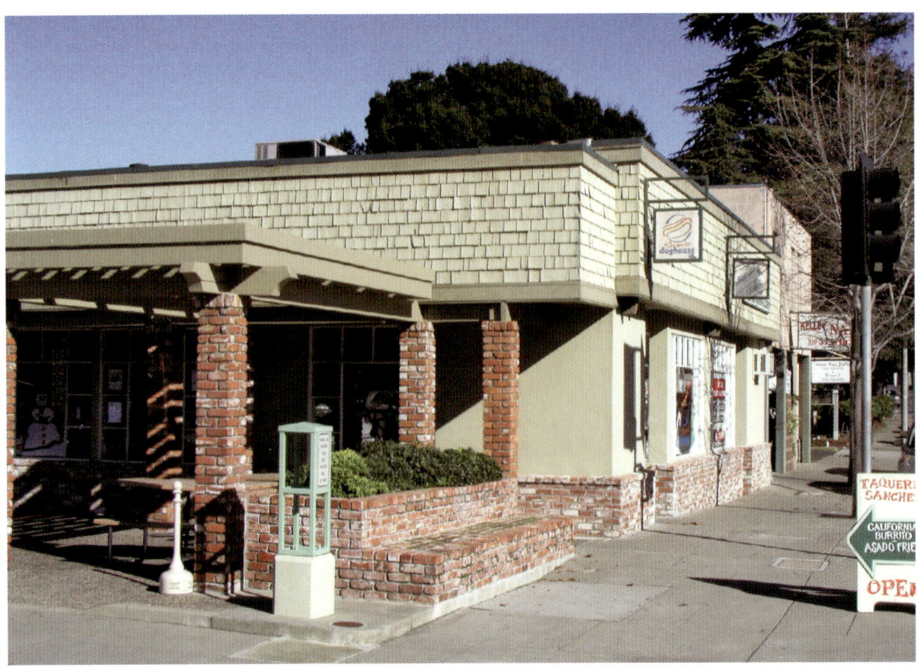

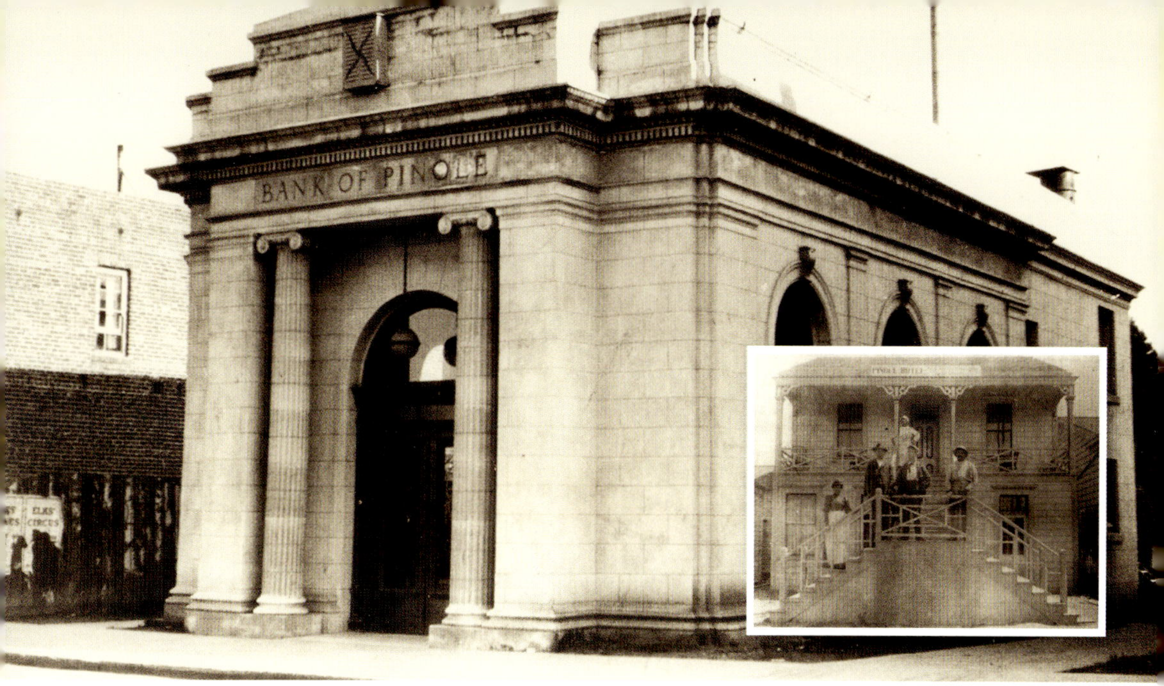

ORIGINAL BANK OF PINOLE: The nineteenth century-built Pinole Hotel (inset) stood on the south side of San Pablo Avenue between Tennent and Fernandez avenues. It burned down in 1914. In 1915, Edward M. Downer, mayor of Pinole, opened the newly constructed Bank of Pinole on this site. Downer, the first official postmaster, transfer agent, and telegrapher of the Southern Pacific's Pinole depot, and co-publisher of Pinole's first newspaper, the *Pinole Weekly Times*, founded the Bank of Pinole in 1905. This building, photographed by Larry Neptune, is one of two in Pinole on the National Register of Historic Places; the Fernandez Mansion is the other. In recent years it has served as a pre-school, youth center, restaurant, and flower shop.

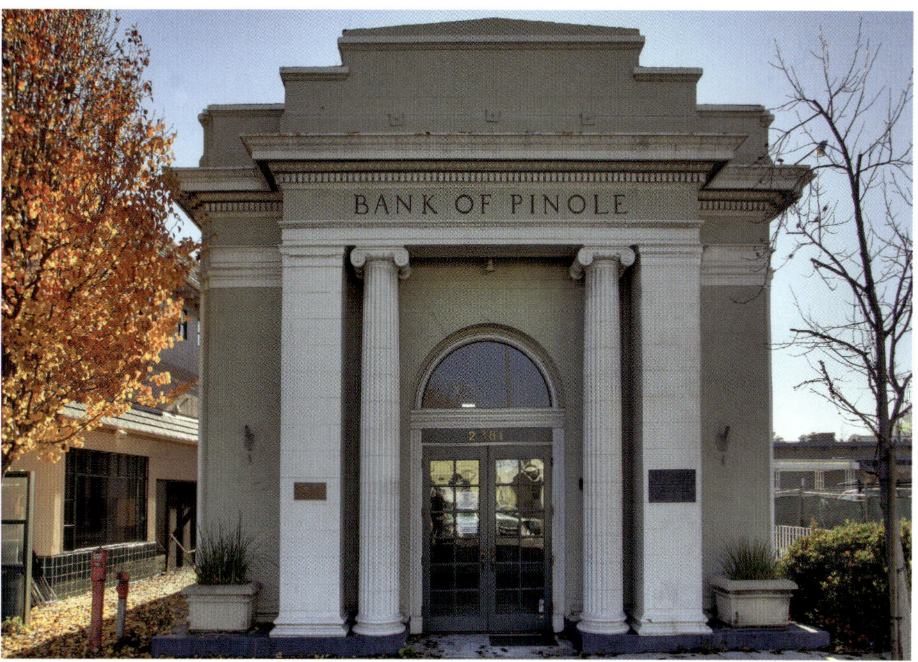

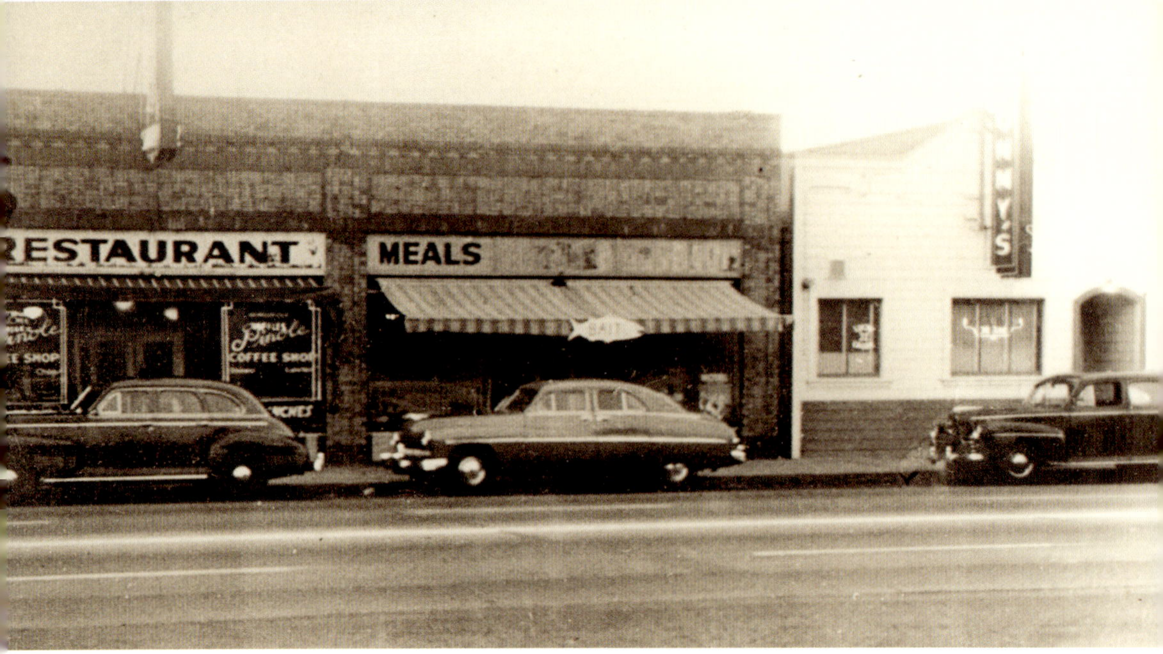

SAN PABLO AVENUE BUSINESSES: Tommy's (far right) anchored a row of businesses, mostly restaurants and bars, on the north side of San Pablo Avenue between Tennent and Fernandez avenues. The above photo, from the late 1940s/early 1950s, shows Deveroux's Pinole Coffee Shop on the left. The space in the middle, next to Tommy's Coffee Cup, had a variety of tenants. It was a restaurant, a pool hall in the 1940s, a bait-and-tackle store in the 1950s, and the Luiz Bike Shop in the 1960s. The Bear Claw now occupies the building Tommy's was in. Lavay's Hair Studio and a new Vietnamese restaurant, PHOnomenal, have added variety to the downtown business district.

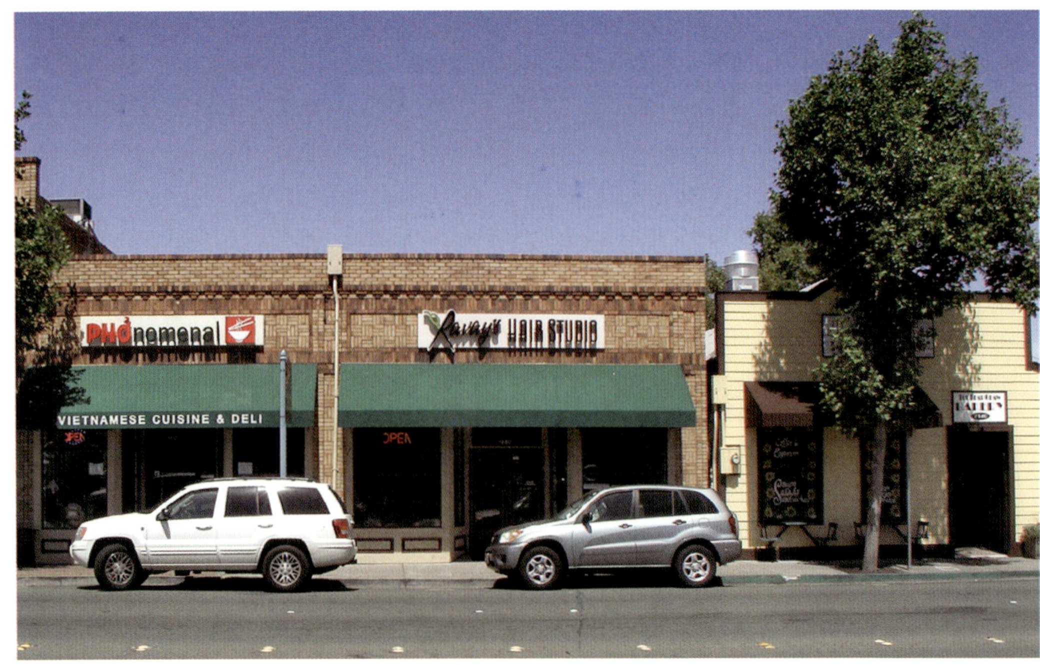

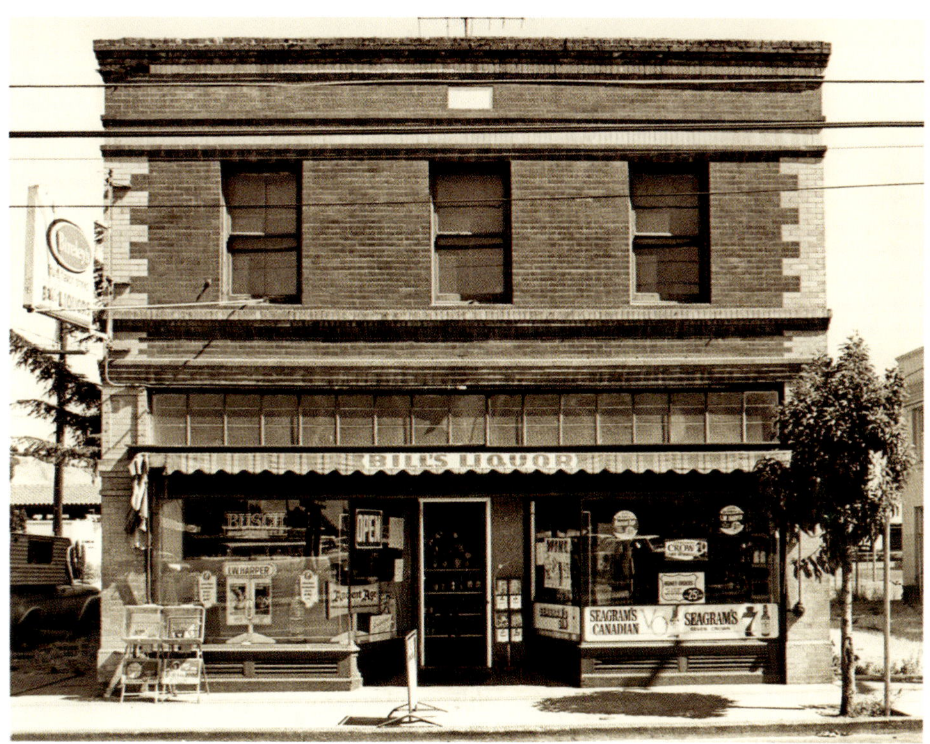

BILL'S LIQUOR/PEAR STREET BISTRO: Carl Ruff built his eponymous building on the southwest corner of San Pablo and Fernandez avenues in 1914; it housed the telephone central and fire-alarm system, as well as a grocery. Louis Ruff took over the business when Carl died and ran it until he died in 1955. His employee, Mel Marcos, took over the business and eventually sold it to Bill's Liquor. The building was demolished after the 1989 Loma Prieta earthquake. The Pear Street Bistro, a popular restaurant and bar, is on this site today.

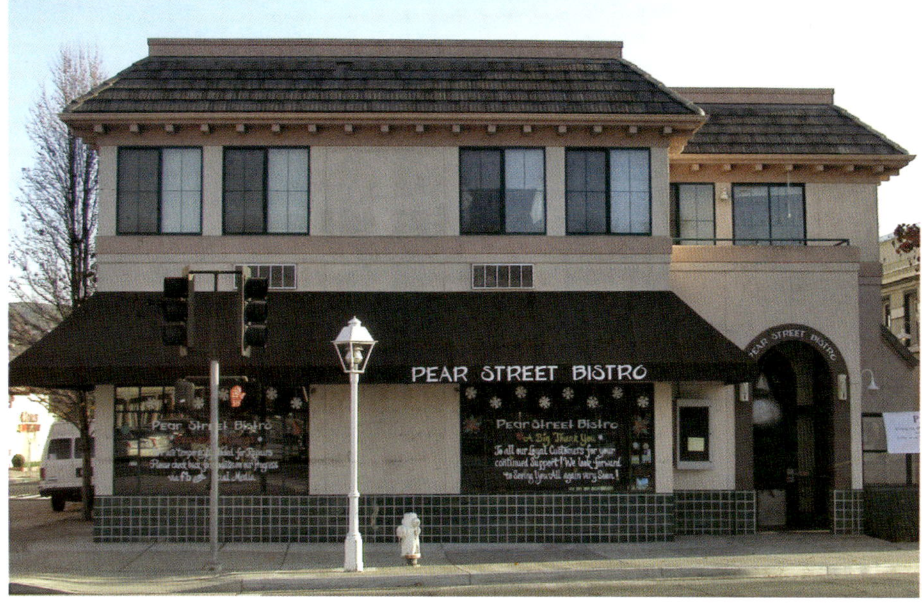

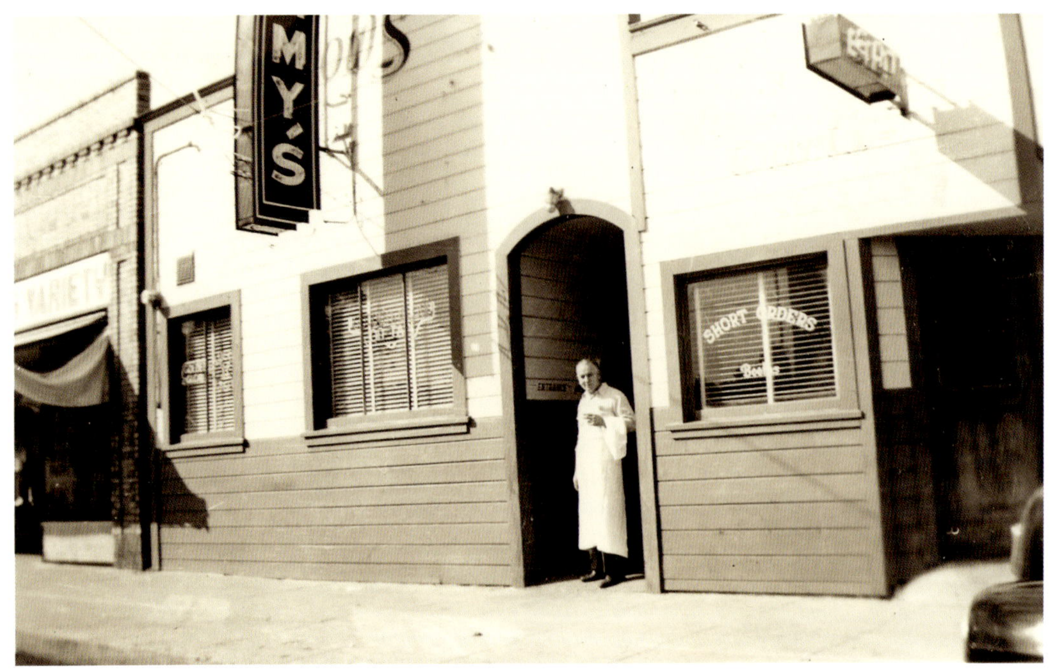

TOMMY'S CAFÉ/THE BEAR CLAW: This Pinole landmark on the north side of San Pablo Avenue has had numerous lives serving Pinole's hungry and thirsty citizens. In 1945-46 it was known as Harry Skow's bar. Gladys Skow, Harry's daughter, and her husband, Tommy Prather (photo above), took over the business, and called it Tommy's Café. People gathered for coffee, conversation, and local news and gossip. It was in the same building that housed the Manuel Marcos Saloon at the turn of the twentieth century. Mike and Terri Stott (photo below), two of Pinole's most civic-minded and generous merchants, opened The Bear Claw Bakery in this building in 1982.

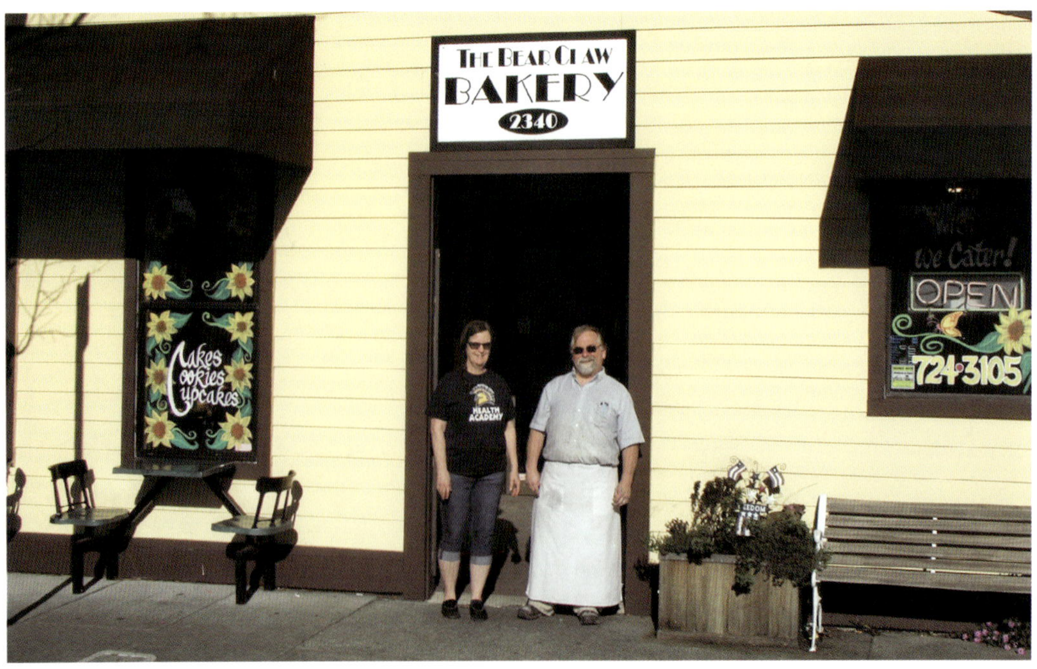

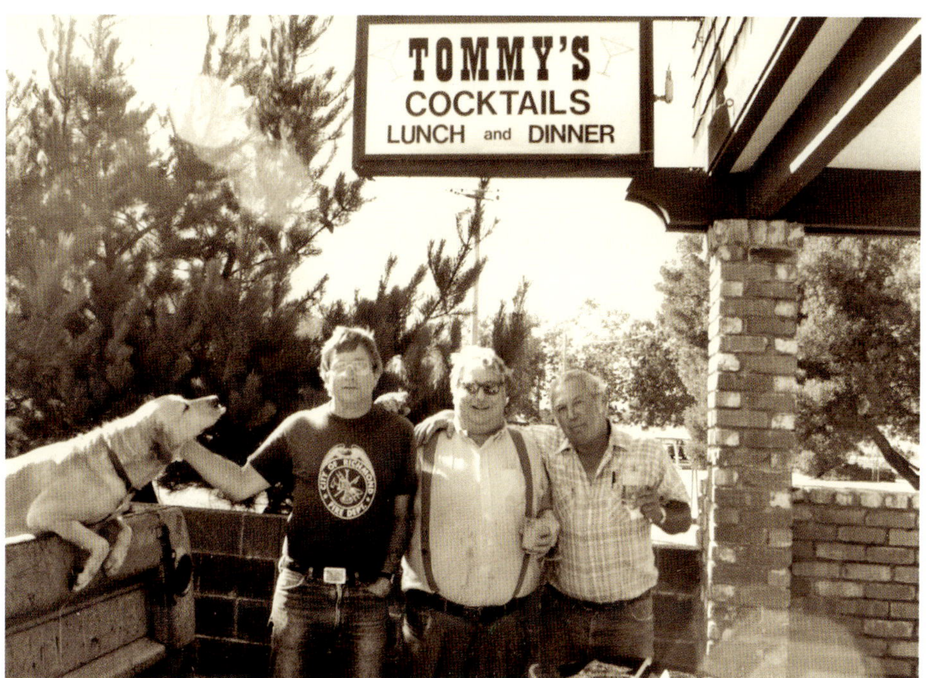

TOMMY'S/TAQUERIA SANCHEZ: Tommy Prather (center, above) was a long-time Pinole resident known for his friendly pranks. He was a 17-year veteran of the Pinole Fire Department, 13 as a captain. Tommy and his wife, Margaret (Faria) Prather, owned Tommy's (formerly the Three Belles), the "Cheers" of Pinole, one of the city's most popular restaurants and bars. The restaurant was open from 1980 to 1999. Tommy died in 1997. George Downs (below), a local restaurateur and chef, owns and operates Taqueria Sanchez on this site today.

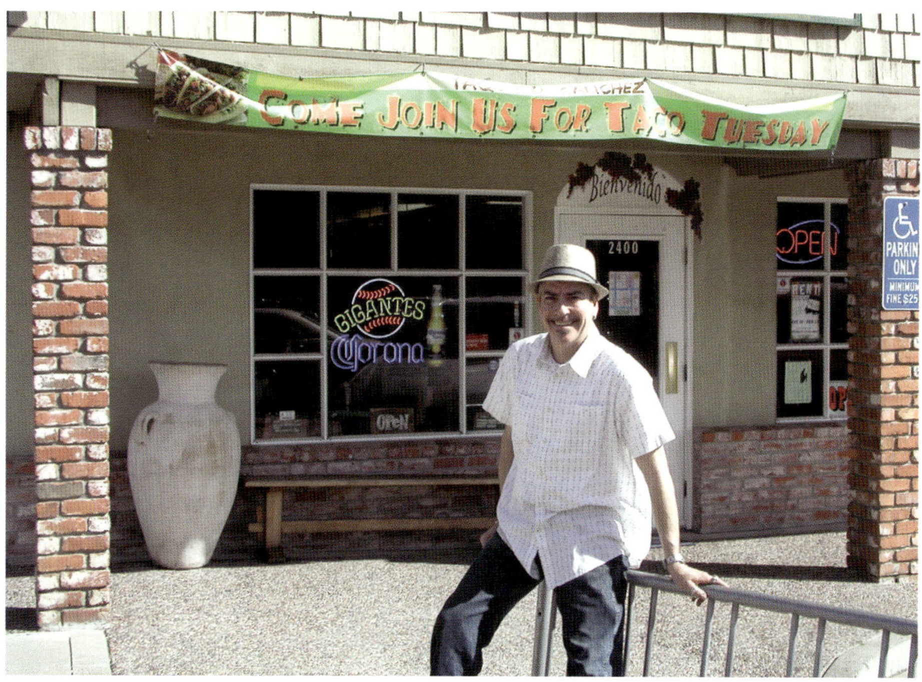

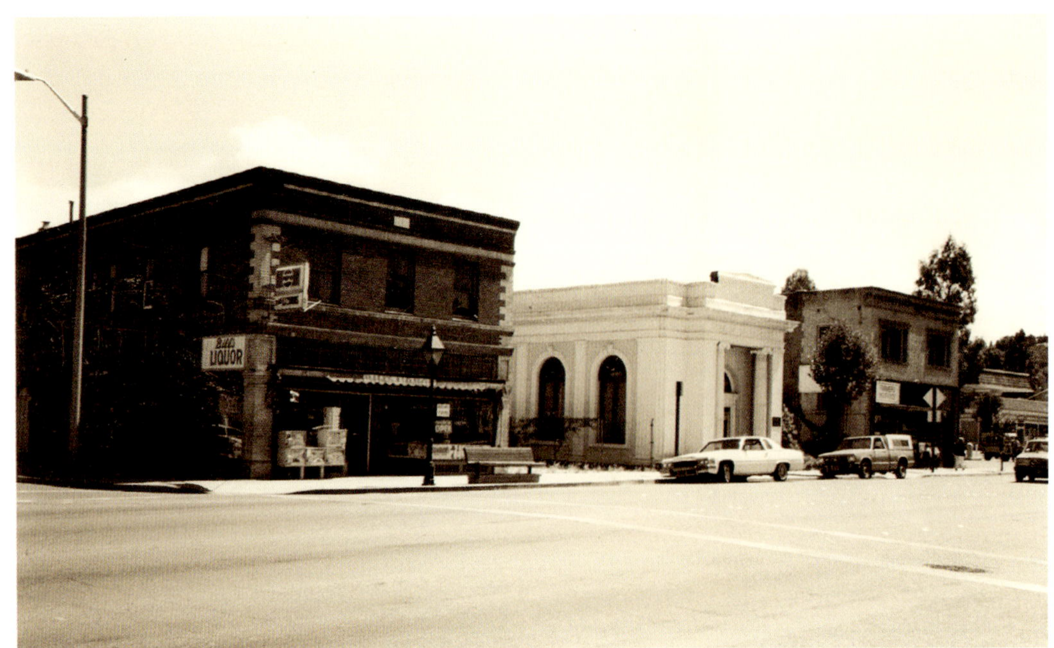

South side of San Pablo Avenue looking west: The Ruff Building, Bank of Pinole, and Downer Building were a focal point of the city's downtown for decades, until the 1989 Loma Prieta earthquake severely damaged the two brick buildings, which were subsequently demolished. The Bank of Pinole survived the quake and is commemorating its 100th anniversary in 2015. Bill's Liquor bought the Ruff Building from proprietor Mel Marcos (who succeeded Louis Ruff in the grocery store), and a Farmers Insurance agency eventually replaced Greenstein's Pharmacy in the Downer Building, which housed the offices of longtime Pinole physician Manuel Fernandez on the second floor. The Pear Street Bistro was built on the lot where the Ruff Building once stood.

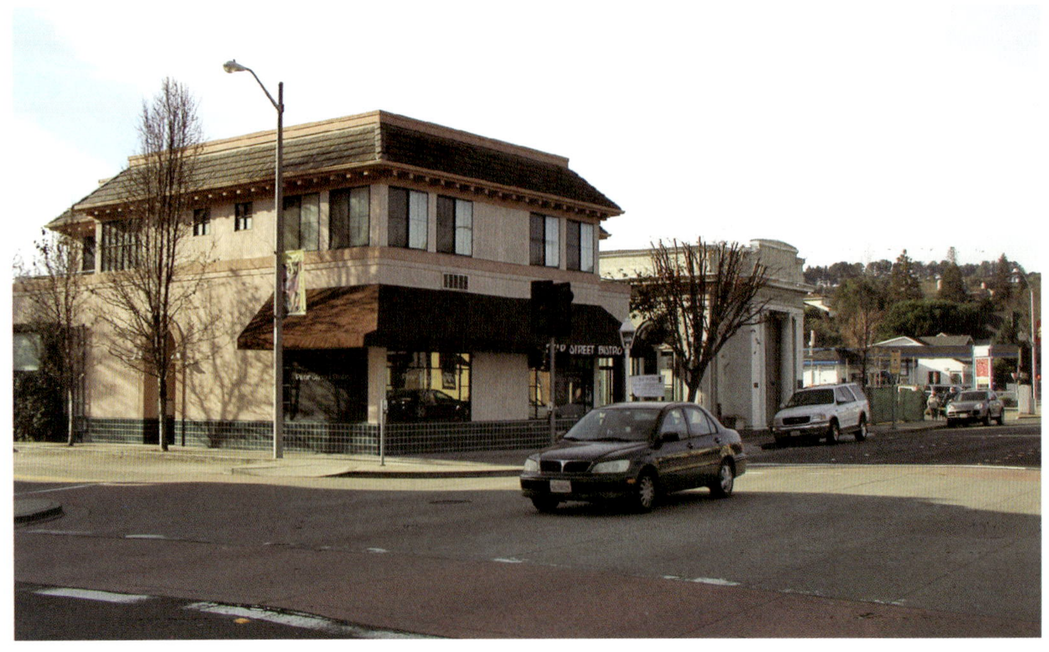

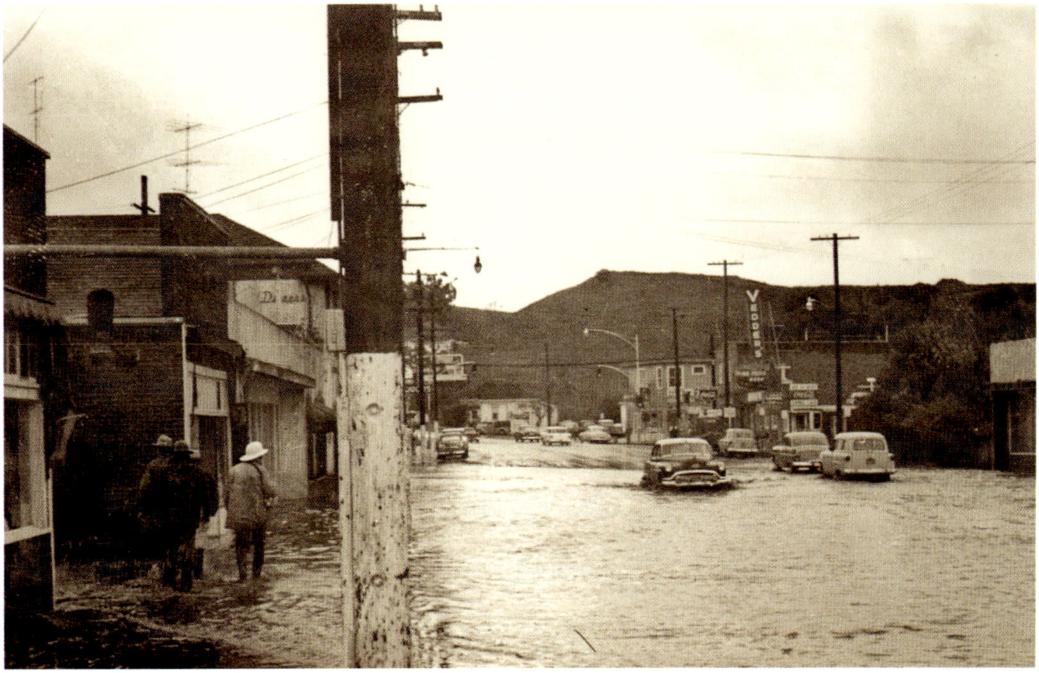

NORTH SIDE OF SAN PABLO AVENUE LOOKING WEST: The flood of 1958 produced many dramatic photos of downtown Pinole. Stores and homes were flooded, as were some cars that tried to navigate through the water. All of the buildings on the south side of San Pablo Avenue in the above photo are gone today. Vedder's, a restaurant, and all of the businesses in the brick building at the northeast intersection of San Pablo and Tennent avenues, are also part of the city's history. The Pinole United Methodist Church now sits atop Shale Hill.

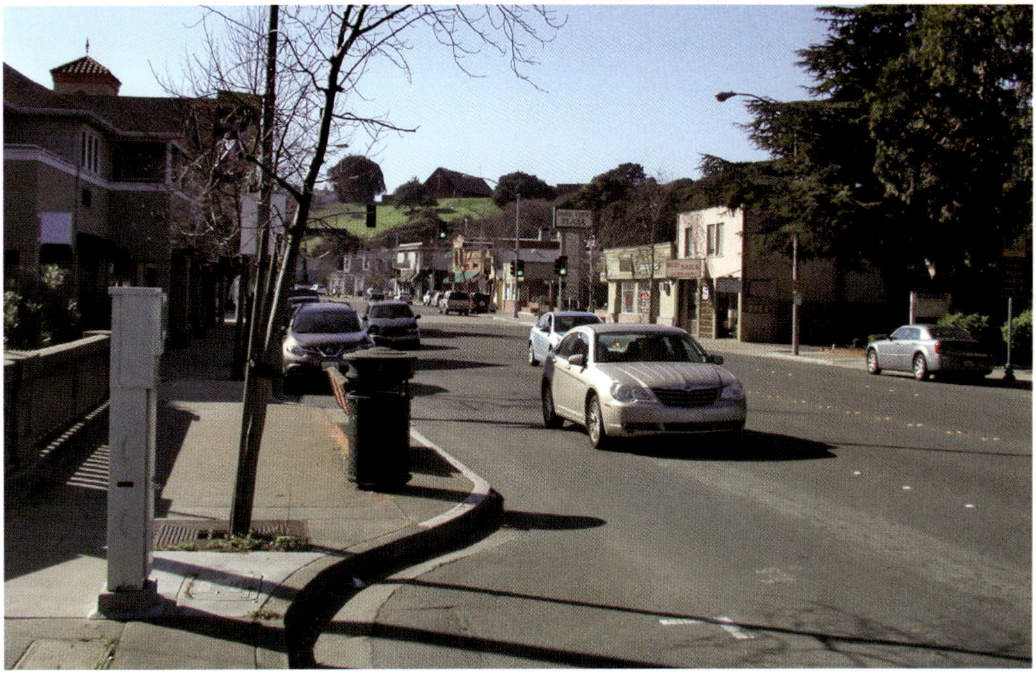

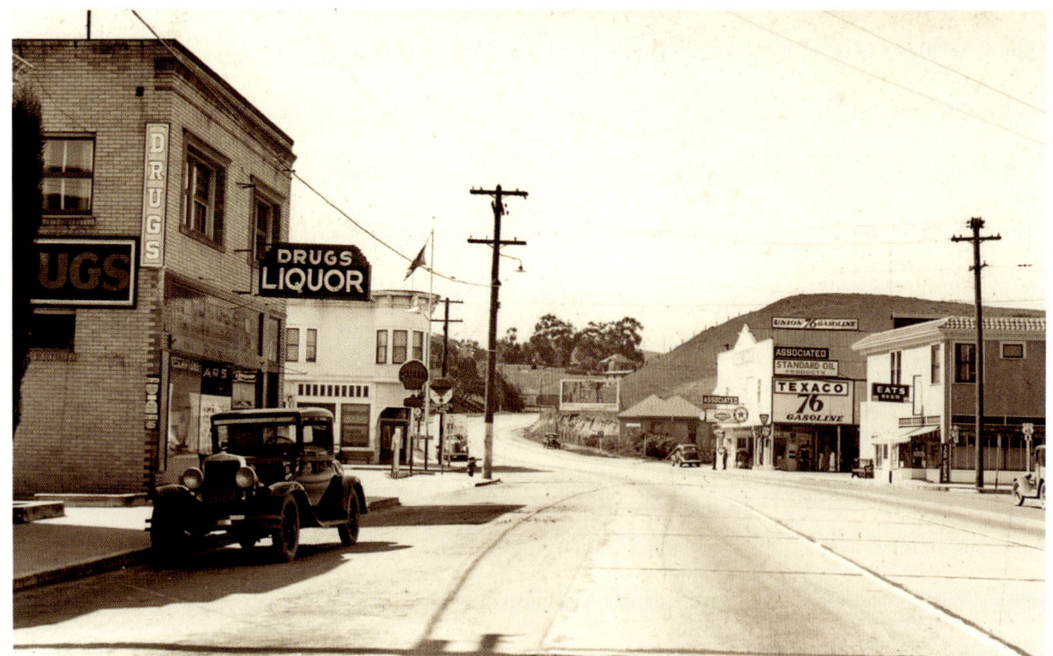

SAN PABLO AVENUE LOOKING WEST FROM BANK OF PINOLE: In 1916, Edward Downer built the two-story brick Downer Building next to his Bank of Pinole near the southeast corner of Tennent and San Pablo avenues. Upstairs were the offices of Dr. Manuel Fernandez. Downstairs was Jacob Greenstein's pharmacy. Also downstairs was a popular soda fountain with its suicide Cokes and great barbequed beef sandwiches. If you had no money, kind-hearted Sally the waitress would let you pay later. Beyond the Downer Building was the Golden West Hotel, with what was to be Antlers Tavern across the street. The Pinole United Methodist Church on Shale Hill had yet to be built.

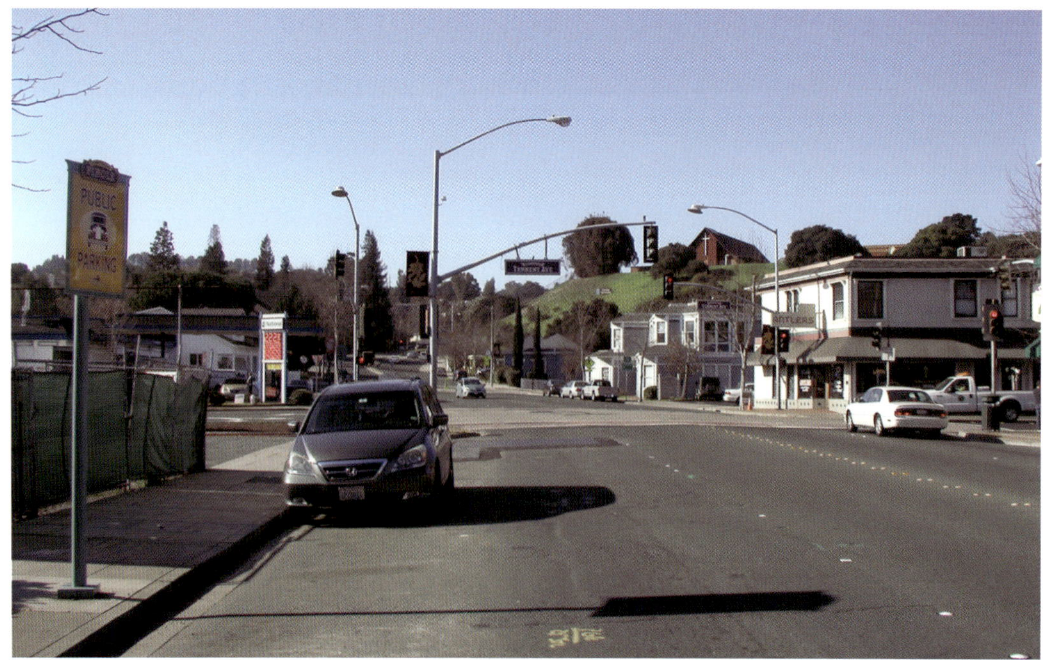

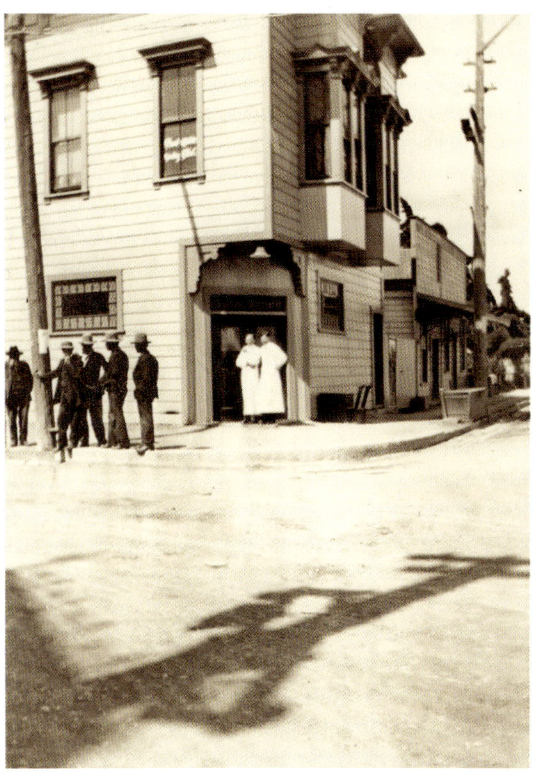

North side of San Pablo Avenue: The Harry Stats Hotel and Saloon on the northeast corner of Tennent and San Pablo avenues was one of many bars in Pinole at the turn of the twentieth century. Mary Nunes bought the wooden building in the 1920s; because of constant fire danger, she replaced it with the brick building there today. Pontes and Barroca's Central Grocery operated there for many years. On April 29, 2011, local restaurateur Tina Holztclaw opened Tina's Place, a destination eatery known for great food, comfortable chairs, great jazz music, and long lines for breakfast and lunch.

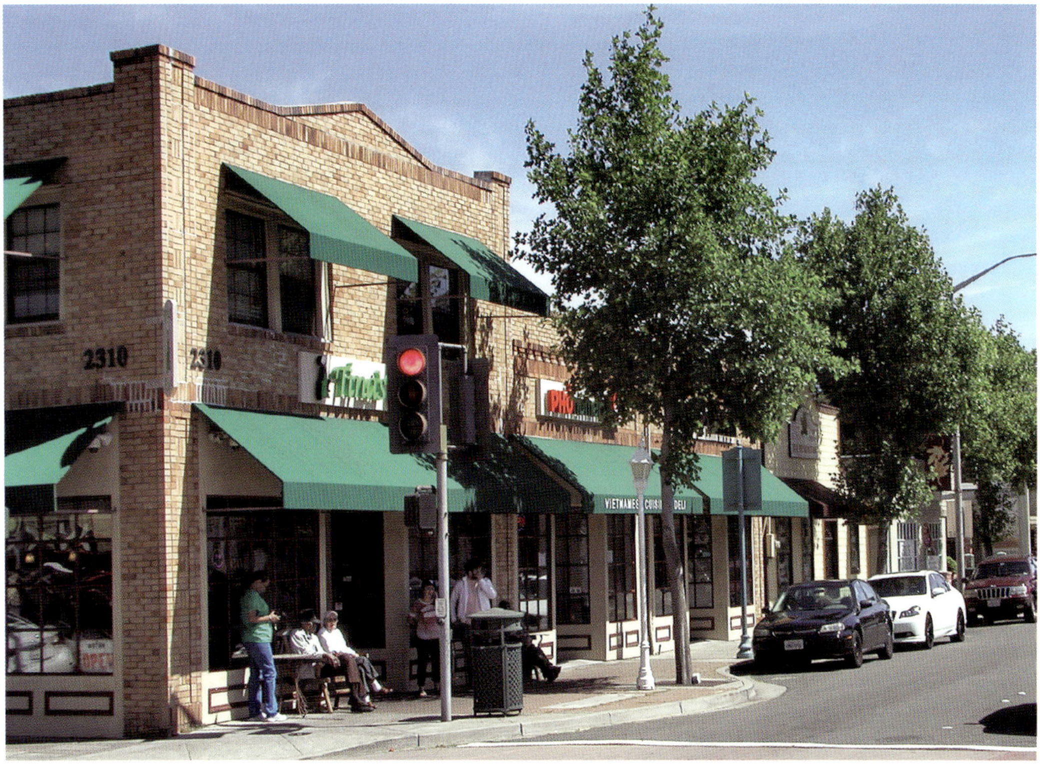

ACKNOWLEDGEMENTS

No project like this can succeed without help from many people. These people were very gracious and forthcoming with information, anecdotes, and/or photographs about a city for which they have great affection. The authors thank them.

Our contributors include: Monica Adler, Dean Allison, Patti Athenour, Donald Bastin, Kathy Bradshaw, Deanna Faria Brownlee, Ed Campbell, Cori Clark, Earl Combs, Contra Costa County Historical Society, Luann Cunningham, Ronnie Dumont, Allen Faria, Stella Faria, Dianne Daiss Felton, Bernie Drouillard, Susan Fernandez, Mike Franklin, Don Hall, Cari Jo Galloway, Carol Jensen, Kibby Kleiman, Stephen Lawton, Mike LeFebvre, Dennis Lorette, Dr. Joseph Mariotti, Norma Martinez-Rubin, Bill McMaster, Jack Meehan, Lee Ann Miller, Robert Morris, Josephine Mulaskey, Larry Neptune, Brian Osman, Kevin Osman, John Paradela, Jim Payne, Walt Peterson, Marilyn Ponting, The City of Pinole, Pinole Fire Department, Jennifer Posedel, Margaret Faria Prather, Gail Price, Shirley Ramos, Bruce Rayburn, Christine Ruiz, Celeste Silvas, Geoff Torretta, Garrison Traver, Chris Treadway, Viola Wessman, and the Facebook group "You Know You Grew Up in Pinole/Hercules if..."

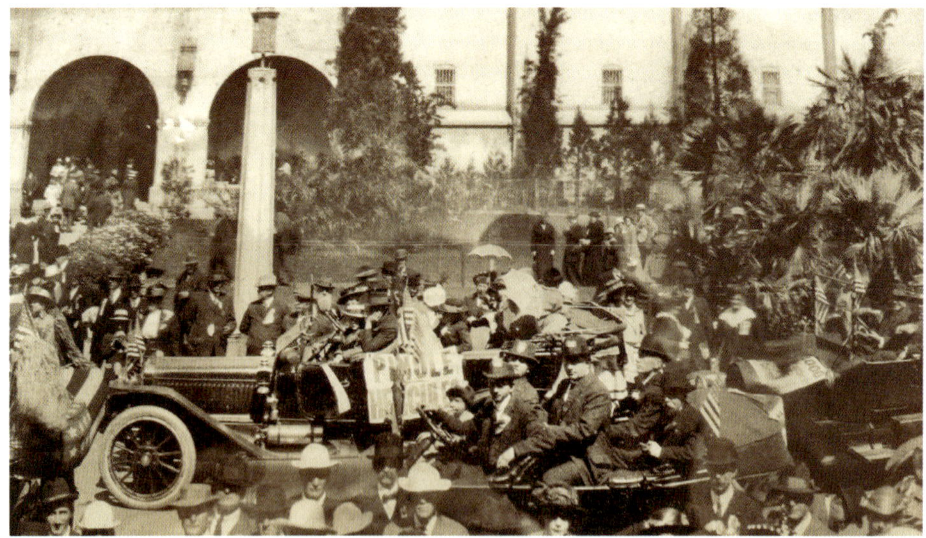

PINOLE-HERCULES DAY AT THE PANAMA-PACIFIC INTERNATIONAL EXHIBITION: The world came to San Francisco between February 20 and December 4, 1915, to celebrate the completion of the Panama Canal and showcase its recovery from the 1906 earthquake. The fair was held along the city's northern shore, today's Marina District. The Palace of Fine Arts was built for this exhibition. April 3, 1915, was Contra Costa County Day; each town and city had its own day. *Photo courtesy Carol Jensen*